Legitimizing Empire

THE ASIAN AMERICAN EXPERIENCE

Series Editors
Eiichiro Azuma
Jigna Desai
Martin F. Manalansan IV
Lisa Sun-Hee Park
David K. Yoo

Roger Daniels, Founding Series Editor

A list of books in the series appears at the end of this book.

Legitimizing Empire

Filipino American and U.S. Puerto Rican Cultural Critique

FAYE CARONAN

University of Illinois Press
URBANA, CHICAGO, AND SPRINGFIELD

© 2015 by the Board of Trustees
of the University of Illinois
All rights reserved
Manufactured in the United States of America
1 2 3 4 5 C P 5 4 3 2 1
∞ This book is printed on acid-free paper.

An earlier version of chapter 1 was previously published in the journal *Philippine Studies*. Segments of chapter 4 and the conclusion were previously published in a chapter in the edited anthology *Transnational Crossroads: Remapping the Americas and the Pacific*.

Library of Congress Cataloging-in-Publication Data
Caronan, Faye
Legitimizing empire : Filipino American and U.S. Puerto Rican cultural critique / Faye Caronan.
pages   cm. — (Asian American experience)
Includes bibliographical references and index
ISBN 978-0-252-03925-6 (hardback)
SBN 978-0-252-08080-7 (paperback)
ISBN 978-0-252-09730-0 (e-book)
1. United States—Relations—Phillippines. 2. Phillippines—Relations—United States. 3. United States—Relations—Puerto Rico. 4. Puerto Rico—Relations—United States. 5. Imperialism—United States.
6. United States—Race relations.
I. Title.
E183.8.P5C375   2015
327.730599—dc23   2014039309

In memory of Avelina Salvador Cruz.
My search for the stories you never told me led me here.

Contents

Acknowledgments ix

Introduction 1

1. Consuming (Post)Colonial Culture: Multicultural Experiences in Travelogues and Novels 21

2. Revising the Colonialism-as-Romance Metaphor: From Conquest to Neocolonialism 47

3. Bastards of U.S. Imperialism: Demanding Recognition in the American Family 73

4. Performing Genealogies: Poetic Pedagogies of Disidentification 105

Conclusion: Imagining the End of Empire 143

Notes 155

Bibliography 169

Index 181

Acknowledgments

The roots of this project reach back to a warm, spring day in Ithaca, New York. While in the Asian American Resource Center reading an assigned article by E. San Juan Jr. about the lasting legacies of U.S. colonialism on Filipinos, I heard some fellow students in the neighboring Latino Studies Resource Center discussing U.S. colonialism in Puerto Rico. Had I chosen to study elsewhere that day, I may never have written this book. Cornell University provided fertile ground for me to understand the related histories and cultures of Filipino Americans and U.S. Puerto Ricans. Claire Conceison, Moon-Ho Jung, and Sunn Shelley Wong showed me how understanding U.S. imperialism was crucial for understanding Filipino America. Mary Pat Brady guided me as I created a comparative framework for understanding U.S. empire through Filipino American and U.S. Puerto Rican literature. I will always be grateful for their attentiveness to my undergraduate research. Their encouragement was pivotal in my decision to pursue graduate school research and an academic career.

At the University of California, San Diego, I had the great privilege of developing my project with experts in the fields of cultural studies, Asian American studies, Puerto Rican studies, and Philippine history. With the guidance of Lisa Lowe, Lisa Sun-Hee Park, Ana Celia Zentella, John D. Blanco, and Vicente Rafael my project transformed from an observation of similarities between Filipino American and U.S. Puerto Rican literature to an interdisciplinary study of what the similarities and differences of these two cultures reveal about U.S. imperialism. The friendships and insights of Margaret Fajardo, Ashley Lucas, Theofanis Verinakis, Tere Ceseña, Monika Gosin, and Theresa Cenidoza sustained me through graduate school. Thuy

Vo-Dang and Cecilia Rivas were invaluable writing partners who helped me revise and keep on schedule. Yen Le Espiritu influenced me the most while in graduate school. I will be forever indebted to her mentorship, which shaped me in so many ways. She encouraged me to branch out methodologically and helped me to design a qualitative study of performance poetry. She advised me on how to juggle a personal life with academic commitments. As I left San Diego, she pointed me in the direction of this book's argument.

A Ford Foundation Postdoctoral Fellowship afforded me time to work exclusively on this book and to consider the relationship between cultural form and critique. Moon-Ho Jung graciously agreed to serve once again as a mentor to me and helped me revise my introduction with this new focus. Rick Bonus and Ileana Rodriquez-Silva offered insightful advice for moving forward during a writing workshop. I am also grateful to the Simpson Center for the Humanities for providing me office space at the University of Washington during my fellowship year.

I am very fortunate to be part of a generous Filipino American scholarly community. Much of this book has been presented at various annual meetings of the American Studies Association and Asian American Studies Association. Comments from Vernadette Gonzalez, Allan Isaac, Lisa Cacho, and Julian Go have been very helpful in enriching my analyses. On several of these panels I presented alongside Dean Saranillio and JoAnna Poblete. I value the friendship, scholarship, and support we've shared over the years. Sharing the transition from graduate students to faculty members with them has made the journey easier knowing that I had friends who could relate to my frustrations and joys. Sharing work with Sarita See, Anthony Ocampo, Jason Magabo Perez, and Gina Velasco in the latter stages of revision alleviated a significant amount of isolation I felt from being physically away from my academic support base on the West Coast. They helped me see the project from a fresh vantage point and to clarify key points that had gotten lost after several revisions. I owe a debt of gratitude to Martin Manalansan, who encouraged me to initially submit my manuscript and guided me through the entire process.

My colleagues at the University of Colorado, Denver, especially Donna Martinez, Jennifer Williams, Rachel Harding, Paula Espinoza, Karen Sobel, Sarah Horton, and Brenda Allen, have been a key support network for me for the past five years. Russell Endo very generously took time out of his retirement to advise and encourage me through all steps of publication.

The University of Illinois Press is really wonderful to work with. They were patient when I needed the extra time and hands on when I needed the handholding. Vijay Shaw, Larin McLaughlin, and Dawn Durante all shepherded the manuscript through different levels of approval. They were all effective and efficient advocates and always kept me in the loop. This book is far better because of the careful attention of the two anonymous reviewers who read this manuscript. I thank them for all their insightful suggestions.

I am grateful to all the performance poets in Los Angeles and New York City who shared their time, stories, and poetry with me: Alan Aquino, Alfie Ebojo, Alison de la Cruz, Americo Caisano, Anthony Morales, Bonafide Rojas, Cheryl Deptowitcz, Cheryl Samson, Dorian Merina, Edren Sumagaysay, Jesus "Papoleto" Melendez, Johneric Concordia, Jose Angel Figueroa, Maegan "La Mala" Ortiz, Marina Ortiz, Mariposa, Nancy Mercado, and Nicole Delgado. They introduced me to a part of Los Angeles I never saw growing up in the suburbs and helped me to navigate the current New York City poetry scene.

The beautiful photograph featured in the introduction is a Diallo Jones-Brown original. It is one in a series he shot at the World War II Memorial on an exclusive trip to Washington, D.C., as a favor to me, a testament to his unbounded generosity to those lucky enough to be his friends. He is one of among many friends who have cheered me on from the sidelines as I worked on this project. I am so lucky, and thankful, to have been blessed with each and every one of you.

My parents, Dionisio and Felicidad Caronan, insisted that I leave the comforts of our California home to study at Cornell, setting me on this path. I thank them for supporting me financially through my undergraduate and graduate studies and for their understanding when I ultimately chose a life different from the one they planned for me. Catherine Lepale and Dennis Caronan are the best older siblings I could ask for. They are always there to lend a sympathetic ear and always ready to help in any way they possibly can. Now that I live far away from them both, spending time with them and their families is something I treasure.

My dear husband, David, supported me emotionally, financially—in every way possible, really—through the end of graduate school, the academic job search, the tenure track, and the writing of this book. His unwavering faith in me helped me overcome my periods of crippling self-doubt. This book would not have been possible without his love and sacrifice.

Finally, thank you to my sweet Azalea, whose hugs, laughter, and smiles were indispensible in finishing the book.

Legitimizing Empire

Introduction

> I was just a poet
> wanting to read a poem
> the first night I came here.
> Since then
> I have become a street poet
> then somebody's favorite urban poet
> a new jack hip-hop rap poet
> a spoken word artist
> a born-again Langston Hughes
> a downtown performance poet
> —Willie Perdoma, "Spotlight at the Nuyorican Poets Café"

Willie Perdomo, a Nuyorican poet, articulates the power of naming in the above excerpt. He represents the disconnect between an author's self-perception and the various ways an author and an author's works are categorized and marketed for a mainstream American audience. The different ways he is packaged as a poet indicate his increasing success and notoriety. He starts off as a street poet, denoting his work to be new, edgy, and gritty. At the end he is a born-again Langston Hughes, a downtown performance poet. Comparing him to Langston Hughes legitimizes his work, placing it within the African American literary canon and larger multicultural American canon. No longer a poet from the anonymous streets, he now represents downtown, a gentrified urban space designed for the pleasure and convenience of young professionals. The process of becoming a legitimate part of American culture and becoming legible within hegemonic narratives of United States multiculturalism entails being co-opted and commodifed by the literary market. Though Perdomo may regard himself as a Nuyorican poet who represents the Puerto Rican experience in New York, his work has been commodified as African American and/or urban poetry. The marketing of his work for consumption by a mass audience eclipses any critique of colonial and racial power. Consuming his work allows individuals to demonstrate their appreciation for multiculturalism and thus their tolerance of differences. In other words, this packaging allows U.S. hegemonic culture to commodify and incorporate Perdomo's work while simultaneously diminishing its critique.

In *Immigrant Acts*, cultural theorist Lisa Lowe argues that Asian American culture is "an alternative formation that produces cultural expressions materially and aesthetically at odds with the resolution of the citizen of the nation" because United States citizenship has historically been defined against Asian immigrants, who were regarded as incapable of assimilating and becoming American.[1] Similarly, the racial logic of U.S. colonialism and the history of the United States in Puerto Rico strategically position U.S. Puerto Rican culture, and artists like Perdomo, to critique U.S. imperialism.[2] A related history of U.S. colonialism in the Philippines likewise positions Filipino American culture to critique U.S. imperialism. Despite the fact that the United States took control of both the Philippines and Puerto Rico in 1898, Filipinos and Puerto Ricans have been differentially incorporated into the United States politically and differentially included in the U.S. cultural imagination. Between 1898 and 1934, Filipinos were classified neither as alien (though some states tried to apply laws targeting aliens to them) nor as United States citizens but occupied a liminal space as U.S. nationals allowed to travel freely within the U.S. empire. Puerto Ricans have been U.S. citizens since 1917, but as commonwealth citizens they are not afforded all of the rights that U.S. citizens residing in the fifty states enjoy. Filipinos and Puerto Ricans have historically been simultaneously a part of and apart from the United States. This is one example of their different but equally tenuous relationships to the United States. Understanding these different relationships and how they change in conjunction with shifting articulations of U.S. exceptionalism provides some insight into the uneven nature of U.S. imperialism as it transitions between covert and overt forms. As a result of this unevenness, Filipino American and U.S. Puerto Rican cultures are at odds with the mythology of U.S. exceptionalism in all the forms it takes: the historical amnesia of U.S. imperialism; the rhetoric of benevolent assimilation that deems the United States as uniquely responsible for spreading democracy and protecting human rights around the globe; and the construction of the United States as an egalitarian society promising social mobility to anyone willing to work hard.

Despite the critique of U.S. imperialism that Filipino American and U.S. Puerto Rican cultures offer, hegemonic narratives of U.S. exceptionalism delegitimize and obscure these critiques. U.S. policymakers and mass media culture strategically deploy the Philippines and Puerto Rico separately to support narratives of U.S. exceptionalism. Narratives that construct the United States as a land of opportunity for immigrants obscure the role U.S. imperialism plays in encouraging migration from the Philippines and Puerto Rico to the United States.[3] Multiculturalism in the United States celebrates superficial ethnic differences in the form of cuisine, costumes, and ethnic performances without contextualizing these differences within histories of unequal global power, like U.S. imperialism, that explain how the communities that practice these differences came to be here in the first place. Constructions of race in the United States rely on simplistic cultural stereotypes applied to different ethnic groups lumped together based largely on geography. U.S. racial stereotypes maintain the racial power hierarchy and the myth of meritocracy by disciplining racialized groups to attribute experiences of social inequality to individual and/or cultural failings instead of to racial and class hierarchies.[4] In this book, I critically juxtapose Filipino American and U.S. Puerto Rican cultures to foreground the critique of U.S. imperialism and global power that these hegemonic narratives delegitimize and obscure.[5] Literary theorist Allan Punzalan Isaac argues that Filipino Americans are not only constructed through racialization in the United States but also through a racialization specific to U.S. imperialism based on the construction of an American Tropics, "a set of regulatory tropes and narratives that reveal a particularly U.S. American imperial grammar that create ethnic, racial, and colonial subjects."[6] For this reason, Filipino American culture can be better understood when read in conjunction with other U.S. colonial cultures.

I rely on Raymond Williams's dual definitions of culture as both the experience of everyday life within a society and the cultural productions that circulate within society.[7] In this book I examine the different ways that Filipinos and Puerto Ricans have been represented to affirm narratives of U.S. exceptionalism in the early twentieth century and today. I discuss how Filipinos and Puerto Ricans were represented to justify U.S. imperialism in the early twentieth century, how recent Filipino American and U.S. Puerto Rican cultures critique these justifications, and how the U.S. cultural market contains these critiques to reaffirm revised narratives of U.S. exceptionalism. In my analysis of Filipino American and U.S. Puerto Rican cultural productions across multiple genres, I contextualize their varying critiques within their conditions of production. As I will demonstrate, their production significantly affects the legibility and audience of a cultural production's critique. In other words, the cultural market actively obscures and marginalizes Filipino American and U.S. Puerto Rican cultural critiques of U.S. exceptionalism in order to legitimate narratives of U.S. exceptionalism and U.S. global power. The remainder of this introduction will further detail how Filipino American and U.S. Puerto Rican cultural critiques are obscured by narratives of U.S. exceptionalism and constructions of race in the United States.

Legitimizing Empire

In the early twentieth century, foreign policy narratives of U.S. exceptionalism centered on the notion of benevolent assimilation. U.S. colonial policies were defined as a project of benevolent assimilation to distinguish the United States' selfless intentions from those of established European empires that exploited their colonies. As a term, *benevolent assimilation* is no longer used to describe U.S. foreign policy, yet a central aspect of benevolent assimilation that defines recent U.S. military interventions as a democratization project remains vital to the construction of U.S. exceptionalism today. Benevolent assimilation entailed the establishment of political institutions modeled after U.S. institutions to teach residents of island territories how to become independent democracies.[8] Metaphorically, benevolent assimilation was culturally represented as Uncle Sam's successful courtships of a female Philippines and Puerto Rico and as Uncle Sam's taking custodial responsibility of infantilized Philippines and Puerto Rico. Both metaphors conveyed the white man's burden to ensure the safety of and care for people of color who are incapable of self-government.[9]

Narratives of U.S. exceptionalism have been institutionally recognized, legitimized, and reproduced. In a discussion of healthcare practices, social theorist Michel Foucault argues that the process of institutionalizing knowledge legitimizes some knowledge and practices while delegitimizing others. For example, institutionalized healthcare recommends practices based on research that meets standards determined by the institution. Under this model, a mother's observations on the best remedies for a common cold or an herbalist's prescription do not qualify as legitimate knowledge because they do not meet institutionalized standards. In this way the institutionalization of knowledge also determines authority, legitimate sources of knowledge, and legitimate narratives. Becoming an institutionally recognized authority often requires training and certification that in turn requires access to certification programs and the resources to pay for these programs.[10] The same process applies to the construction of the history of U.S. imperialism.

Though there was much public and congressional debate in the early twentieth century over whether or not the United States should retain overseas colonies, by midcentury U.S. historians legitimated U.S. exceptionalism's claim that the United States' territorial expansion differed completely from self-interested European empires.[11] The institutional legitimization of benevolent assimilation disregarded the brutal, self-interested colonial policies implemented early in the administration of these islands by the United States. Millions of Filipinos fought against U.S. colonization and died between 1900 and 1915. U.S. Congress refused to grant Filipinos U.S. citizenship on the grounds that they were racially inassimilable, and though it granted citizenship to Puerto Ricans, it did not accord Puerto Ricans with all the rights of citizens residing in states.[12] Philippine and Puerto Rican economies did not foster domestic growth for the benefit of Filipinos and Puerto Ricans but instead were developed with U.S. economic and business interests in mind.[13] The Supreme Court ruled that the rights accorded in the U.S. Constitution need not follow the flag to overseas U.S. territories.[14] Due to their academic credentials of historians' representing U.S. imperialism through a narrative of U.S. exceptionalism, the court's objectivity remained largely unquestioned until the movement for ethnic studies programs began in the 1970s.[15]

Instead, the institutionalized narrative of U.S. colonialism in the Philippines and Puerto Rico is as follows: As the United States acquired noncontiguous and overseas territory at the turn of the twentieth century, there were heated arguments among legislators over the ultimate fates of these territories, demonstrating the United States' thoughtful hesitance to become an imperial power. Would the Philippines and Puerto Rico become states as territories had previously? Could the native populations of these territories become American? Were they capable of democratic self-government? If the answer to all these questions was no, could the United States govern these territories without repudiating its anticolonial roots and becoming just another imperial world power?[16] To address the seeming contradictions of the United States' possession of overseas territory and government of people without their democratically given consent, the United States constructed itself as a different kind of empire. The United States was not a conqueror but a liberator freeing territories from previous colonizers. It was not a colonizer but a teacher demonstrating how democracies are built and run. Overseas U.S. territories were first and foremost a burden, not a benefit. As the first successful democracy, the United States had the responsibility to export this system of government around the world.[17] Recent iterations of U.S. exceptionalism still underscore the United States' unique global responsibility to help establish new democratic nations.[18]

The notion that the United States is only an imperial power when absolutely necessary is another significant aspect of the narrative of U.S. exceptionalism. Whereas other imperial powers retain colonies indefinitely for their own interests, the United States establishes democratic institutions, teaches the native population democracy, and leaves as soon as it deems the natives fit to govern themselves. The U.S. colonial era in the Philippines and Puerto Rico officially ended shortly after World War II. One of the United States' significant rationales for participating in the war was its aim to fight against German and Japanese territorial expansion, to challenge German and Japanese imperialism in Europe and Asia.[19] In order to avoid the appearance of hypocrisy after the allied powers won World War II, the United States decided that Filipinos and Puerto Ricans were ready for self-government and set into motion processes that led to the Philippine independence in 1946 and the establishment of Puerto Rico as a U.S. commonwealth in 1952.

The successful implementation and end of benevolent assimilation in the Philippines and Puerto Rico underpins the narrative of U.S. exceptionalism, which is institutionalized, legitimized, and reproduced by public education curriculum in the United States. Young students are taught that the United States reluctantly intervenes in the other nations' affairs only to ensure the development of democracy. The U.S. colonial governments in the Philippines and Puerto Rico are rarely mentioned specifically, but if these islands are referenced, they are examples of U.S. democratizing or development successes.

Representing the end of U.S. imperialism obscures the ways in which the United States maintained and even expanded its global power without direct political control over territories after World War II.[20] The United States agreed to grant the Philippines independence only with strings attached. The Bell Trade Agreement ensured U.S. economic interests by restricting the Philippine government from completely controlling the country's economy and by ensuring preferential treatment for U.S. businesses. The U.S.–Philippines Military Bases Agreement allowed the United States to maintain its military presence there.[21] Puerto Rico was never granted complete political independence: U.S. commonwealth status allows only for local self-government subject to U.S. congressional approval. Though Puerto Ricans have a delegate in U.S. House of Representatives, they cannot vote on approving bills into law. This means that should the Puerto Rican government pass legislation that the U.S. Congress disapproves of, the legislation can be struck down. Basically, commonwealth status continues the unequal status of Puerto Ricans vis-à-vis the United States that began when Puerto Ricans were granted citizenship. Independence and the conferral of commonwealth status marked an official end to U.S. colonialism in the Philippines and Puerto Rico, but Filipino American and U.S. Puerto Rican cultures represent the consequences of the uneven relationship between the U.S. and its former colonies and illuminate what remains the same in Puerto Rico, despite their status change.

In her study of women's health policies in Puerto Rico before and after the U.S. colonial period, anthropologist Laura Briggs argues that globalization is an ambiguously defined successor to colonialism that often does reproduce the racist, sexist, and exploitative policies of its predecessor.[22] Briggs contends that Puerto Rico is a perfect site for studying the reproduction of empire in the age of globalization because of its continuing subordinate relationship to the United States. The cultural productions I analyze in this book demonstrate how colonial inequalities and hierarchies are reproduced in the era of globalization. I build on Briggs's assessment that a study of Puerto Rico provides important insight into the transformation of U.S. imperial power and argue that a study of the Philippines alongside Puerto Rico provides insight into the different forms the U.S. imperial power takes.

The Philippines and Puerto Rico represent two models of U.S. colonial and neocolonial power. This is demonstrated from the divergent colonial paths laid out for them by U.S. colonial policy within two decades of being incorporated into the U.S. empire.[23] These divergent paths determine how the Philippines and Puerto Rico are represented for a mainstream American audience. U.S. imperialism in the Philippines and Puerto Rico cannot be regularly acknowledged together because doing so would reveal a sustained U.S. imperialism that discredits the narrative of U.S. exceptionalism. The fact that the "end" of the U.S. colonial era in the Philippines and Puerto Rico are different indicates the malleable nature of U.S. imperialism. When the United States engages in large-scale military interventions aimed at changing governments or building democracies, the Philippines is acknowledged as a successful example of such an endeavor. During World War II, as France lost control of Vietnam, the U.S. State Department's Subcommittee on Territorial Problems perceived France as a failed colonial power for leaving Vietnam politically undeveloped. To counter France's failure, the subcommittee presented the United States' "successful" development of the Philippines into an independent democracy as an example for other empires to emulate.[24] President George W. Bush also openly acknowledged the Philippines as a past U.S. colony during a visit to the Philippines in October 2003.[25] In a speech during this visit, he insinuated that Iraq, like the Philippines, would be a "successful" U.S. intervention.

As a U.S. commonwealth, Puerto Rico cannot serve the same narrative function as the Philippines. It is a successful U.S. colony not because it attained political independence but because its relationship to the United States has ensured Puerto Rico economic success and stability in relation to other Caribbean islands and Latin American countries. Instead, the ambiguity of Puerto Rico's commonwealth status makes it a perfect example for U.S. "stealth imperialism."[26] Puerto Rico is recognized as an independent entity by worldwide sports and cultural organizations, providing Puerto Rico the semblance of sovereignty and belying Puerto Rico's economic dependence on the United States. U.S. imperialism takes a covert form when the United

The Philippine and Puerto Rican pillars at the World War II Memorial in Washington, D.C. Photo by Diallo Jones-Brown.

States exerts its international influence through economic aid to third-world countries with the contingency that these countries accept security assistance in the form of military training. During the Cold War, while the United States actively disavowed its history and practice of imperialism, Puerto Rico was a "symbolic showcase" for the United States, serving as a model for the success of U.S. developmentalist policies for the third world.[27] The showcasing of Puerto Rico took advantage of its ambiguous status to encourage independent Latin American countries to accept conditional economic aid from the United States. Thus, Puerto Rico serves as a model for the building of a covert U.S. empire, one without official colonies.

One of the rare times that the Philippines and Puerto Rico are represented together is at the U.S. World War II Memorial in Washington, D.C. The memorial consists of fifty-six off-white stone pillars adorned with green wreaths. Each pillar bears the name of a state or a territory that sent troops who died in combat during the war. The pillars form an oval around a pool that features several fountains. On either side of the pool is an arch. On one arch is etched "Atlantic" and on the other arch is etched "Pacific," denoting the two theaters in which the United States fought. At this memorial, the Philippines pillar is situated adjacent to the Puerto Rico pillar. Here at this memorial the two are recognized as somehow belonging to the United States. They are represented in the same way that states are represented. One might argue that the similar representations indicate that Filipino and Puerto Rican sacrifices during World War II are recognized as just as significant as those by mainland U.S. citizens. Despite the representation of equality here, Filipino veterans of World War II were denied military benefits equal to their fellow U.S. soldiers for decades.[28] Although Puerto Ricans are, to this day, U.S. citizens who answer the call to serve and die for their country, they cannot vote for their commander in chief. Thus, even at the U.S. National World War II Memorial, the Philippines and Puerto Rico are only visible to affirm another narrative of U.S. exceptionalism, the notion that everyone in the United States is equal. And yet the fact that the Philippines and Puerto Rico are not only visually recognized here as a part of the United States but also are set together opens up the possibility of understanding U.S. history differently by critically juxtaposing Philippine and Puerto Rican history.

The Politics and Economics of Cultural Representation

Why do Filipino Americans and U.S. Puerto Ricans challenge narratives of Philippine and Puerto Rican history in the realm of culture where their narratives may be dismissed as fiction? Sociologist Avery Gordon argues that culture "enable(s) other kinds of sociological information to emerge" because it "has not been restrained by the norms of a professionalized social science and thus it often teaches, through imaginative design, what we need to know but cannot quite get access to with our given roles of method and modes of apprehension."[29] That is, culture provides a space where critiques of institutionalized narratives, such as that of U.S. exceptionalism, can emerge.

Filipino American and U.S. Puerto Rican cultures challenge institutionalized narratives of U.S. exceptionalism by representing the contradictions between the rhetoric of benevolent assimilation and implemented colonial policies to depict the enduring influence of U.S. imperialism for Filipinos and Puerto Ricans. The critique of U.S. exceptionalism can be found in Filipino American and U.S. Puerto Rican cultures across genres, by both renowned and unknown cultural producers, at times subtle and at times explicit. Despite the sustained critique that Filipino American and U.S. Puerto Rican cultures offer, U.S. hegemonic culture still manages to privilege and reproduce narratives of U.S. exceptionalism. The Philippine-American war and the Philippines' status as a U.S. territory for nearly half a century are often forgotten. Puerto Rico's continuing status as a U.S. commonwealth also does not often enter public discourse. These blind spots in U.S. history enable the narrative of U.S. exceptionalism to continually justify numerous U.S. interventions around the globe, including current U.S. interventions in the Middle East. These elisions and the continuing currency of the rhetoric of U.S. exceptionalism suggest that Filipino American and U.S. Puerto Rican cultural critiques have been contained.

Filipino American and U.S. Puerto Rican critiques of U.S. exceptionalism are articulated from a position of significantly less power than institutional narratives of U.S. exceptionalism. Filipino American and U.S. Puerto Rican cultural producers are not institutionally recognized as authorities on the history of U.S. imperialism and thus their narratives are not accorded the same level of legitimacy as U.S. exceptionalism. They do not have the resources that the U.S. nation-state has at its disposal to disseminate the historical narratives they construct in their work. Their narratives of the Filipino and Puerto Rican experience are not validated by public-school curricula. Thus, while culture provides Filipino Americans and U.S. Puerto Ricans a site from which to challenge hegemonic culture, these challenges often remain confined to the realm of culture. Foucault describes such narratives as "subjugated knowledges" that are often local and discontinuous because of their institutionalized illegitimacy.[30] Having not met the standards set by institutional gatekeepers for what is considered to be history, narratives challenging U.S. exceptionalism often find expression only as cultural productions where they can be easily dismissed as fiction.

Though culture is a site where hegemonic, institutional narratives can be challenged, it is also a site where such narratives are reinforced. The continuing viability of the narrative of U.S. exceptionalism requires the careful strategic representation of U.S. foreign interventions not only in public-school history books but also in culture. As cultural studies scholars have previously demonstrated, culture is not simply a space of democratic expression. Rather, how history is represented in national memorials and museums is the subject of contentious debate, especially in permanent exhibits because the historical narratives within also become permanent and effectively legitimized. Exhibits that deviate from the narrative of U.S. exceptionalism meet with fierce opposition. This is particularly true at the Smithsonian museums in Washington, D.C. The 1991 "West as America" exhibit at the National Museum of American Art featured artwork from the westward expansion. Instead of reiterating the tale of brave U.S. pioneers taming and settling the supposedly "wild West," the exhibit reinterpreted the paintings by questioning the positionality of the artists and illustrating how these images obscure the violence of conquest and racism to equate the United States expansion to the west with progress.[31] Political opposition to the exhibit resulted in the rewording of certain captions and the cancellation of subsequent showings of the same exhibit in other cities.

A similar controversy ensued with the Smithsonian National Air and Space Museum exhibit of the Enola Gay, the U.S. Air Force aircraft used to drop the atomic bombs on Japan to end World War II. The original exhibit offered a perspective on World War II foregrounding the United States' use of violence during the war. Among the artifacts of the original exhibit were pictures of the physical and bodily damage sustained by the Japanese after the United States dropped atomic bombs on Hiroshima and Nagasaki. The widely circulated image of the atomic bombings shows the resulting mushroom cloud from a distance. Although the mushroom cloud does suggest mass death, it does not portray the human suffering of the Japanese civilians in the same way that graphic pictures would. Politicians objected to the graphic nature of the photographs and exerted pressure to prevent the circulation of these images emphasizing the violence the United States inflicted on Japanese civilians. The exhibit was revamped. The text accompanying the displays was rewritten, and the ground level photographs of Japan after the bombing were removed.[32] This intervention reflects the refusal to acknowledge U.S. military violence that runs contrary to the narrative of U.S. exceptionalism.

In 2006 the Smithsonian Asian Pacific American program commemorated the centennial of Filipino migration to Hawaii with an exhibit on the century-old Filipino American experience entitled "Singgalot: The Ties that Bind." The exhibit mentioned the Philippine American War but never characterized it as a revolution or as the Filipinos' fight for independence. It also foregrounded the colonial relationship between the Philippines and the United States as it related to the migration of Filipinos to the United States. Rather than focus on the Philippines as a U.S. colony the exhibit focused mainly on the struggles against racism that Filipinos in the United States have faced and the progress Filipino Americans have made from being U.S. colonial subjects to becoming U.S. citizens. In this sense, the exhibit parallels the thread of U.S. exceptionalism that emphasizes the Philippines' progress from U.S. colony to independent nation and fits neatly in narratives of the United States progressing beyond its racist past.

Puerto Rico's relationship to the United States has not been featured in the Smithsonian. Between September 2008 and January 2009, the international gallery at the Ripley Center housed an exhibit called "Posters from the Division of Community Education of Puerto Rico, 1949–1989." These posters were created in the first few decades of the commonwealth era as part of a program encouraging the creation of art for social change. Though this program was similar to the Works Progress Administration's Federal Arts Project established by President Franklin Roosevelt, descriptions of the exhibit on the Smithsonian's Web site make no mention of this. Puerto Rico is described as a commonwealth, but not as a commonwealth of the United States.

These examples demonstrate how hegemonic culture, like all culture, is never static. It is constantly reconstituted in reaction to alternative cultural narratives, choosing aspects of alternative cultural narratives to incorporate and discarding those aspects that too explicitly contradict its own narratives. Cultural theorist Raymond Williams warns that cultural incorporation is powerful because it feels like recognition by hegemonic culture.[33] The reality is that incorporation by hegemonic culture is more akin to a revision and repackaging to de-emphasize critique and instead reaffirm hegemonic cultural narratives. The ways Filipino Americans and U.S. Puerto Ricans are racially categorized demonstrates how dehistoricizing Filipino and Puerto Rican communities in the United States serves to affirm the narrative of U.S. exceptionalism that constructs the United States as a land of equal opportunity.

Hegemonic Narratives of Racial Stereotypes

In the United States, Filipino Americans are racially categorized as Asian Pacific Islander American. Puerto Ricans can choose from different racial groups but are categorized as Latino. These categories are not neutral. They are imbued with meaning based on stereotyped assumptions about cultures that homogenize different ethnic groups from a shared geographical space. Since the mid-twentieth century, Asian Americans have been stereotyped as the model minority, constructed as self-sufficient, quiet, hard working, and successful individuals. Asian American scholars have pointed out that the model-minority stereotype emerged in response to international criticism of U.S. racism during World War II and domestic criticism of U.S. racism during the civil rights movement.[34] Asian American scholars have demonstrated the myriad ways that the model-minority stereotype is a myth: Many Asian Americans live in poverty. Statistics used to support Asian American success often focus on family income, not on per capita income. Asian Americans are paid less than their white counterparts in the same professions. Despite these rebuttals, the model-minority myth retains currency in U.S. culture because it supports the hegemonic narrative that the United States is a meritocracy where social mobility is possible.

This stereotyped and homogenous understanding of Asian Americans as model minorities obscures Filipino American specificity. Though Filipino Americans are often considered to embody the model minority, studies on the educational outcomes of second-generation Filipino Americans suggest otherwise. U.S.-born Filipino Americans are less likely to be admitted into college and to receive a college degree than East Asian Americans.[35] Furthermore, the different racialized experiences of Filipino Americans lead many to disidentify as Asian Americans and identify instead as Latinos, citing a closer cultural affinity with Latinos, given Spanish colonialism.[36]

The Puerto Rican experience is likewise marginalized by stereotypes of Latinos in the United States. At an event commemorating the life and works of Nuyorican poet Pedro Pietri in Harlem in 2006, green construction paper was passed out to everyone in attendance. On one side of the paper was a number; on the other side was a line of Pietri's well-known "Puerto Rican Obituary." Everyone in the audience was to participate in a group reading of Pietri's poem, reading their given lines in chronological order. When the time came for the reading, Jesus Papoleto Melendez, master of ceremonies for the event, asked the crowd, "Does everyone have their green card?" The predominantly Puerto Rican audience erupted in laughter. For Puerto Ricans, U.S. imperialism affords the benefit of U.S. citizenship and the ability to travel and migrate to the United States without restriction and thus Puerto Ricans do not need green cards. Laughter in response to this question recognizes one of the most significant differences between the Puerto Rican experience and that of other Latino groups. In the United States, undocumented immigrants are stereotyped as being Latino. Historically, this stereotype resulted in the deportation to Mexico of not only undocumented immigrants but also of documented immigrants and U.S.-born citizens during Operation Wetback and similar state government programs.[37] Today, this stereotype plays a major role in the passage and support for laws that rely on the racial profiling of suspected undocumented immigrants, legislation such as Arizona's SB 1070 and the subsequent copycat laws enacted in other states.[38] That the Puerto Rican audience that night could laugh at being asked if they possessed a green card recognizes the relative security that Puerto Ricans enjoy compared to that of other Latino groups. For some the laughter might articulate anger at how Puerto Ricans might be subject to questions of immigration status due to their racialization. For others the laughter might be a way of distancing themselves from other Latino groups, asserting their superiority due to their citizenship.[39] Though Puerto Ricans might be racially profiled in similar ways, their lack of a green card or their failure to carry the proper documentation on them at all times will not result in consequences as serious as those for other Latino groups, including deportation and separation from family.

Despite how the legacy of U.S. imperialism has distinguished Filipinos and Puerto Ricans from other ethnic groups in the United States within their designated racial categories, these differences are often obscured by homogenous constructions of Asian American and Latino culture. Stereotypes of the Asian American as model minority and the Latino as suspected undocumented immigrant actively prevent interracial identification. With its origins in the civil rights movement, the model-minority stereotype aims to discipline minority groups fighting for government policies to correct historic inequalities by insinuating that it is not racial inequality that prevents success but individual irresponsibility and laziness.[40] Asian American success without government assistance is represented as evidence of racial equality, pitting them against other minority groups. In many ways undocumented immigrants are the antithesis of the model minority. They are represented as interlopers who steal jobs from Americans, do not contribute taxes to the U.S. government, and drain resources from U.S. social services.[41] These opposing stereotypes discourage these two racial groups from recognizing any commonalities they might share. Asian Americans are incentivized to accept the "good" stereotype and perform the model minority, and their valorization leads to resentment from other racial groups. This resentment hinders the ready recognition of the common colonial history that Filipino Americans and U.S. Puerto Ricans share. This is not to say that identification between Filipino Americans and U.S. Puerto Ricans based on cultural similarities and a shared colonial history does not occur, but that the homogenous stereotypes of Asian Americans and Latinos work to prevent such identifications and in the process obscures U.S. imperialism.

In her critique of the conceptual and theoretical basis of Asian American literature as a genre, Susan Koshy argues that "[t]he unique specificities of the colonial relationship between the U.S. and the Philippines, the topos of return that haunts Filipino American writing, and the continuities between Filipino and Filipino American writing create a distinctive literary formation that does not conform to prescriptions about Asian American writing derived from Japanese American and Chinese American literature."[42] Current Asian American paradigms inadequately account for the United States' imperial imprint on the Philippines. The overdetermined emphasis on assimilation in popular, mainstream Asian American literature obscures the influence of U.S. imperialism on the Filipino American experience and culture.[43] Due to U.S. colonialism in the Philippines, assimilation to U.S. culture begins before Filipino immigrants leave their homes, and the widespread belief that the United States and U.S. culture are superior encourages immigration to the United States. In terms of policy, neocolonial agreements such as the U.S.–Philippines Military Bases Agreement allowed for specialized Filipino migration streams to the United States. In sum, what is generally understood as the model-minority Asian American immigrant experience—determined, hard working Asians escape from poverty in their homelands to find success in United States, where opportunities abound—completely obscures the role that U.S. imperialism plays in Filipino migration to the United States.[44] In his examination of the different stages of Puerto Rican literature in the United States, cultural theorist Juan Flores identifies two distinguishing characteristics of Puerto Rican American writing. These include the obsession "with the United States, whose presence not only lurks, allegorically, as the awesome colossus to the north but is manifest in every aspect of [Puerto Rican] national life" and its "association to Puerto Rico's national literature."[45] It is not surprising that these distinguishing features of U.S. Puerto Rican writing correspond with the characteristics of Filipino American writing that Koshy identifies. U.S. imperialism looms large in both Filipino American and Puerto Rican writing in the United States, testifying to its important role in shaping Filipino American and U.S. Puerto Rican subjectivities.

Literary scholar Allan Punzalan Isaac's *American Tropics* responds to the calls of Koshy and Flores to analyze these two groups outside of their designated racial groups. He demonstrates how racial formation in the United States renders both Filipino American and U.S. Puerto Ricans invisible. Thus, the homogenous and stereotyped construction of race in the United States obscures U.S. imperialism and works in tandem with the narrative of benevolent assimilation to uphold the hegemonic narrative of U.S. exceptionalism. By exploring the productivity of analyzing Filipino American, U.S. Puerto Rican, and Pacific Islander literature comparatively, Isaac works to unravel a narrative of U.S. exceptionalism. This book contributes to the growing scholarly project that situates Filipino Americans and U.S. Puerto Ricans within cultures of U.S. imperialism instead of within multicultural narratives of Asian American and U.S. Latino ethnic nationalism.

Cultural studies scholar Jodi Kim identifies multiculturalism as co-optation of the social, political agenda of the civil rights movement. Inclusion into a multicultural society, she notes, takes the place of true political inclusion that empowers people of color in the United States.[46] Striving toward multicultural inclusion encourages people of color in the United States to familiarize themselves with their authentic ethnic culture in order to celebrate their difference. In her seminal work *Immigrant Acts*, Lisa Lowe demonstrates how reading beyond the hegemonic narrative of the clash between assimilated second-generation Asian Americans and their immigrant parents' authentic cultures reveals the complexity of Asian America and an Asian American culture that is fundamentally at odds with American culture.[47] The difficulty of reading beyond the hegemonic narratives of Asian American culture and multiculturalism lies in Asian American identification with these narratives.[48] The disciplinary nature of the model-minority narrative creates Asian American desire to embody that narrative. The desire to belong and contribute to U.S. multicultural society encourages Asian Americans to embody an authentic Asian ethnic identity. Cultural studies scholar Kandice Chuh identifies the desire to embody the authentic model-minority Asian American as the obstacle to a critical understanding of the constructedness of Asian America. She posits conceptualizing Asian American studies as a "subjectless discourse" in order to foreground how the Asian American subject has been constructed through hegemonic U.S. racial, gender, class, and sexual ideologies.[49] In his application of Chuh's concept to Filipino American studies, Allan Isaac summarizes how Chuh's approach demonstrates how categories of identity, such as Asian American or Filipino American, are actually categories of critique.[50] Thus, deconstructing the Filipino American identity reveals U.S. constructions of race, class, gender, sexuality, and imperialism. I contribute to this argument by juxtaposing the categories of Filipino American and U.S. Puerto Rican to reveal a more comprehensive critique of U.S. exceptionalism.

In the remaining chapters of this book I analyze how Filipino American and U.S. Puerto Rican novels, documentary films, and activist poems critique narratives of U.S. exceptionalism and how these critiques are contained by the U.S. cultural market. Each chapter of the book analyzes cultural representations of U.S. exceptionalism that justified U.S. imperialism in the Philippines and Puerto Rico, Filipino American and U.S. Puerto Rican cultural critiques of these representations, and how these critiques are incorporated and/or marginalized by U.S. hegemonic culture.

In chapters 1 and 2 I analyze Filipino American Jessica Hagedorn's *Dogeaters* and U.S. Puerto Rican Esmeralda Santiago's *América's Dream* beyond the limiting frames of minority literary canons and center the novels' critiques of U.S. benevolent assimilation and its enduring legacies in the Philippines and Puerto Rico. Generally, these novels are categorized and thus understood within the canonized literature of their larger racial categories. That is, *Dogeaters* and other Filipino American works are categorized as Asian American literature, whereas *América's Dream* and other U.S. Puerto Rican works are categorized as U.S. Latina/Latino literature. I demonstrate how removing *Dogeaters* and *América's Dream* from their canons and reading these novels in tandem center a comprehensive critique of U.S. benevolent assimilation and continuing U.S. power in the Philippines and Puerto Rico.

Chapter 1, "Consuming (Post)Colonial Culture," interrogates the narrative of U.S. exceptionalism that characterizes U.S. imperialism as economic development benefiting its colonies and the world.[51] This narrative represents U.S. colonization of the Philippines and Puerto Rico as economic emancipation from the exploitative policies of the Spanish empire. Instead, the United States would aid these islands in developing their economies in their own best interests.[52] This particular aspect of benevolent assimilation claimed that any economic benefit to the United States was merely a byproduct of the economic developments to be introduced for the good of island natives. Hagedorn's *Dogeaters* and Santiago's *América's Dream* trace the continuities between the colonial and the postcolonial Philippines and Puerto Rico through their representation of the tourism industry. I contextualize their critique of the tourism industry within a comparison of the colonial representations in the 1899 travelogue *Our Islands and their People* to representations of these islands in the popular travel guide series *Lonely Planet*. Tracing colonial representations from the U.S. military to postcolonial representations from the tourism industry parallels the shift in the articulation of U.S. global power from more traditional forms of imperialism (such as holding island territories) to the neocolonial model of power that is more reliant on free trade to advance U.S. global interests. The continuities in the representations between the military travelogue and the recent travel guides underscore that the Philippines and Puerto Rico remain economically dependent on foreign currency. Juxtaposing the Philippines' and Puerto Rico's current reliance on tourism underscores that regardless of their current political status, the United States did not develop these island economies to become independent. The continuing currency of colonial stereotypes of the islands facilitates the Philippines' and Puerto Rico's continued consumption by foreigners and the continued importance of attracting foreign investment to compensate for poorly developed domestic economies. These colonial stereotypes are challenged in Hagedorn's *Dogeaters* and Santiago's *America's Dream* even as their representations of daily life in the Philippines and Puerto Rico confirm the lack of economic opportunities and domestic development. Ironically, these critiques can be undercut by the packaging of canonized novels as multicultural escapes that appeal to the same desire for exotic experiences that tourist guidebooks appeal to.

Chapter 2, "Revising the Colonialism-as-Romance Metaphor," examines how Hagedorn and Santiago challenge representations of benevolent assimilation as a consensual heterosexual relationship. Their novels rewrite the metaphor of colonialism as a romantic relationship to one that represents U.S. neocolonialism as rape. Such a revision represents the complex and entangled power relationships that resulted from the transitions of the Philippines and Puerto Rico from United States colonies to territories to self-governance. Reading the similar manner in which these authors update this metaphor to articulate these islands' current relationship to the United States underscores that the different levels of political sovereignty granted to the Philippines and Puerto Rico mask their continuing nonconsensual subordination to the United States. In revising this metaphor, Hagedorn and Santiago also highlight how metaphors of colonialism as romance and as rape both reduce women to objects to either possess or protect. By authorizing the raped women as active subjects, the authors question the gendered implications of the woman-as-nation metaphor and imagine a different role for women within anti-imperialist possibilities. However, their rearticulation of U.S. neocolonialism as rape is obscured by current debates over what constitutes legitimate rape in the United States and by marketing that privileges the narrative of women of color escaping the oppression of their traditional culture.

In chapter 3, "Bastards of U.S. Imperialism," I analyze two documentary films that use their personal stories of family illegitimacy as a metaphor for the illegitimacy of Puerto Rican and Filipino histories. I conceptualize these narratives of "empire's bastards" as a critical resurrection of the metaphor of benevolent assimilation as paternal benevolence that represented Uncle Sam as the guardian of wayward Filipino and Puerto Rican children. Extending this metaphor forward in time, the disavowal of U.S. imperialism in mainstream narratives symbolizes Uncle Sam's disavowal of these children, rendering them illegitimate. Juxtaposing how the United States' colonial relationship with both the Philippines and Puerto Rico is disavowed despite their different political statuses today demonstrates how deeply the United States desires to deny its imperialism. The United States will disavow its past colonies that are now independent as well as its current territories unless there is a politically compelling reason to take credit for them. Both documentary films *Yo soy Boricua, pa'que tu lo Sepas!* (I'm Puerto Rican, Just So You Know!) and *Memories of a Forgotten War* attempt to legitimize the history of U.S. colonialism in the Philippines and Puerto Rico, and its narrators publicly claim their places within their families. Though both documentaries use similar frames to set up their representation of marginalized histories, the more mainstream *Yo soy Boricua, pa'que tu lo Sepas!* reproduces and affirms U.S. multicultural narratives, whereas the experimental *Memories of a Forgotten War* demands U.S. recognition and accountability for colonial violence in the Philippines. *Yo soy Boricua, pa'que tu lo Sepas!* more easily affirmed narratives of U.S. exceptionalism and thus its critiques were more easily overlooked. *Memories of a Forgotten War*'s more forceful critiques were fundamental to the film's main narrative and could not be easily dismissed. I argue that these differences reflect variances in production, marketing, and ultimately the dissemination of the documentaries.

In chapter 4, "Performing Genealogies," I analyze the community work of Filipino American activist performance poets in Los Angeles and U.S. Puerto Rican activist performance poets in New York City. Most of these poets were born and raised in the United States and are explicitly critical of U.S. imperialism. The establishment of public education systems in the Philippines and Puerto Rico was of utmost significance for the project of benevolent assimilation. Though public education was touted as necessary for the democratization of these islands, it also helped secure ideological consent for U.S. imperialism by reproducing histories that naturalized the United States' presence in the Philippines and Puerto Rico. Filipino American and U.S. Puerto Rican activist performance poets realize that the importance of education for colonial projects points to the important role that education can play for decolonizing projects. They construct a genealogy of global power by centering global inequalities caused by colonial projects and globalization. Instead of privileging narratives of national progress in their construction of history, these performance poets privilege individual narratives usually disregarded by mainstream historical narratives. Reading Filipino American and U.S. Puerto Rican activist performance poet critiques together provides a comprehensive view of U.S. global power in the Atlantic and the Pacific and demonstrates how Filipinos and Puerto Ricans challenge racial categories in the United States. These activist performance poets deploy their genealogies when teaching in classrooms and in the community to encourage disidentification with hegemonic U.S. narratives and instead identify across racial and ethnic categories. Such disidentification enables interracial and interethnic coalitions for social change. Like the critique in *Memories of a Forgotten War*, these performance poet activists' critiques are explicit and cannot be readily dismissed or incorporated into U.S. hegemonic narratives. As a result, their popularity remains largely limited to Los Angeles or New York City, and their critiques are marginalized.

Raymond Williams argues that though most counterhegemonic work is historical, this work seldom connects those excluded histories to the present and thus makes little impact. According to Williams, connecting the past to the present is vital because it is at these points of connection "where a version of the past is used to ratify the present and to indicate directions for the future, that a selective tradition is at once powerful and vulnerable. Powerful because it is so skilled in making active selective connections, dismissing those it does not want as 'out of date' or 'nostalgic,' dismissing those it cannot incorporate as 'unprecedented' or 'alien.'"[53] For the remainder of this book, I will demonstrate how this is precisely how hegemonic culture operates in its processing of Filipino American and U.S. Puerto Rican cultural productions. It selectively incorporates parts of these productions that affirm narratives of U.S. exceptionalism. Cultural studies scholar Jodi Kim argues that Asian American culture refuses to comply with hegemonic U.S. narratives. Filipino American and U.S. Puerto Rican cultures do not actively comply with hegemonic U.S. narratives. However, the packaging of Filipino American and U.S. Puerto Rican cultural productions for mainstream American audiences often obscures the critical narratives within to affirm hegemonic narratives of U.S. exceptionalism. U.S. hegemonic culture maintains the narrative of U.S. exceptionalism by incorporating Filipino American and U.S. Puerto Rican cultures while marginalizing their critiques that underscore the contradictions between the rhetoric of U.S. exceptionalism and the practices of U.S. imperialism. *Legitimizing Empire* explores the power hegemonic culture has to legitimize U.S. global power by delegitimizing Filipino American and U.S. Puerto Rican cultural critiques.

1. Consuming (Post)Colonial Culture

Multicultural Experiences in Travelogues and Ethnic Novels

> [T]he reading of ethnic literature can be seen to set a stage for the performance of difference—race relations are made manageable and students are able to "relate" to diverse and highly differentiated experiences by reducing difference to individual encounters via ethnic "texts"; that is, complex differences crosshatched by gender, class, race, ethnicity, sexual orientation, and so on, are subordinated to the general category of experience of the unfamiliar.
> —David Palumbo-Liu, *The Ethnic Canon*

In his introduction to *The Ethnic Canon*, David Palumbo-Liu argues that the formation of the ethnic literary canon coincides with the corporate recognition of the changing demographics of the U.S. workforce. The implementation of ethnic studies curricula and the teaching of the ethnic canon at universities can thus be understood as perfunctorily incorporating ethnic differences to manage an increasingly diverse U.S. workforce.[1] Uncritical additions of diverse cultural narratives do not transform our understanding of U.S. history and society but serve instead to affirm and institutionalize the hegemonic narrative of the United States as a colorblind, multicultural, egalitarian society where one's success can be directly attributed to one's effort. Scholarship on multicultural education compares simplistic additions of ethnic and racial diversity to tourism.[2] This comparison underscores how both multicultural education and international travel are ways of offering "authentic" cultural experiences to U.S. consumers interested in accumulating multicultural capital, touted as a key asset in today's job market.[3] It also demonstrates how ethnic cultures are simplified and commodified for consumption by a mainstream U.S. audience.

In their commodification of ethnic cultures, ethnic novels and contemporary travel guides are today's equivalent to the photographic catalogs of the United States' new island territories at the turn of the twentieth century. In this chapter I analyze three different sets of texts: *Our Islands and Their People* (a set of turn-of-the-century travelogues commissioned by the U.S. military), the popular travel guide *Lonely Planet*, and the novels *Dogeaters* and *América's Dream*. These cultural productions all serve to deliver the colonized other to a mainstream U.S. public that is specific to its particular historical context. The military-funded travelogues are products of the traditional colonial form that U.S. global power took at the turn of the century. These were government-produced books aimed to familiarize the American public with the United States' intentions for its new island territories, demonstrating direct government involvement in manufacturing consent for U.S. imperialism. The travel guides and ethnic novels likewise manufacture consent for U.S. global power, but they are products of the form U.S. global power took after World War II, one that was no longer dependent on direct political control but on unequal economic and military agreements to secure U.S. global interests. Thus, the travel guides and novels reproduce narratives of U.S. exceptionalism and affirm U.S. global power independently, without overt ties to the U.S. government. Instead, the narratives they produce are shaped by the cultural market. The novels and the travel guides I analyze are mainstream cultural representations, but they reproduce hegemonic narratives of U.S. exceptionalism in distinct but related ways. As cultural products, the novels and travel guides are widely understood as enabling consumers to experience the "authentic" postcolonial other. Travel guides recommend itineraries and activities that allow the consumer to experience postcolonial culture firsthand, whereas ethnic novels are marketed as representing "authentic" stories of the postcolonial others. In this sense, the ethnic novel delivers the postcolonial other for consumption by a mainstream U.S. audience while the travel guides recommend how best to consume the postcolonial nation.[4]

Our Islands and Their People, like the more recent *Lonely Planet* guides, represent the Philippines and Puerto Rico for consumption. *Our Islands and Their People* note what industries are best suited for the new island territories and evaluate the island populations as potential workers to attract U.S. capital investment. The *Lonely Planet* guides represent the islands' unique cultural attractions and natural wonders to entice the Western tourist. I begin this chapter by arguing, through a comparative analysis of *Our Islands and Their People* and the *Lonely Planet* Philippines and Puerto Rico guides, that the tourist industry reproduces colonial stereotypes and hierarchies. The continuity of these representations from the colonial to the postcolonial period in the Philippines and Puerto Rico suggests a lack of self-sustaining economic development under U.S. colonial rule. Such development was touted as economic emancipation in contrast to the Spanish empire's explicit economic exploitation of the islands and part of the packaging of U.S. imperialism as benevolent assimilation.[5]

Whereas *Our Islands and Their People* and *Lonely Planet* center the tourist perspective in their representations of the Philippines and Puerto Rico, the perspectives of tourist industry workers themselves are represented in the novels *Dogeaters* and *América's Dream*. Hagedorn's and Santiago's representations (respectively) of Filipino and Puerto Rican interactions with foreign tourists and the tourist industry bring into question the social consequences of economic reliance on international tourism. Through the characters of Joey in *Dogeaters* and América in *América's Dream* I analyze the authors' representations of tourism to demonstrate how both authors foreground the continuity of limited economic opportunities for Filipinos and Puerto Ricans in the colonial and "postcolonial" era. In representing this continuity Hagedorn and Santiago critique the construction of U.S. imperialism as the economic emancipation of the Philippines and Puerto Rico and the promise of foreign tourism as an easy way for the islands to develop their respective economies.

Dogeaters and *América's Dream* can be read as a critique of how the Philippines and Puerto Rico were economically exploited by U.S. colonialism and thus left vulnerable to economic exploitation by global capitalism in various forms, including unequal trade relations with the United States, World Bank structural adjustment programs, and foreign tourism. However, the novels' representations of the tourist industry can also be read simply as an account of inherent third-world corruption and poverty because the hegemonic narrative of U.S. exceptionalism either touts the benefits of U.S. colonialism in the Philippines or Puerto Rico or neglects this history altogether. Without the historical context of U.S. imperialism and within the culturally American assumption that success correlates with hard work, it is a logical conclusion to blame Filipinos and Puerto Ricans for their own lack of economic development. I close the chapter by analyzing how the marketing and canonization of these novels facilitate the erasure of the historical contexts of the novels and enable readings of these novels as authentic voices of diversity for consumption by an American society that values multiculturalism. As a result, this framing perpetuates hegemonic narratives of U.S. exceptionalism and predisposes readers to approach the novels in the same way that tourists use travel guides—as a mechanism for the consumption of multicultural diversity.

How to Consume the Empire

Travelogues explicitly produce knowledge about foreign places and people for those who have yet to encounter them physically. Travel guides recommend itineraries and inform potential tourists of what to expect when they travel. However, these travel narratives offer seemingly objective information about places and people from particular privileged vantage points. For instance, *Our Islands and Their People* is a two-volume 1899 travelogue of the United States' newly acquired empire of islands in the Pacific and Caribbean created from images taken by photographers commissioned by the U.S. military.[6] It is not surprising, then, that such representations of Filipinos and Puerto Ricans supported U.S. military and economic interests on these islands by introducing U.S. citizens to America's new overseas empire and explaining the benefits of possessing these islands. Recent travel guides to the Philippines and Puerto Rico are not explicitly linked to nor do they explicitly represent U.S. foreign interests, but they are representative of U.S. global power in the post–World War II, "postcolonial" era of globalization, after the United States granted the Philippines and Puerto Rico varying degrees of political sovereignty.

Due to the lack of self-sustaining economic development during U.S. colonial rule, the Philippines and Puerto Rico were still economically dependent on the United States despite being granted some degree of political sovereignty. This in turn required the Philippines and Puerto Rico to seek out foreign sources of economic aid as U.S. global power transitioned away from the colonial model. Mass tourism offered the possibility of attracting foreign sources of income. For Puerto Rico, the advent of the mass tourist industries coincides with the advent of Puerto Rico's commonwealth status in the mid-twentieth century.[7] In the Philippines, attracting tourists first became a priority during martial law, as the American war in Vietnam neared conclusion.[8] The Philippines benefited economically from providing support for U.S. military involvement in Vietnam. In both cases, the departure of U.S. economic support made it necessary for these islands to find other sources of foreign income. Tourism was one of these sources. Today, travel and tourism represents a small but significant fraction of the Philippines' and Puerto Rico's GDP, 11.3 percent and 7 percent respectively in 2013.[9] However, their commitment to investing in and developing their international tourist industries illustrates the importance both islands place on tourism for their economic development. As a former U.S. colony and a current U.S. commonwealth, the Philippines' and Puerto Rico's development of their tourist industries can be understood as postcolonial strategies for fostering economic growth after centuries of economic subordination to colonial powers. Apparently, the United States had not followed through on emancipating the Philippines and Puerto Rico from colonial economic exploitation through self-sustaining economic development.

The *Lonely Planet* guidebooks thus represent the re-articulation of colonial power hierarchies in an era of postcolonial globalization because tourism is one way that cash-strapped postcolonial countries exploit themselves to re-attract capital from former imperial powers. These guidebooks package the Philippines and Puerto Rico for the consumption of individual tourists, whereas *Our Islands and Their People* packaged these islands for consumption to benefit U.S. business interests. The illusion of choice in the current era of globalization masks how globalization reproduces colonial inequalities between wealthy former empires and poor former colonies. The Philippines and Puerto Rico choose to develop their tourist industries because this seems to be an easier way to bring in foreign money than borrowing money from international institutions at high interest rates. Tourists from wealthier former imperial powers can choose to visit poorer former colonies because they have the resources to travel with ease internationally, whereas it is difficult financially and logistically for many residents of former colonies to visit wealthier, former imperial powers. In this way, the *Lonely Planet* guidebooks' recommended consumption of the Philippines and Puerto Rico and *Our Islands and Their People's* recommended consumption of the islands similarly facilitate the economic exploitation of the islands.

Here I examine *Lonely Planet* travel guides because they are produced by the world's largest travel publishing company. The guides' success and popularity led the British Broadcasting Corporation to first purchase a 75 percent stake in the company in 2007 and ultimately the entire company in 2011.[10] Their offices are located in the United Kingdom, the United States, France, and Australia—all developed countries. A majority of the authors of *Lonely Planet: Philippines* and *Lonely Planet: Puerto Rico* are from the United States.[11] Thus, these representations are mediated through the economically privileged perspective of individuals who are (for the most part) from former colonial powers. Given these circumstances, the similar representations of Filipinos and Puerto Ricans in *Our Islands and Their People* and the *Lonely Planet* guidebooks are not surprising because both encourage the consumption of the islands. *Our Islands and Their People* argues—by emphasizing the new colonies' development and business potential—that these islands should be U.S. colonies. The *Lonely Planet* guidebooks for these islands provide historical, natural, culinary, and other pleasurable reasons to visit. The similar representations in the *Lonely Planet* guidebooks and *Our Islands and Their*

People also suggest that little has changed in the Philippines and Puerto Rico in the past century, minimizing the enduring consequences of U.S. colonialism except those that benefit the Western tourist.

The introduction to *Our Islands and Their People* indicates travel as a key objective: "The object of this book, therefore, is to present as perfect and complete a view of the late Spanish Islands and their people as the *tourist, traveler or pleasure seeker* could obtain by visiting them in person."[12] This travelogue clearly links travel to colonialism by encouraging travel to the islands while itemizing the benefits for the U.S. of maintaining an island empire. Discussion for each territory delineates the benefits of its occupation, describing the climate and what crops would be successful there, indicating inexpensive, available land, and even including methods for cultivating crops. *Our Islands and Their People* and *Lonely Planet: Philippines* represent the Philippines as an unexplored frontier. In an explicit pitch to U.S. entrepreneurs, the authors state that "[i]n a commercial sense, [the Philippine islands] are probably worth more than any other region of the same size in the world. In spite of the average density of the population, which is three times greater than that of the U.S., there are vast districts of wild lands, wholly unoccupied and nominally owned."[13] Likewise, the *Lonely Planet: Philippines* represents the Philippines as an exotic paradise that is for the most part untouched. This guide reproduces the rhetoric of Westward expansion:

> The best thing about traveling in the Philippines is the sense that there are still discoveries to be made, sometimes just around the corner. With so many islands and so few visitors (at least in comparison to some other Southeast Asian nations), the Philippines is one of the last great frontiers in Asian travel. For those willing to adapt to the challenges of travel here, there are plenty of rewards . . . extraordinary rice terraces, tropical rainforests, underground rivers, soaring limestone towers, uninhabited "Robinson Crusoe" islands, and cascading waterfalls. And that's just above the ocean surface![14]

Adventurous travelers are urged to challenge themselves by discovering firsthand the "last great frontier." Both texts evacuate the Philippines of people to construct an image of empty lands waiting to be developed or discovered by the reader.

Our Islands and Their People and *Lonely Planet: Puerto Rico* also describe Puerto Rico using the rhetoric of westward expansion. *Our Islands and Their People* emphasizes empty, fertile lands to encourage the entrepreneur to invest labor and capital in Puerto Rico: "In every one of the principal islands there are vast tracts of unoccupied lands as fertile as the sun ever shone upon, and these may be purchased, now before the general era of improvement sets in, for a mere song in comparison to their real value."[15] *Lonely Planet: Puerto Rico* encourages tourists to travel beyond the cities by promising that those "who venture into the island's mountainous interior or explore its undeveloped southern and western coasts are coming across stately hill towns where the locals in the plaza seem to have been feeding the same pigeons for decades."[16] This text constructs Puerto Rico as still undeveloped but markets the untouched lands for U.S. tourists, not U.S. entrepreneurs. The author constructs the locals as anachronistic, quaint people more suited for tourist consumption than their own economic production.

Representations of the Filipino people in these texts are not similarly enthusiastic. In *Our Islands and Their People*, the U.S. military perceived Filipinos as a primitive, savage people. Comparing Filipinos to Africans, the authors conclude that "[f]or all the practical purposes of civilization, the mirthful, easy going African is superior to these treacherous and bloodthirsty hybrid Malays. They have been pirates from the earliest eras and the vengeful disposition is written indelibly on their sullen faces."[17] The fact that the Filipinos resisted U.S. colonization could only have reinforced the U.S. military's violent characterization of Filipinos. Representations of Filipinos as uncivilized savages were common at the turn of the century and were used as evidence that Filipinos could not govern themselves or be American. *Lonely Planet: Philippines* does speak well of the Filipino people, but only tentatively. The guide reassures the tourist by stating, "There is no reason to be overly nervous about visiting the Philippines, [as] most Filipinos are honest folks who will go out of their way to help a traveler."[18] Qualifying their endorsement of Filipinos with the word "most" accounts for what the guide categorizes as "dangers and annoyances." Among the dangers the guide identifies are political instability in the Muslim south and the impoverished rural areas. The guide fails to mention that these dangers are exacerbated by the neocolonial attempts on the part of the United States to militarily pacify the Philippines' Muslim minority and the devastating effects of neocolonialism on the Philippine economy. Under "annoyances" the guide states that "the prostitution scene [is] quite disturbing, particularly if you are unlucky enough to see evidence of the Philippines' bustling child prostitution industry (in places like Angeles)."[19] The authors describe another, gender-specific, annoyance: "Filipino men are unfailing in their efforts to charm women, especially foreign women."[20] These excerpts ignore how U.S. colonialism contributes to a particular sexual economy in the Philippines. The authors omit that Angeles was once home to the United States' Clark Military Base. The guide's description of how Filipino men attempt to woo foreign women ignores the sexual economy created by the U.S. base. Historically, many Filipino women attempted to woo U.S. servicemen in the hopes of leaving the Philippines. Today, Filipino women continue to view U.S. men as a possible way out of dire economic circumstances in the Philippines. Mail-order bride industries take advantage of such women. There are separate travel guides and group tours designed to help the Western man find the Filipina of his dreams.[21] Articulating the gendered annoyance of the Filipino man wooing the Western woman and the prostitution industry without the colonial understandings of race and sexuality represents the Philippines as an inconvenience, if not a possible danger, for Western female tourists and naturalizes the sexual tourism market for white Western men.

On the other hand, *Our Islands and Their People* and *Lonely Planet: Puerto Rico* both represent Puerto Rico as a place of racial harmony. *Our Islands and Their People* states that there is "a population of over 800,000, there are 70,000 negroes and 250,000 mulattoes. These conditions within themselves show the absence of all prejudices on account of color. But the African race is declining, and will eventually either disappear or be amalgamated with the white race."[22] *Our Islands and Their People* assumes that the existence of a sizeable mulatto population translates to the absence of racism and assures the U.S. reader that the black population will vanish, thereby minimizing the possibility of future race trouble the United States might encounter there. Similar evaluations of race in Puerto Rico are later made in U.S. congressional debates by those supporting legislation to grant Puerto Ricans U.S. citizenship. Such supporters successfully argued that Puerto Ricans could be assimilated into the United States because they were nearly white.[23] *Lonely Planet: Puerto Rico* reiterates the image of Puerto Rico as a mixed-race society, without qualifications, by describing the "strong and recognizable vestiges of Amerindian ancestors, Spanish *conquistadores* and West African slaves, as well as the political and economic influence of the USA."[24] Like *Our Islands and Their People*, *Lonely Planet* constructs Puerto Rico as a place of cultural and physical mixing. The different marketing purposes of these two texts accounts for the different emphasis placed on Puerto Rico's cultural mix. The black population was minimized at the turn of the century so that Puerto Rico could be imagined as part of the United States, whereas all components of Puerto Rico's racial mix are acknowledged today to package Puerto Rico as a racially exotic destination for tourists seeking authentic cultural experiences. Interestingly, *Lonely Planet: Puerto Rico* does not include the United States as part of this cultural mix, suggesting to the U.S. tourist that they can have the conveniences of home (the use of U.S. currency, not needing a passport for travel) and still experience the exotic other.

The Philippine and Puerto Rican *Lonely Planet* travel guides are a particularly fruitful site for investigating the contradictions of neocolonialism because they market the Philippines and Puerto Rico as exotic and culturally authentic but simultaneously convenient for the Western tourist. On the one hand, as illustrated in my previous analyses, the effects of U.S. colonial rule on culture must be minimized in order to emphasize that these islands can offer a culturally exotic experience. On the other hand, the conveniences that the Philippines and Puerto Rico offer emphasize the legacy of U.S. colonialism. As a U.S. commonwealth, Puerto Rico offers far more conveniences for the U.S. tourist than the Philippines does as a former colony. In describing what items are necessary for the tourist to bring to Puerto Rico, *Lonely Planet: Puerto Rico* advises, "Not much, really. One of the great joys of Puerto Rico's tropical climate and status as a U.S. commonwealth—as well as its position as the economic center of the Caribbean—is that travelers do not need to lug in a lot of clothes, gear, supplies, medicines, favorite foods, etc."[25] The U.S. tourist does not need a passport or visa, can drive around Puerto Rico with their driver's license, and can even avoid the hassle of currency conversion. Emphasizing the conveniences created by U.S. colonial rule encourages the tourist to focus on the privileges that the history of U.S. imperialism imparts rather than on how U.S. imperialism has affected and continues to affect those living in the Philippines or Puerto Rico.

This continuity between representations of the Philippines and Puerto Rico in *Our Islands and Their People* and the *Lonely Planet* guidebooks minimizes the importance of U.S. colonialism on the islands and demonstrates how the function of these islands remains unchanged between the colonial and postcolonial era. Both sets of texts encourage the consumption of these islands in their recommendations of how its U.S. readers can make best use of their resources to maximize their own benefits in terms of business profits or multicultural experiences. The travel guides reduce U.S. colonial and neocolonial influence on these islands to conveniences that do not affect the authentic, exotic cultures. These enduring representations are challenged in Hagedorn's *Dogeaters* and Santiago's *América's Dream*. Travelogues and travel guides do not include a local voice, emphasizing only what the locale offers. In contrast, these novels privilege the local perspective in order to demonstrate the power inequalities that colonialism and tourism create in the former colonies and thus underscore the lack of economic development for the benefit of the native population during U.S. colonial rule.

Tourism's Reproduction of Colonial Inequalities

In *Dogeaters* and *América's Dream*, Jessica Hagedorn and Esmeralda Santiago complicate and challenge popular hegemonic representations of peoples and places found in *Our Islands and Their People* and *Lonely Planet*. Hagedorn and Santiago, by representing the local perspective of tourist-industry workers in the Philippines and Puerto Rico, respectively, foreground the colonial inequalities that international tourism reproduces. In *Dogeaters*, set in Manila toward the end of martial law, Joey Sands is a mestizo whose father is an African American serviceman and whose mother is a Filipino prostitute. Joey's livelihood likewise depends on prostitution to wealthy, male, international tourists. In *América's Dream*, the main character América works as a hotel maid on the island of Vieques. She juggles the pressures of a runaway daughter, an alcoholic mother, and an abusive, possessive boyfriend.

Representations of the tourist industry center on the prostitution industry in *Dogeaters* and on the hotel business in *América's Dream*. What might account for the different emphasis in representing these tourist industries? The *Lonely Planet* guide for the Philippines identifies prostitution as an annoyance, suggesting that the practice is widespread. The *Lonely Planet* guide for Puerto Rico does not similarly cite prostitution as a problem. The different relationships the United States established with Puerto Rico and the Philippines may offer an explanation. When the United States made Puerto Ricans U.S. citizens in 1917, the island also became subject to the United States' domestic prostitution policy that resulted in stricter regulation and punishment of prostitution. Colonial authorities imprisoned and administered invasive medical examinations to women they believed were prostitutes. Different prostitution policy applied to U.S. possessions.[26] These regulations were the beginning of a long history of strict sanctions against prostitution in Puerto Rico.[27] In contrast, from 1901 to 1917 the U.S. colonial government in the Philippines maintained a red-light district to meet the needs of their military forces and contain the spread of venereal disease through regulation. After the red-light district closed, prostitution continued around U.S. military bases in the Philippines despite efforts to regulate it.[28] However, after the Philippines became independent, prostitution increased significantly. Before World War II only five cabarets operated outside the U.S. military base in Subic Bay. The nominal activity at the base required only a minimum of troops. During the Vietnam War, U.S. military bases in the Philippines were not only essential for military operations but also became important rest-and-recreation facilities for U.S. troops fighting in Vietnam. Prostitution-related businesses such as bars, nightclubs, massage parlors, and hotels sprang up around the bases, offering their services to an average of nine thousand military personnel nightly.[29] The profitability of prostitution and its contribution of foreign currency to the economy influenced the development of the Philippine tourism industry. During the 1970s, then-president Ferdinand Marcos made developing the tourism industry one of his priorities. Sex tours were developed to entice male travelers to the Philippines. Under the direction of José Aspiras during martial law the Department of Tourism explicitly marketed Philippine women to tourists through promises of "a tanned peach on every beach." Such sexualized marketing led to an increase in sex tourism and pedophilia tours.[30] Under Marcos's martial law, prostitution increased significantly and continues to be a visible service industry today.[31]

Santiago's representation of the Puerto Rican tourist industry in *América's Dream* centers on a hotel. This particular focus is also indicative of the close economic relationship between the United States and Puerto Rico. As a U.S. commonwealth, Puerto Rico's economy is integrated with the U.S. economy and its debt is part of the U.S. debt. Puerto Rico has not needed to borrow money from the International Monetary Fund for development. Rather, attractive tax incentives entice U.S. companies to invest and establish offices and factories in Puerto Rico. Puerto Rico's commitment to developing its tourist industry has resulted in increased construction of hotels. The Puerto Rican Tourism Development Act of 1993 declared that on the island of Puerto Rico 90 percent of tourism income is tax exempt, and tourism income is completely tax exempt on Vieques and Culebra. Capitalizing on these tax exemptions, international hotel franchises based in the United States, such as Ritz-Carlton, Wyndham, Marriot, Embassy Suites, and Hampton Inn, have built luxury hotels in Puerto Rico to attract wealthy tourists.[32] In 2008 alone, $1.3 billion from private investors produced 5,400 new hotel rooms.[33]

Thus, the aspects of the Philippine and Puerto Rican tourist industry that *Dogeaters* and *América's Dream* foreground represent two models of economic development influenced by these former colonies' relationship to the United States. The Philippines, as an independent postcolonial economy in need of foreign currency, is articulated by prostitution in *Dogeaters*. Puerto Rico's incorporation into the U.S. economy is articulated in the figure of the hotel in *América's Dream*. Accordingly, my analysis of these two novels explores these representations of tourism and how they emphasize the privileged position of tourists and the subservient position of locals, similar to the former colonial hierarchy of the colonizer in a privileged position over the colonized. As Mary Louise Pratt observes in *Imperial Eyes*, this hierarchy produces stereotypes of "the rough and humble peasant gladly sharing his subsistence with the enlightened man of the metropolis whose essential superiority is accepted."[34] Both novels represent tourists' expectations of the Philippines and Puerto Rico and illustrate how the locals' willingness to meet tourist expectations reinforces these stereotypes and reproduces colonial inequalities.

América's Dream opens by explicitly representing América's subservient position within the tourism industry: she is "on her knees, scrubbing a toilet at the only hotel on the island."[35] The hotel is located on the island of Vieques, home to a U.S. naval base at the time. The base served as a weapon-storage facility and a site for bombing exercises.[36] Setting the first half of the novel on Vieques, itself a flashpoint of U.S. colonial rule, suggests a connection between América's subservience and U.S. colonialism. Santiago underscores América's subordination within the tourism industry and hotel employment hierarchy by representing her in the kneeling position and emphasizing the difficult and dirty work of "scrubbing a toilet." Revolving the main character's life around a hotel reflects the dominance of the hotel industry in recent Puerto Rican economic development. The explosive growth of the hotel industry increases the probability that a Puerto Rican local's livelihood will come to depend on a hotel. These hotels, symbols of privilege and wealth, become important interfaces between the poor locals and privileged tourists.

In *Dogeaters*, Hagedorn focuses on sexual tourism in the Philippines under martial law. The book's representation of sexual tourism critiques President Ferdinand Marcos's political use of tourism to legitimate his imposition of martial law, which facilitated U.S. neocolonial influence in the Philippines.[37] During Marcos's rule the Philippines was marketed in any way necessary to attract foreign tourists, to the detriment of the local population. Hagedorn represents the ease with which a tourist can obtain sex-related services to exemplify the exploitation of the Philippines' sexual tourist workers. An American military serviceman with whom Joey Sands is engaged in a short-term sexual relationship asks Joey for a sex show as a favor for a friend. To this Joey replies, "You want boys, girls, or both? Maybe you want children?"[38] Tourists can expect a varied sexual menu that fulfills all of their fantasies, even pedophilic ones. Joey's matter-of-fact manner in presenting him with these choices suggests that these services are routine. This sexual transaction, much as hotels in *América's Dream*, portrays tourists' privilege. Their economic privilege allows them to pay any price to obtain any desired pleasure. Such privilege has also enabled exploitative colonial and neocolonial economic policies in "postcolonial" countries like the Philippines. Given the low wages that jobs in other industries offer, the economic benefits of pleasuring tourists constrain locals to economic choices in the service industry.

In her ethnography on Filipina workers in the Clark Special Economic Zone (the former Clark U.S. military base that has been converted into a leisure escape for the wealthy) American studies scholar Vernadette Gonzalez argues that cheap Filipina labor is the site where the continuities between the colonial period and neocolonial period become visible. Filipino tourist officials laud the trainability of Filipina workers, who are very willing to accommodate the needs of their employers' clients.[39] The privilege that tourists to the Philippines enjoy depends on the trainability of Filipino workers, and they are trainable precisely because of their economic vulnerability caused by neocolonial economic policies. In postcolonial countries the tourism industry is constructed as a benevolent creator of sorely needed job opportunities. However, catering to tourists' needs and desires creates employment opportunities for locals, but these jobs are labor intensive, menial jobs. Hotels offer positions for waiters, bellhops, and chambermaids. Sexual tourism creates jobs for prostitutes and pimps. These service positions are similar to those offered to native populations in a colonial context. Thus, development of the tourist industry results in native populations remaining in positions of servitude.

Both novels use tourism explicitly to link colonial and neocolonial inequalities in Puerto Rico and the Philippines. The link between colonialism and tourism is made in *América's Dream* through the figure of La Casa del Francés, the hotel where América works while she is in Puerto Rico. She has worked there "since [Don Irving] bought the decaying plantation house and converted it into a hotel."[40] In his analysis of tourism to third-world countries, David Harrison observes a trend where old colonial buildings, such as abandoned sugar mills in the Caribbean, are renovated into hotels. This transformation suggests that tourism in the neocolonial era replaces commodities that were of economic importance during the colonial era.[41] The plantation house's conversion to a hotel, rather than the construction of a new hotel, suggests a superficial shift that does not undermine the original economic foundation.[42] Tourism, like colonialism, leaves Puerto Rico dependent on an external source of economic prosperity. The figure of the charming plantation house also illustrates the desire to idealize the "good old plantation days," thereby fulfilling the desires of tourists from former colonial powers to celebrate colonial legacies while omitting history because the workers in the fields have been displaced to urban factories or tourism jobs.

Puerto Rico's colonial and neocolonial economies both exploit the working class. In *América's Dream* the unbroken continuity of exploitation from Spanish colonialism to U.S. colonialism to the U.S. commonwealth period is represented through América's maternal lineage. América traces her ancestry to a Frenchman who brought his wife and her servant, Marguerite, to Puerto Rico. His wife died shortly after she arrived in Puerto Rico, and Marguerite helped the Frenchman overcome his despair over the loss of his wife. Eventually, the two became romantically involved, but when the Frenchman passed away he left Marguerite with only an illegitimate child. América is Marguerite's great-great-great-great-granddaughter. During the early colonial period, settler colonists often pursued romances with native women because of the lack of foreign women, and natives were knowledgeable in the preparation of local foods and medicines and could thus care for their masters in times of illness.[43] The native Taíno population in Puerto Rico was wiped out by disease shortly after Columbus's arrival in the Caribbean. There was no ready population of native women to serve as European concubines. Servants like Marguerite fulfilled the role of caretaker and lover for early colonists. Marguerite could not legitimately claim her lover's land and only managed to survive by maintaining her position as housekeeper for the plantation's new owner: "Over the years, La Casa changed hands many times, and each time, one of Marguerite's descendants, a woman with a child and no husband, appeared at the back door claiming to be the housekeeper. No one questioned her right to clean its hallways, tend the courtyard, dust its rooms, scrub its tubs, polish its tiles."[44] Dubbing the ability to perform housework "a right" is ironic but also illustrates the lack of opportunities that exist for poor women, especially those unmarried, both now and under colonial rule. Santiago's use of irony highlights the masculine perspective of La Casa's various owners. La Casa's male owners tacitly recognized Marguerite's descendants' ownership rights by allowing them to perform menial housework. Passing the job of housekeeper from one generation to the next suggests that Puerto Rico's passage from colonial possession to commonwealth made little difference in the lives of the Puerto Rican working class because tourism recreates a hierarchy reminiscent of those inscribed by its former colonizers.

Joey's ancestral lineage in *Dogeaters* likewise expresses the continuity of economic exploitation of Filipino workers in the colonial and neocolonial periods. Exploitation resulting from sexual tourism subject both Joey Sands and his mother to similar forms of oppression. Joey's livelihood depends on sexual tourism. His steady clients and one-night stands are all wealthy men who bring him to hotels and bachelor apartments. The three times we see him involved in short-term sexual relationships, he is always with a foreigner: an American, an Australian, and a German. Joey describes his mother as "a legendary whore": "[She was] disgraced, abandoned, just like the movies. Driven to take her own life. My father was not the first man to promise her anything that's for sure."⁴⁵ Like Joey, his mother sold her body to survive. Although the identity of his father is never revealed, various references to Joey as a "little GI baby" and descriptions of his "tight kinky curls" imply that his father is an African American U.S. serviceman.⁴⁶ Between 1946 and 1992 U.S. military bases remained active in the Philippines, and prostitution near these bases was commonplace. The reference to Joey as a GI baby implies that his mother was one of these prostitutes. Persistently limited economic opportunities in the Philippines creates a second generation of prostitutes: identifying Joey as a GI baby born to a Filipina prostitute servicing U.S. military bases in the Philippines is a remnant of colonial rule, and Joey's becoming a prostitute for international tourists explicitly links the exploitative conditions of the colonial and neocolonial economy.

Tourism also leaves intact the hierarchy that privileges the colonizer over the colonized. The novels represent two distinct viewpoints: the perspective of tourists who occupy a position of privilege and the perspective of locals who occupy a subservient position. Within the categories of tourist and local are myriad perspectives of class, gender, ethnicity, and sexual preference. In fact, a majority of tourists to the Philippines do not arrive from the United States but from neighboring Asian countries and Australia.⁴⁷ However, the emphasis in both novels on foreign tourists from Western countries underscores that the international tourist industry exploits the Filipino and Puerto Rican laboring classes in ways similar to colonialism. This emphasis also explicitly critiques the erasure of colonialism in current travel guides like *Lonely Planet*. Interactions between tourist-industry employees and foreign tourists in *América's Dream* and *Dogeaters* focus on wealthy foreigners' privileges and their exploitation of tourist workers Joey and América. An examination of these foreign tourists' perspectives reveals how tourists' expectations, which are often created by or reinforced by travel guides, affect Puerto Rico and the Philippines, thus illustrating how these two countries cater to tourists' needs at their own expense.

Catering to Foreign Desires

Both novels explicitly represent Puerto Rico's and the Philippines's own complicity in their respective subordination by conforming to tourists' expectations. Prioritizing tourism and other industries aimed at injecting these economies with foreign currency is often done at the expense of developing the economy in the best interests of resident Puerto Ricans and Filipinos.

In *América's Dream*, América's lover, Correa, works at a beach guardhouse, stopping tourists and taking down their personal information before allowing them onto the public beach. However, América realizes that "the road and parking are not the only ways to get to the beach. You can walk to it from other beaches, from the town, and, on horseback, from the wild vegetation surrounding it. She thinks the tourism office goes through all the trouble of taking down people's information to make tourists feel safe."[48] Tourists value safety while traveling, so any perceived danger can decrease the number of tourists visiting a country. Therefore, countries dependent on tourism need to simultaneously create for tourists a sense of security and an adventurous escape from everyday life. The presence of a guardhouse at a beach implies that the beach may otherwise be dangerous, adding a sense of risk to tourists' excursions. América's reaction to the guardhouse illustrates that the guardhouse serves no real purpose but to fulfill the tourists' desires to feel safe. In this scene, Santiago argues that Puerto Rico allocates resources to build and maintain a guardhouse that merely represents security. By dubbing the guardhouse "a waste" Santiago implies that these resources ought to be used in a more productive manner, perhaps to benefit Puerto Ricans. Allocation of funds to tourism rather than to services for Puerto Ricans illustrates that tourists' desires take precedence over locals' needs. In *Dogeaters* the Philippine government also complies with tourists' expectations: "The Manila International Film Festival is the First Lady's latest whim. She orders the city and slums rejuvenated with fresh coats of paint, windows and doorways lined with pots of plastic flowers, the streets swept and reswept by women in red and yellow sweatshirts with 'Metro Manila Aide' printed in big black letters on the back and front. Even Uncle's shack gets the treatment."[49] Here, Hagedorn deploys sarcasm to critique the film festival, a fictionalized version of an actual international film festival hosted by First Lady Imelda Marcos. The novel intentionally represents the international film festival to reveal corruption and inequity under Marcos's rule. The International Film Festival was expected to attract many tourists to the Philippines. The novel's First Lady creates a façade of cleanliness and order to produce a pleasing, modern atmosphere for tourists. Instead of substantively addressing the problem of poverty in Manila, symbolized by the slums, "coats of paint" superficially cover up the problem. Ironically, the workers wear "Metro Manila Aide" sweatshirts, suggesting that their work is for metro Manila's benefit. In reality attracting tourists takes precedence over addressing local issues, which would best be met by actual aid for the city. In this case, the novel clearly blames the U.S.-supported Marcos administration for disregarding the needs of poor Filipinos.

Hagedorn's sarcastic critique continues as she depicts how the construction of a cultural center for the Manila International Film Festival exemplifies total disregard for locals:

> The workers are busy day and night, trying to finish the complex for the film festival's opening night, which is scheduled in a few weeks. Toward the end, one of the structures collapses and lots of workers are buried in the rubble. Big News. Cora Camacho even goes out there with a camera crew. "Manila's Worst Disaster!" A special mass is held right there in Rizal Park, with everyone weeping and wailing over the rubble. The archbishop gives his blessing, the First Lady blows her nose. She orders the survivors to continue building: more cement is poured over dead bodies; they finish exactly three hours before the first foreign film is scheduled to be shown.[50]

Again, Hagedorn fictionalizes past events to critique the Marcos administration. In 1982, Imelda Marcos inaugurated the Manila Film Festival, which she felt necessitated the building of a film palace. The rushed construction resulted in an avalanche that killed at least six people.[51] In *Dogeaters*, Hagedorn depicts how the unconcerned First Lady views the tragedy as a nuisance. Although the media label the avalanche "Manila's worst disaster," no concrete measures are taken to make amends for it or to prevent such a disaster from happening again. Instead, a façade of concern performed for the media, represented by the archbishop's blessing and the First Lady's blowing her nose, constitute the official response to the tragedy. The sarcastic tone of the passage underscores the public officials' insincerity.

Later, the First Lady, without addressing worker safety, orders the survivors to continue construction. Narrowly escaping death once, these survivors' lives are again endangered. Despite the hazardous conditions, they manage to finish building the Film Palace on time; the implication is that that the International Film festival is more important than its builders' lives. Most egregious is that cement is poured over the dead bodies with the archbishop's hasty benediction in place of proper burials, signifying the worthlessness of their lives. These dead workers represent the Philippines' willingness to sacrifice Filipino lives for tourism.

During martial law, Marcos directed resources toward tourism and left more pressing domestic concerns such as labor laws, land reform, and environmental issues unaddressed. President Marcos wished to present the Philippines as a modern nation to encourage foreign investment.[52] Arturo Escobar's discussion of development in *Encountering Development* notes that the first world's emphasis on development compelled many in the third world to devalue their own culture, believing their traditions somehow prevented development.⁵³ Development was equated with modernization, and local cultures were cast aside in the name of progress and Western culture. Hagedorn captures this sentiment in *Dogeaters* by representing the Manila International Film Festival that showcases no Filipino films but instead features films from the West. Colonizers assume their culture to be superior to that of the colonized in some way. This assumption of superiority often is the justification given for colonization and becomes internalized by the colonized. The choice to show foreign films reveals not only the government's desire to attract tourists but also colonialism's internalized oppression that leads Filipinos to devalue their own cultural productions.

In prioritizing the tourism industry, the Puerto Rican and Filipino governments devalue the lives and needs of their own people and enable tourists to likewise devalue the local population, especially those who are tourist-industry workers. In *América's Dream*, América is in contact with tourists at the hotel on a regular basis. As she performs her housekeeping duties, "she notices how they look right past and pretend not to see her. She feels herself there, solid as always, but they look through her, as if she were a part of the strange landscape into which they have run away from their everyday lives. Those who do see her, smile guardedly, then slide their gaze away quickly, ashamed, it seems, to have noticed her."⁵⁴ América is rendered invisible because recognizing her subjectivity also requires that the tourists recognize their own privilege.⁵⁵ Santiago represents how those confronted with their own privilege become uncomfortable with guilt and avert their eyes. The guilt these tourists feel upon realizing that one's privilege relies on the subordination of others is the same guilt experienced by some colonial civil servants, who assuaged their guilt by attempting to better understand and preserve the local culture.⁵⁶ In the novel, tourists avoid this discomfort and guilt by framing América as a contented worker. They "tell her how charming it is that she sings" boleros, ballads, and cha-cha-chás as she works.⁵⁷ These songs are commodities of the local culture tourists traveled to find. Instead of focusing on the role they play in América's subservience, tourists readily consume her songs. Santiago depicts hotel guests observing América as she cleans the rooms in the morning, "hum[ming] a bolero or a salsa tune, seemingly lighthearted."⁵⁸ The word "seemingly" casts doubt on the tourists' interpretation of América. Whether or not América's mood corresponds with her actions does not matter to tourists, who view her only as a commodity.

Tourists objectify not only tourist-industry workers but the local population as well. América is commodified both at and away from work. As she walks around Vieques, "[a] público passes in the opposite direction, and the driver waves at her. It is an air-conditioned van for twelve passengers, full of tourists gawking at the lush vegetation and doubtless at the brightly dressed woman walking along the road. She tries to ignore their rude stares, the feeling that to them she represents the charm of the tropics: a colorfully dressed woman walking along a sunlit road."[59] The tourists do not consider that their stares may cause América discomfort. In attributing the rude behavior to multiple tourists, Santiago emphasizes that it is common behavior for tourists to be inconsiderate to the local population. Comparable to "lush vegetation," the tourists objectify América through their desire to experience "the charm of the tropics" while on vacation. Santiago marks the tourists privilege in relation to América: they are able to travel comfortably in an air-conditioned vehicle while América walks on a hot day under the sun.

In *Dogeaters,* the German filmmaker Rainer, one of Joey's lovers, similarly objectifies Joey, symbolized by the pictures that Rainer takes of him, both real and imaginary: "I feel his eyes boring into me, watching every move as I eat, as if he'll never get enough. 'It's a picture I take with my mind, so I won't forget you.' I wish he'd stop. I don't mind when he takes *real* pictures of me with that fancy camera of his, which he's done all week: *Joey Swimming. Joey and Cup of Coffee. Joey Lighting a Cigarette. Joey Bored. Joey Brooding.*"[60] In *Tender Violence,* American studies scholar Laura Wexler argues that photographs taken of domestic images in U.S. colonies served the interests of U.S. imperialism. In the above excerpt, Rainer chooses to take pictures of Joey engaged in ordinary activities, not ones that reveal his own consumption of Joey's body. Through Rainer's photographic choices, Hagedorn critiques the subjects that tourists tend to choose for their pictures. Tourists desire to capture locals performing everyday tasks, like eating, sleeping, playing, or talking. They take pictures of everyday leisure tasks, not the also-everyday task of factory work, or cleaning hotels as a maid. Rainer does not take photographs of Joey at the club where they met, where Joey usually finds his clients. Taking a picture of Joey in the club would also be no less real than a picture of Joey bored. However, a picture of Joey at the club would capture Rainer's sexual objectification of him, thus revealing the exploitive hierarchy of tourism. Instead of capturing Joey's character, the pictures reduce Joey to a flat, two-dimensional reproduction, a commodity representing "authentic" Filipino life to take home as a souvenir. Tourism allows privileged foreigners to objectify and exploit tourist workers, just as colonialism did.

Returning the Colonial/Tourist Gaze

Our Islands and Their People and the *Lonely Planet* travel guides for the Philippines and Puerto Rico are written from the perspective of the privileged foreign consumer that reduces these islands and their people to commodities. Hagedorn and Santiago subvert this hierarchy by returning their gaze. Their characters are not merely helpless victims of the tourist industry but have agency, however limited, within the power hierarchy created by international tourism. In both of the novels, the characters are subjects who objectify tourists, who exploit tourists' expectations. Through América's position as a hotel maid, Santiago also challenges tourists' negative stereotypes of Puerto Rico and the third world in general.

Santiago represents the exploitation of tourists' desire for security and safety while they travel. Correa's job at the guardhouse at one of the islands' popular beaches requires that he sign the visitors in and out as they arrive or leave the public beach area. There is no fee for the tourists' use of the beach, so Correa often benefits from worried tourists. In one scene a tourist inquires if paying a parking fee is required. "'If you want to pay . . .' Correa grins, and the woman pulls out two folded dollar bills from her pocket and hands them to him. The tourists think if they tip the guard, he'll keep an eye on their cars."[61] Correa's statement is at once suggestive and subtly threatening. Santiago implies that Correa will not exert extra effort to give paying individuals preferential treatment, but tourists expect their car will be left unsupervised if they do not pay.

In contrast, Santiago subtly subverts the hierarchy produced by tourism through América's perspective. Santiago inverts Western stereotypes of hygiene. Developing countries, like those in the Caribbean, are often stereotyped as dirty and unhealthy in contrast to developed countries in North America and Europe. However, América subverts this stereotype by illustrating that tourists are unsanitary and that she is responsible for maintaining a clean environment. While cleaning a room, she finds two used condoms on the floor. She reflects: "That's one thing she has never understood about Yanquis. They do things like leave their used condoms on the floor, or bloody sanitary pads, unwrapped, in the trash cans. But they throw a fit if there's hair in the shower drain, or if the toilet is not disinfected. They don't mind exposing other people to their germs, but they don't want to be exposed to anybody else's."[62] América is aware of the tourists' double standards, expecting their rooms to meet their expectations of cleanliness but at the same time demonstrating little regard for the local hired help with their unsanitary carelessness while on vacation.

Like Santiago, Hagedorn likewise represents the manipulation of tourists. In contrast to América, Joey's interactions with tourists are much more intimate and involved. Joey is an entrepreneur within the Philippine tourist industry and must attract clients to ensure his livelihood. In her study of the heritage industry in Sitka, Alaska, anthropologist Celeste Bunten argues that indigenous tour guides develop a commodified persona, a marketable identity for use when working with tourists.[63] Bunten emphasizes that the construction of a commodified persona is an emotionally protective practice. Tourist-industry workers, like Joey, perform their commodified persona on the job and thus separate their real selves from that work. That is, Joey the individual is separate from the commodified persona he sells. This separation allows Joey and his pimp, Andres, to exploit tourists seeking sexual services. When some Australians enter the club, Joey and Andres observe and analyze the men to best market their services: "Middle-aged, okay bodies. They've never been here before. They hesitate—they could turn around and leave and never come back. Andres sizes up the situation. They aren't servicemen. They look classy, yet casual. What Andres calls 'old money'—his favorite kind."[64] As savvy businessmen, their analysis of potential customers determines how they will approach the situation and the commodified persona they will perform. Their ability to read and manipulate their clientele illustrates their understanding of the tourist market. In this case, Andres greets the Australians with the utmost courtesy, using his best English. As expected, this causes the Australians to relax and engage in conversation with Andres at the bar: "Andres stands under a poster of a matador and bull, brought to him all the way from Barcelona by one of his rich lovers. He is chatting amiably with the Australians, asking innocent little questions: *Where are you from? Really? And how do you like Manila?* The Australians loosen up. One of them, the older one, eyes me boldly. I ignore him, smiling to myself. Andres will pick just the right moment to make his introductions."[65] The image of the matador and the bull on the wall serves two purposes. The poster displays a scene readily identified with Spain, a subtle reference to Spanish colonial influence on the Philippines. Hagedorn's reference to Spanish colonialism in the inert form of a poster also illustrates how colonial legacy in the Philippines is packaged culturally, without referencing the violence of Spanish conquest and occupation. Simultaneously, the image symbolizes the power struggle between Andres and the Australians. Although the bull may have more brute strength (representing the Australians' greater economic resources), the matador controls the situation with his distracting red cape, representing Andres' ability to play on the Australians' sexual desires. Joey likewise takes advantage of the situation. The older Australian's bold stares suggest that he is the aggressor. However, his aggression does not equate with power and control. Rather, Joey controls the situation by acting disinterested and forcing the Australian to actively pursue him. By describing how Joey waits for the calculated "right moment" to meet the Australian, Hagedorn illustrates Joey's agency to better negotiate his sexual transactions.

Hagedorn depicts how the development of a commodified persona not only results in simplified constructions of native identity but also stereotypical constructions of foreign tourists. Joey compares Rainer to "God the Father, lost in paradise. He can't get over how perfect I am; he can't get over the perfection of his own creation. He falls in love with me. They always do."[66] The transition from describing Rainer as an individual "he" to the plural "they" signifies the unimportance of Rainer's individuality to Joey. What is important is that Joey can exploit the tourists' expectations to live a life of luxury temporarily. These expectations are premised on the colonial assumptions about the colonized. Filipinos can be considered a colonial "creation" because of the benevolent assimilation policies aimed to help the Philippines become an American-style democracy.[67] That is, Filipinos are created in the image of Americans. Allan Isaac argues that this scene inverts the narcissistic imperial gaze.[68] What the colonizer and foreign tourist desires is their own reflected selves. Joey inverts the power dynamic within his relationship with Rainer by performing a commodified persona that caters to these desires to maximize his benefit.

Political groups also capitalize on tourists' desires. During martial law Marcos expanded the Philippine tourist industry, hoping to establish the legitimacy of his rule. Political groups opposed to martial law targeted tourism to undermine Marcos's rule.[69] Hagedorn reveals the irony of Marcos's failed plans for tourism in a description of Manila's beautification for the International Film Festival as "painted scenery in a slum no one's going to bother visiting—but what the hell, we all get a big bang out of it."[70] Marcos did not address domestic concerns, and so slums arose; instead, he simply covered up these problems to attend to his priority of attracting international tourists. Hagedorn depicts how Marcos's political opposition reacted by targeting tourists to create the image of the Philippines as a dangerous environment, discouraging tourism. Referring to the efforts to beautify Manila as "a big bang," Hagedorn simultaneously critiques Marcos's efforts as a local joke and alludes to an explosion during the 1980 American Society of Travel Agents World Congress held in the Philippines. In his speech, Marcos emphasizes peace and order in the Philippines to encourage tourism to the Philippines. An explosion occurred at the end of his speech. Shortly thereafter, organizers cancelled the conference.[71] These opposition groups successfully turned what was Marcos's political stage into their own. Knowing the importance of safety and security to tourists allowed these political groups to use them as political leverage. Instead of showcasing a safe, orderly Philippines, the conference highlighted the instability of Marcos's government. Hagedorn illustrates how such acts of political terrorism work to subvert the hierarchy that seeks to privilege tourists. In a role reversal, the lives of the tourists become as politically expedient a tool as the lives of the locals buried in the collapsed Film Palace.

Representations of tourist-worker perspectives in *Dogeaters* and *América's Dream* emphasize that these workers are not merely victims of the international tourist industry but that they have the agency to exploit tourist expectations to their own individual advantage. However, this limited agency does not provide a long-term escape from neocolonial economies that continue to exploit working-class Filipinos and Puerto Ricans. Neocolonial economies like the Philippines and Puerto Rico focus on developing industries like tourism that will help infuse their economies with foreign currencies. However, focusing on these industries does not create domestic economic growth that enables social mobility. Tourism may help the Philippine and Puerto Rican economies, but tourism does not allow for development that can transform the unequal colonial relationship that the tourism industry reproduces.

In *Dogeaters*, Joey Sands constantly yearns to escape his life as a prostitute in Manila. However, prostitution also offers him a way out of Manila. He hopes that "[s]ome foreign woman will sponsor me and take me to the States. Maybe she'll marry me. I'll get my green card."[72] After returning to the United States, one of Joey's clients sends him a postcard of Las Vegas. Joey considers writing back and asking his client to send for him. Unlike Filipinos, Puerto Ricans are U.S. citizens. As a U.S. citizen, América manages to achieve that which Joey most desires—she leaves Puerto Rico for New York City. However, despite the fact that América enjoys the benefits of travel to the United States as a U.S. citizen, her move changes the economics of her situation very little. She temporarily works as a nanny before resuming employment as a hotel maid in New York City. Here, Santiago shatters the illusion of the United States as a land of unlimited opportunity and economic mobility. The conditions América faces upon migrating to the United States suggests that Joey would encounter similar limitations if he had the opportunity to migrate there. After all, the postcard Joey receives is from Las Vegas, the only state where prostitution is legal. Thus the characters of Joey and América illustrate how working-class Filipinos and Puerto Ricans travel internationally under circumstances far different from those that bring international tourists to their islands. They travel as laborers, not as tourists. Both characters gesture at how working-class Puerto Ricans and Filipinos are unable to escape their conditions of oppression as colonized people even after their homelands become politically sovereign or upon their own emigration. By tracing the continuity of conditions for Filipinos and Puerto Ricans from the colonial to the postcolonial period, Hagedorn and Santiago argue that the global capitalism, which encourages postcolonial nations to prioritize tourist-industry development over development for the needs of local residents, reproduces colonial inequality. The difference is that postcolonial governments today exploit their own resources and people to participate in the global capitalist economy.

Conclusion

The similarities in rhetoric between *Our Islands and Their People* in 1899 and today's *Lonely Planet: Philippines* and *Lonely Planet: Puerto Rico* underscore the similar ways that Filipinos and Puerto Ricans are packaged for a Western audience. In 1899 and today the Philippines and Puerto Rico are marketed to Western countries for consumption, first as colonies abundant with resources for the U.S. empire, and later as tourist sites abundant with exotic culture and untouched environmental wonders and yet simultaneously convenient. The conveniences—the use of English in both the Philippines and Puerto Rico, and the use of the dollar and lack of customs hassles in Puerto Rico—point to prior or current U.S. colonial policies while at the same time erasing the negative effects of U.S. colonialism. Hagedorn and Santiago contest representations of the Philippines and Puerto Rico by contemporary tourist texts and explicitly link the inequalities caused by colonialism and by tourism in the neocolonial period.

Like *Our Islands and their People* and the *Lonely Planet* guidebooks, *Dogeaters* and *América's Dream* are produced and published in the West, specifically in the United States. Being based in the United States allows Hagedorn and Santiago to contest colonial/tourist representations of the Philippines and Puerto Rico in the space where these representations are produced. The novels' critiques of tourist texts are readily available to those considering travel to the Philippines and Puerto Rico who purchase travel guidebooks for these islands. Unfortunately, availability does not ensure that this critique is given the same legitimacy as travel narratives. Though *Dogeaters* and *América's Dream* offer representations of the Philippines and Puerto Rico, as novels these books are marketed as fiction, not a reliable source of useful information about these islands. Prospective tourists to the Philippines or Puerto Rico would not likely pick up a work of fiction as a research aid for their travels.

Even if the novels were lent equal credence to travel guides or hegemonic historical narratives of the Philippines and Puerto Rico, the critiques by these authors can still be overlooked. They connect the colonial and neocolonial periods in subtle ways—through the characters' ancestry and through colonial buildings or institutions now repurposed for tourists. Without a prior knowledge of U.S. colonialism on these islands, readers can attribute the exploitation that Joey and América face solely to Filipino and Puerto Rican greed. Such a characterization falls neatly into a narrative of U.S. exceptionalism. Filipinos and Puerto Ricans do not know how to manage a democratic society properly on their own, and it is foreign investors in the tourism industry who are philanthropically bringing development to these islands.

The inclusion of Jessica Hagedorn and Esmeralda Santiago in the U.S. multicultural literary canon likewise contributes to the containment of their critiques. Lisa Lowe describes how the canonization of minority literature can serve to contain critiques of U.S. hegemonic culture when such literature is understood only in relation to the majority Anglo-American canon. When minority literary canons are read as a supplement to the majority literary canon, they reproduce notions of multicultural assimilation, notwithstanding the fact that minority literature often can be read also as a challenge to U.S. hegemonic culture.[73]

The popularity and canonization of Hagedorn and Santiago increases the readership of their work, which in turn increases the reach of their representations of U.S. imperialism and neocolonialism. The packaging of the novels *Dogeaters* and *América's Dream* actively obscures this critique. In her analysis of the marketing and perception of ethnic novels, Lori Ween argues that paratexts, including a novel's marketing, jacket art, and reviews, play a much more significant role in framing the public's understanding of a novel.[74] The back cover summary of *Dogeaters* illustrates how an ethnic novel can be packaged as a fun escape into an otherworldly Philippines. The summary description begins with "Welcome to Manila in the turbulent period of the Philippines' late dictator. It is a world in which American pop culture and local Filipino tradition mix flamboyantly."[75] A *San Francisco Chronicle* quote on the front cover dubs the novel a "surrealistically hip epic of Manila," while on the back the *Philadelphia Inquirer* states, "At the end, you emerge from its intense, dreamlike world feeling as if you've been to the Philippines."[76] The last quote from the *San Diego Union* claims that in the novel "Hagedorn transcends social strata, gender, culture, and politics in this exuberant, witty, and telling portrait of Philippine society."[77] Taken together, the reviews allow the novel itself to be packaged as an ideal tourist vacation. It's fun. It's immersive. You will not be overwhelmed with cultural or political hierarchies that result in class and gender inequalities. The novel rises above that fray. Though the summary description references American pop culture, it does not mention how U.S. imperialism enables the popularity of American culture in the Philippines. The packaging suggests that *Dogeaters* and other immigrant novels that represent their countries of origin target the same audience as *Lonely Planet* because both genres offer their American audiences a safe, convenient escape into a different world whose persistent poverty can be blamed on corrupt, postcolonial governments without implicating its audience.

Whereas the packaging of *Dogeaters* contains the novel's critique by framing it as a fun, literary escape akin to an exotic vacation, *América's Dream*'s packaging contains its critique of U.S. imperialism by highlighting its affirmation of the narrative of U.S. exceptionalism that casts the United States as the masculine savior of oppressed women around the world. Chapter 2 will deconstruct the metaphor of colonialism as romance.

2. Revising the Colonialism-as-Romance Metaphor

From Conquest to Neocolonialism

> The metaphor that substitutes rape for colonialism depends on a "code of recognition." Indeed the violence of an imperialism that penetrates and possesses territories, the violation of the colonized, their powerlessness and voicelessness, and the web of desires binding the colonizers and the colonized, can all be recognized in this metaphor.
> —Monique Y. Tschofen, "Post-Colonial Allegory and the Empire of Rape"

Esmeralda Santiago's *América's Dream* and Jessica Hagedorn's *Dogeaters* each contain a particularly brutal rape scene. Not all literary representations of rape are necessarily metaphors for foreign invasion and subjugation, but given the history of U.S. colonialism in Puerto Rico and the Philippines, I argue that the rape victims in these two novels represent their respective island nations. Colonialism has long been understood through gendered and sexualized rhetoric. Masculine explorers conquer native lands, laying claim and penetrating its innermost territories. Through the act of civilizing the land and its natives, European powers reproduced their own cultures and societies.[1]

At the beginning of the twentieth century, U.S. policymakers in favor of and also against the annexation of island territories used heterosexual relationships as a metaphor for the colonial relationship between the United States and its new island territories.[2] U.S. imperialism advocates depicted island territories as females successfully courted by the United States and in need of U.S. protection in their argument that these island territories consented to their colonial subordination. Imagining colonialism as a consensual heterosexual relationship implied that both colonizer and colonized knowingly chose to be together. Gendering the U.S. colonizer as masculine savior and the feminine island colonies as damsels in distress naturalized the unequal nature of the colonial relationship. The female colony knowingly subordinates herself to the imperial power in return for protection and economic resources. Puerto Rico was more regularly represented as a submissive native woman because the United States did not meet with long-term resistance as it had in the Philippines.[3]

What pro-imperialist factions in the United States represented as heterosexual romance, anti-imperialists represented as shotgun or ill-advised marriages, implying the United States' unwise decision to assume unnecessary responsibilities.[4] Anticolonial nationalist movements revise the metaphor to equate colonialism with rape. The metaphor of rape has been deployed in cultural productions time and again to represent colonial conquest, in part because rape captures both the physical destruction that occurs during conquest and the long-term psychic destruction brought on by conquest.[5] The emotional devastation of rape articulates the complex consequences of conquest and subsequent colonial rule. The potency of this metaphor depends on an emotional response to protect the nation's women. In their discussion of how women are positioned in the nation-state Floya Anthias and Nira Yuval-Davis argue that "the nation as a loved woman in danger or as a mother who lost her sons in battle is a frequent part of a particular nationalist discourse in national liberation struggles or other forms of national conflicts when men are called to fight 'for the sake of our women and children' or to 'defend their honour.'"[6] The discourse effectively imbues a nation's people with personal responsibility for preventing the rape of their mother country by outside forces. The metaphor of colonialism as rape has figured prominently in recent high-profile cases wherein U.S. military personnel are accused of rape in the Philippines and Korea.[7] The metaphor of rape as colonialism demonstrates Anne McClintock's argument that all nationalisms depend on constructions of gendered difference. Though women play a significant role in anticolonial nationalist resistance and postcolonial nation building, they are often not represented at the leadership level. For this reason McClintock argues that women are treated as objects in nationalist discourse, not as actors.[8] What women signify (the domestic space, the national family) represents nationalist ideologies.

In *América's Dream*, the rape victim is América. Santiago's naming of the rape victim "América," marking clearly the hispanicized pronunciation of "America," refers to the United States' Spanish Caribbean territory, Puerto Rico. In *Dogeaters*, the rape victim is Daisy Avila, the daughter of Philippine senator Domingo Avila and the recent winner of the teen Philippine beauty queen contest. One of Daisy's responsibilities as a Philippine beauty queen is to represent the Philippines. Hagedorn's naming here is likewise

Uncle Sam as the Philippines' masculine savior. Louis Dalrymple. "He Can't Let Go." *Puck*, November 23, 1898. Found in Abe Ignacio et al., *The Forbidden Book: The Philippine-American War in Political Cartoons* (San Francisco: T'boli, 2004).

significant. A daisy is a flower associated with purity and innocence, while Avila is a fortified city in Spain. Taken together, her name and role as beauty queen indicate that she symbolizes the woman-as-nation who is to be protected from foreign advances. Given the symbolic equation of América with Puerto Rico and Daisy with the Philippines, what do their rapes represent? I argue that in these novels the reading of rape as a straightforward metaphor for colonial conquest is insufficient. Instead, Santiago and Hagedorn rewrite colonial narratives of rape to represent neocolonial subjugation. Through the abusive relationship between América and her lover, Santiago represents how Puerto Rico's economic incorporation into the U.S. economy is obscured by the rise of a cultural nationalism predicated on the disciplining of Puerto Rican women. Hagedorn encapsulates the violent suppression of political opposition during martial law under former President Marcos through the rape of a Philippine teen beauty queen. The United States supported President Marcos and his imposition of martial law until the mid 1980s.

The rapists in both novels are not Americans but Puerto Rican and Filipino men. Therefore, there is a danger of reading América and Daisy's rapes as indicative of the oppressiveness of traditional, patriarchal Puerto Rican and Filipino culture, as opposed to representing the effects of neocolonialism. Hegemonic cultural constructions of rape and of U.S. exceptionalism make the former reading more likely than the latter for an American audience. In the United States, debates over what constitutes rape continue to privilege some acts of sexual violation as legitimate rape. Research on rape reporting argues that rapes that meet the following criteria are most likely to be reported: The victim is female. Her assailant is a male stranger who uses weapons to subdue her. The victim physically resists and there is physical evidence of this resistance. The rape occurs in a public space or in the woman's home as a result of unlawful entry.[9] Rapes that take place under these circumstances are most likely to be reported because they are legitimate rapes by U.S. cultural standards. Racial bias also influences the legitimacy of rapes. Interracial rapes are more readily believed than rapes where the victim and the assailant are of the same race. On the whole, white women are more likely to report rapes than women of color because women of color who are rape victims are more likely to feel unsupported by the criminal justice system.[10] Neither of the two rapes in these novels is interracial. In *Dogeaters* Daisy Avila is raped by Philippine military servicemen in a secret location; in *América's Dream* América is raped by her longtime boyfriend in the hotel room of a family she is babysitting for. Though both rapes are brutal, neither rape is reported—not to the government, not to friends, not to family members. Since these rapes do not conform to U.S. cultural perceptions of rape, they cannot be and so are not publicly legitimated.

Neither do these rapes conform to the classic metaphor of colonialism as rape because these metaphorical rapes have been rewritten to articulate neocolonial power. Both Hagedorn and Santiago represent two rapes in their novels: the unnoticed rape of Puerto Rico and the Philippines and the physical rapes of female characters. The latter rape cannot be fully understood without the former. In the following section I will discuss how Hagedorn and Santiago represent the rape of Puerto Rico and the Philippines through scattered references to United States bases, commodities, movie stars, and news. Such references implicitly convey to the reader the extent to which the United States military and markets have penetrated both areas. This critique of neocolonial power is precarious because it disappears in the absence or erasure of the history of U.S. colonialism in both the Philippines and Puerto Rico.

I will then demonstrate how Santiago and Hagedorn rewrite colonial narratives of rape not only to articulate the complexities of U.S. neocolonialism but also to authorize the raped-woman-as-nation as an active subject. Allegorizing colonialism as rape objectifies women in order to communicate anticolonial nationalist ideology. The metaphor implies that women need male protection and do not have the agency to protect themselves. Women are not national subjects in their own right. Such representations elide the contributions that women make in anticolonial nationalist resistance.[11] These representations take rape as the main action of the national narrative with only two possible outcomes: either the rape of the woman-as-nation is successfully prevented by resistance forces, enabling a patriarchal elite to establish a sovereign nation, or the rape is not averted, symbolizing the unstoppable power of cultural, economic, or political imperialism. Both outcomes leave the woman-as-nation as only an object, and as such she cannot fend off imperialism but can only hope to be saved. As an object, she has no place in imagining a future for the nation, whether or not her rape is prevented. In contrast, I argue that Santiago and Hagedorn authorize América and Daisy respectively through the violence both use eventually to fight back against their rapists. Though these scenes may be read simply as Filipino and Puerto Rican women rising up against corrupt, patriarchal Philippine and Puerto Rican societies, read within the representation of the subtle yet pervasive nature of U.S. influence in the novels the rape victims defensive violence becomes a challenge to continuing U.S. neocolonialism.

The marketing of the novels obscures the gendered critique of neocolonialism that emerges in the authors' updated revision of the metaphor of heterosexual relationship as colonialism. I end this chapter by considering how the narrative of ethnic-women empowerment on the cover of *América's Dream* relies on stereotypes of oppressive, ethnic patriarchy that ultimately reaffirms the hegemonic image of the United States as the masculine savior of oppressed ethnic women. The novel is packaged to erase empire and reproduce U.S. exceptionalism.

A Colonial Web of Desires

In the opening quote to this chapter, Tschofen identifies desire as a product of the colonial encounter that adheres to the imperialism-as-rape metaphor. Chapter 1 examined how colonial travelogues articulated U.S. colonial desires in Puerto Rico and the Philippines through its representations of these islands as alluringly exotic and profitable. Modern-day travel guides also market Puerto Rico and the Philippines as desirable and convenient destinations for the Western leisure traveler. However, creating desire for the United States in Puerto Rico and the Philippines is also a key component in ensuring U.S. neocolonial hegemony. Desire for U.S. commodities, movie stars, and the like becomes emblematic of consent in these regions to be subordinated to the United States. In describing the backdrops for the action of *América's Dream* and *Dogeaters*, both authors convey the extent to which the United States has penetrated Puerto Rico and the Philippines not only militarily and economically but also psychologically.

The novels' numerous references to the U.S. military are reminders not only of the United States military conquests of Puerto Rico and the Philippines but also that the United States retains considerable influence over both areas despite the fact that these former colonies are technically self-governing. Rio, a character in *Dogeaters*, describes the hospital that houses her sick grandfather as a "shabby American Hospital with its drab green walls, drab green smells, and the hovering presence of the hospital's supervising staff of melancholy American doctors. Like my grandfather, they are leftovers from recent wars."[12] This description captures the lingering nausea of rape, in this case the lingering institutional United States presence across the Philippines even after colonial occupation. The repetition of the words "drab, green" in conjunction with the "hovering presence" of the hospital staff give the hospital a supernatural, haunted feel. The passage illustrates the process of historical amnesia. The hospital's patients remain from recent, nameless wars, referencing not only the Japanese invasion of the Philippines, but also to the 1898 Philippine–American war that began U.S. intervention in the Philippines and enabled the establishment of American hospitals there. Hagedorn repeats the motif of military haunting of the Philippines later in the novel, when Joey Sands asks some of his U.S. military clients, "'Is that your ship?' I point to the ghostly carrier floating in the middle of the dark sea."[13] The carrier looms not only as a reminder of military influence both past and present, but also as a threat. At any time the carrier can turn on the local Filipino population should any activity threaten U.S. interests.

Santiago likewise points to the history of the U.S. military in Vieques, the backdrop for the first half of the novel. As América walks around the island, an omniscient narrator conveys the differing layers of colonial histories on the island: "when the U.S. Navy appropriated two-thirds of the island for its maneuvers, the great sugar haciendas disappeared and the tall stacks that dotted the island were bulldozed out of the way. This is history, and América doesn't think about it as she walks the slope of the narrow road."[14] The great sugar haciendas the narrator refers to hearken back to Spanish colonial rule, when the Puerto Rican economy centered on the production of sugar. The appropriation of the island for U.S. military maneuvers, a euphemism for military bomb testing, demonstrates the United States' control of Puerto Rico.[15] However, just as in *Dogeaters*, the narrator does not specify the origins of the colonial relationship between Puerto Rico and the United States. Instead, the narrator dubs this background to be a history that does not even register for locals like América. In both novels U.S. neocolonialism is so pervasive that the characters no longer perceive U.S. military and economic presence as out of place.

Not only is the military presence in the Philippines and Puerto Rico the coercive arm of U.S. neocolonialism in these areas, but it also enables the free flow of U.S. commodities into these areas. The abundance of U.S. commodities in Puerto Rico and the Philippines indicates the ubiquitous presence of U.S. imperialism. Both authors reference the U.S. Navy PX, small stores on military bases that provide American goods for the men and women stationed at the base. In *América's Dream*, América's boyfriend, Correa, gives her a gift from the PX after severely beating her a few days earlier. Although "Correa is not a soldier, a veteran, or an employee of the U.S. Armed Forces . . . somehow Correa can shop at the Navy PX."[16] Likewise, the reference to the PX in *Dogeaters* also implies illicit dealings. Joey buys new speakers for CocoRico, the club where he works. The speakers "look good—beautiful, black and cool," and to top it off Joey "bought them hot from some American guy with connections at the PX."[17] Both quotes represent the desire for U.S. commodities. The authors intentionally point out that these commodities were purchased from a military base, suggesting that the value of these commodities' is enhanced by their origin. This explicit link between the military and the desire for U.S. commodities reveals how U.S. military bases enable the penetration of U.S. commodities into local markets.

Military imperialism is not the only method by which U.S. goods penetrate into Puerto Rico and the Philippines. Hagedorn conveys the workings of cultural imperialism in *Dogeaters* by creating a world that is thoroughly obsessed with American movie stars and their movies. She emphasizes the popularity of epic American films like *The Ten Commandments* in a character's casual observation that the film "played to packed houses in Manila for what seemed to be an eternity."[18] After watching another American film, *All that Heaven Allows*, two characters discuss the acting in the movie and marvel at Gloria Talbot's "cool indifference, the offhand way she treats her grieving mother. Her casual arrogance seems inherently American, modern, and enviable."[19] *The Ten Commandments* and *All that Heaven Allows* are classic American movies whose popularity cannot be attributed to their recent release. The popularity of such classic films underscores Filipinos' inherent fascination with all aspects of U.S. culture, not just contemporary culture. Another character dreams of riding in a car "like in those American commercials where the road is endless and smooth, empty of other cars, trucks, buses, jeepneys, pedicabs, barefoot boys riding slow, plodding *carabao*.[20] These representations of the United States mediate a sense of what is American for the Philippine public, and Americanness is constructed in opposition to the Philippines. Unlike the Philippines and Filipinos, the United States as a nation and Americans as a people are modern and enviable. This obsession for anything and everything American captures rape's psychological violence: the devaluation of self and the belief that such violence is necessary, even desirable.[21]

Both *América's Dream* and *Dogeaters* convey the obsession with American name brands in Puerto Rico and the Philippines. Hagedorn lists the items that one woman buys for a party to be held at the American consul: "Del Monte De Luxe Asparagus Spears, two bottles Hunt's Catsup, one jar French's Mustard, Miracle Whip Sandwich Spread, Kraft Mayonnaise, Bonnie Bell Sweet Sliced Pickles, Jiffy Peanut Butter, packages of Velveeta, party-size bags of Cheez Whiz, one box of Nabisco Ritz Crackers, and several boxes of Jell-O gelatin."[22] Specifying the name brands of the items illustrates the importance placed on these particular brands. It is not enough to buy mayonnaise, but one must buy Kraft Mayonnaise, especially when entertaining. In *América's Dream*, everyday items are also referred to with their brand names, not generically. In describing the breakfast that América makes for her daughter, Rosalinda, Santiago refers to it specifically as "Rice Krispies with sliced banana," not merely as cereal with sliced banana.[23] Her mother drinks "a frosty Budweiser," not just beer.[24] América drinks Coke, not soda.[25] These may seem like small points, but taken together, specifying the U.S. brand name instead of referring only to the item's regular name demonstrates how integrated brand-name products are in the lives of Puerto Ricans and reveals the saturation of U.S. commodities in Puerto Rican markets.

These references to U.S. military, cultural, and economic imperialism in Puerto Rico and the Philippines are lodged in the background of these novels but play an important role in contextualizing the action of the novels. Santiago and Hagedorn give the historical background of conquest in these descriptions, thus articulating the symbolic rape and domination of Puerto Rico and the Philippines by the United States. Just as the trauma of rape remains after the act, U.S. colonialism permeates everyday life of Puerto Ricans and Filipinos over time. These implicit, symbolic rapes sets the stage for the physical rape scenes in the novels.

The Taking of América, Whenever and However

Through the metaphor of rape, *América's Dream* not only foregrounds the violence inflicted on Puerto Rico since it became a U.S. possession but also critiques the Partido Popular Demócratico's role in thwarting Puerto Rican political nationalist movements and replacing them with a cultural nationalism that is complicit with U.S. interests in Puerto Rico. Luis Muñoz Marin, governor of Puerto Rico and head of the Partido Popular Demócratico when the island became a commonwealth, believed that Puerto Rico's economic progress depended on continued association with the United States, but he felt that Puerto Rico needed to develop a strong cultural nationalism to be recognized as an independent entity internationally. To these ends, Muñoz Marin implemented Operation Bootstrap and Operation Serenity. Operation Bootstrap was designed to urbanize Puerto Rico in order to attract U.S. corporations to open factories on the island, facilitating the further incorporation of Puerto Rico into the U.S. economy, whereas Operation Serenity advocated for the preservation of a distinct Puerto Rican culture. Muñoz Marin defined culture in the broadest sense. For him Puerto Rican culture included the attitudes, habits, and values of the Puerto Rican community. Taken together, the two programs disconnected Puerto Rican's strong cultural nationalism from calls for political sovereignty and allowed Muñoz Marin to emphasize that culture was to be separated from political status.[26]

Hence, whereas the colonialism-as-rape metaphor requires an American man, symbolized by United States, to rape a woman—Puerto Rico, as represented by América—here América's Puerto Rican boyfriend Correa rapes her.

"Correa" translates into English as "belt" or "leash." Thus Correa's character can be read as the mechanism that disciplines América-as–Puerto Rico to comply with subordination to U.S. interests. Santiago therefore encapsulates the semblance of political rule Puerto Rico is given as a commonwealth.

A brief account of América's life before Correa arrives on the scene describes her neighborhood:

> [B]efore it got built up, . . . every house was set back behind broad yards, surrounded by mango, breadfruit, and avocado trees. Before urbanization. They didn't have running water then, or electricity. The road was a dusty path in winter and a treacherous, muddy trail when it rained.
>
> Correa had come to the barriada with the contractors improving the roads, stringing electric wires from tall poles, digging up ditches to lay pipes for running water and sewers. Correa was a man, Odilio Pagán a boy, and América a girl who hadn't seen much. La conquista, the seduction, didn't take long."[27]

Mention of mango, breadfruit, and avocado trees emphasizes how abundantly fertile the neighborhood's land is. Describing the "broad yards" indicates that neighborhood residents all owned ample property and benefited from the productivity of the land. This description advertises América's neighborhood as perfect and ripe for exploitation. Its inaccessibility stands as the only obstacle to harnessing this vast, fertile land. Development promises to defeat this obstacle. One of the touted benefits of colonization was the promise of progress, in this case urbanization. Muñoz Marin implemented Operation Bootstrap in order to develop the Puerto Rican economy through urbanization and industrialization. Before Operation Bootstrap the Puerto Rican economy centered on agrarian capitalism.[28]

Operation Bootstrap also facilitated the further incorporation of Puerto Rico into the United States economy after World War II by creating incentives for U.S. businesses. Santiago articulates Muñoz Marin and the Partido Popular Demócratico's complicity with U.S. interests in the above excerpt. Development marks Correa's arrival in América's life, as development signaled Puerto Rico's economic integration into U.S. industry. Before Correa came, América's neighborhood lacked the luxuries of industrialization. Along with taming the wilderness by bringing the order of civilization, Correa also claims América. Development is superimposed with the image of sexual conquest. This moment is described in the passage as "La conquista, the seduction." It appears that Santiago is offering a translation here. In Spanish, *conquista* can mean both conquest and seduction. By choosing to translate *conquista* as only seduction, Santiago deftly demonstrates how from the U.S. perspective conquest can be understood only as consensual romance. Constructing conquest as romance easily masks the workings of power and subordination.[29]

Correa embodies both Operation Bootstrap and Operation Serenity. He is the agent who not only brings urbanization to América's neighborhood but also marks boundaries of acceptable behavior for América. These boundaries reflect the rigorous requirements of Puerto Rican cultural nationalism and point to how Puerto Rico is complicit in its own subordination. Correa considers América's associations with anyone who can help her gain a sense of independence unacceptable. He disapproves of América working closely with the Leveretts, an American family from New York vacationing in Puerto Rico, because he equates the United States with independent-minded women. He does not allow América to go to New York because Puerto Rican women who go to the United States "come back behaving like Americanas, and he doesn't like Americanas. 'Our Portorras,' he says, 'the old-fashioned ones I'm talking about, know how to treat a man, they know the meaning of the word *respect*. Our women,' he tells his friends, 'are well trained.'"[30] The refusal to let América go to the United States reflects how members of the Puerto Rican diaspora in the United States are considered already culturally tainted, and the anxiety over América's exposure to U.S. ideas reflects the goal of Puerto Rican cultural nationalism to disassociate the United States from Puerto Rican cultural identity.

Santiago references more than just allegorical violence in portraying América as a battered woman. The disconnection between cultural nationalism and political resistance in Puerto Rico tangibly affects working-class women like América. In the nation-state, women are expected to reproduce not only the nation's citizens but also national culture.[31] Fervent Puerto Rican cultural nationalism disciplines Puerto Rican women to adhere to "traditional" Puerto Rican culture. Thus, women in Puerto Rican literature are either depicted as defenders of Puerto Rican cultural values or as the individuals who bring shame to the family through sexual immorality, which is seen as a consequence of U.S. modernization.[32] In other words, the woman either conforms or does not conform to Puerto Rican traditional, patriarchal values. Such a dichotomy renders feminists in Puerto Rico culturally suspect. The link between female empowerment and national cultural erosion erects further barriers to the empowerment of women like América. Correa's violence toward América illustrates the violence against women inherent in normalizing patriarchy as a vital component of a distinct Puerto Rican culture.

As América works more for the Leveretts, her exposure to what Correa dubs "Americana" behavior increases, and she becomes culturally suspect. By taking care of the Leverett children in her spare time, América also augments her hotel-maid wages, increasing her economic independence from Correa. The Leveretts pose a threat to Correa because América chooses to spend her free time working for them instead of serving him. This threat brings Correa to the hotel where América looks after the Leverett children in a bid to reassert his power over América. Here, both children sleep peacefully: "Kyle turns over, holds his teddy bear closer [and] Meghan sucks on her thumb."[33] The first signs of Correa's aggression immediately follow this portrayal of youthful innocence. He "shoves [América] onto the bed, climbs on top of her, scratches her with clawed fingers, bites her thighs, her belly, her breasts."[34] His violence transforms him from man to savage animal. His nails become claws and he bites her everywhere uncontrollably. By juxtaposing the image of sleeping American children and América's rape, Santiago emphasizes how easily the United States can claim innocence from so-called Puerto Rican domestic problems when these problems are not contextualized within a history of U.S. imperialism. The fact that América's rape does not conform to the narrative of a classic rape further delegitimizes both the literal and metaphoric violence. América is raped by her boyfriend, whom she knows to be violent and controlling. Women who are raped by their husbands or boyfriends of many years are often accused of enabling their own rapes by tolerating domestic abuse.[35] Metaphorically, the hegemonic rape narrative further places the blame on Puerto Rican patriarchal culture that violently exploits América-as-Puerto Rico.

Santiago critiques Puerto Rico's semblance of sovereignty through América's frequent assertions of independence. Throughout the novel, América repeatedly states, "It's my life," although it becomes increasingly clear she has no control over her life. The text interweaves this mantra with the violence Correa inflicts on América to inhibit her freedom. When the Leveretts offer América a job in their Westchester, New York, home, she first considers what Correa's reaction to the job offer will be, knowing that he would not approve of such a move. She fears most the violence she knows he will use to keep her in Vieques. Considering his reaction before contemplating what benefits and opportunities the job offers her illustrates how Correa's violence dictates and controls América's actions. After ruminating on his violence, she declares, "I'll not show up for work one day, and a week later they'll get a postcard with a picture of a tall building or something. No one has to know my business. It's my life." Although she claims control over her life, her desire to leave without warning does not result from a need for privacy but from her fear of Correa's violence.

América's limited economic opportunities and the routine physical and psychological abuse she endures illustrates how U.S. imperialism's symbolic rape of Puerto Rico makes this colonized space so unbearable for Puerto Ricans that the United States becomes a place of freedom for them. Just as battered women often constantly return to the men who oppress them because they believe the violence is their own fault, Puerto Rican emigrants flee to the land that actively enables their oppression.[36] After her brutal rape, América asserts her subjectivity by escaping Correa and leaving for the United States to be the Leveretts' domestic worker. Even though U.S. imperialism creates the conditions that necessitate Puerto Rican migration, read simply, the positioning of the United States as safe haven for a battered América reinforces constructions of U.S. benevolence, gender equality, and oppressive third-world patriarchies. These hegemonic cultural narratives obscure the reading of América's rape as a metaphor for U.S. neocolonialism.

Further buttressing the construction of irrational and oppressive third-world patriarchies, Correa's violence still inhibits América even after she flees to New York and establishes an independent life. As she speaks to her mother on the phone, the mere mention of Correa's name is enough to bring on "a chill, a thud at the pit of her stomach."[37] Even when her distance from Correa decreases the possibility of his violence, she still fears him. In spite of this uncontrollable fear, she assures herself by once again claiming "I'm alone, and it's my life, and I'm not going to let them spoil it anymore."[38] To the contrary, this scene illustrates that América's life is still not her own because her fear controls her. The mainland United States offers no comfort for América. However, this scene can be understood as not merely upholding hegemonic understanding of the oppressive third world and U.S. benevolence. Read within the context of Operation Serenity and Operation Bootstrap, Correa's desire to still control América in the United States underscores how Operation Serenity's cultural nationalism functions as a disciplinary mechanism for the Puerto Rican diaspora, particularly females. Also, América's move to the United States does not result in her own socioeconomic mobility. In the United States she is still a domestic worker and is no more immune to fear or economic subordination in the United States than she was in Puerto Rico. Santiago depicts the continuity of América's fear and disadvantaged economic position to comment on how Puerto Rico's colonial legacy follows those in the Puerto Rican diaspora who came to the United States as laborers.

For Santiago, escaping Puerto Rico is not the answer to ending the destructive effects of U.S. colonialism once and for all. *América's Dream* imagines a different future for the woman-as-nation. As América plans to escape from Correa's violent love once more, she decides to "change her name to Margarita, in honor of her great-great-great grandmother. Her last name will be Guerra, for war."[39] A common practice of decolonization is to renounce names imposed by the colonizing power. America was the name given to the "New World" in honor of Amerigo Vespucci. Therefore her name, América, bears the weight of colonial history. She breaks the shackles of patriarchy by refusing to be named after a man, and she breaks the shackles of colonialism by refusing her given name. Instead, she chooses the name of a matrilineal ancestor, suggesting that her struggle is as much for the past as it is for herself. Her surname of choice, Guerra, foreshadows the violent measures necessary in order for her to successfully win her independence from Correa. Santiago explicitly maps out a feminist agenda here. Instead of representing the Puerto Rican nation, América actively chooses to represent exploited Puerto Rican women.

In América's final confrontation with Correa, Santiago implies that gendered colonial violence can be opposed only with violence. After he locates her in the United States, it seems certain that Correa will murder América: "He comes around to face her, and she can't recognize him. No, this can't be him, this can't be, his green eyes so dark, so savage. There's no love there. It's hate she sees, hate that she feels as she uses her last bit of strength to kick him hard in the one place she knows she can hurt him, between his hairy legs. He doubles over with a groan, and she kicks again, connects against his lowered face this time, and he turns and falls. There's a crack, like a twig breaking."[40] A sense of denial pervades this passage. The repetition of the word "can't" illustrates that América cannot accept that she mistook his violence for love all those years. In place of her lover is a savage, dark-eyed animal. At this point, the myth of romance disappears. The appearance of love gives way to the reciprocal hate she uses to attack him. América directs her first violent act against Correa at his sexual organs. This act is in direct opposition to the image of América as a willing sexual partner, emphasizing her refusal to be victim once more to rape for either nationalist or colonial purposes. To insure her own safety, she must kill Correa, because merely injuring him would guarantee further violence. Understood through the woman-as-nation metaphor, América's defensive violence translates to insurrection, a crime often punishable by death. América-as-Puerto Rico murders Correa and in doing so destroys the image of Puerto Rico as a lover who willingly subordinates herself to U.S. neocolonial interests. She also attacks the patriarchy inherent in Puerto Rican cultural nationalism. Santiago argues for a complete revolution in giving América-as-Puerto-Rico agency, one that authorizes Puerto Rican women to challenge their subordination.

América's Dream represents rape as an allegory for both the United States' colonial exploitation of Puerto Rico and the complicity of Puerto Rican cultural nationalism in Puerto Rico's subordination. The novel imagines a future where Puerto Rico fights for independence and puts an end to these abuses. The novel complicates this ideal vision of fighting for complete independence. At the end of the novel América asserts once more, "It is, after all, her life, and she's the one in the middle of it," while examining the scars Correa left on her face in the mirror of a New York hotel where she now works.[41] Her scars remind her of how she fought and won her independence, but she is still subordinated by the U.S. economy working as a hotel maid. The novel ends with a warning that revolution is not complete without economic independence because imperialism can assume an economic guise. If Puerto Rico would ever became a sovereign nation, it still runs the risk of remaining politically and economically dependent on the United States. The Philippines' continuing dependence on the United States is a perfect case in point, to which I will now turn.

Martial Law–Sanctioned Rape

The United States granted the Philippines independence in 1946, but the United States continued to protect its interests in the area by supporting a Filipino government sympathetic to U.S. interests and insisting on uneven economic and political agreements. U.S. intervention in early Filipino presidential elections further solidified U.S. influence. The United States supported President Marcos's imposition of martial law and was aware of Marcos's plans for martial law five days before it started.[42] U.S. businesses in the area sent Marcos a telegram expressing their support. In these ways and others, U.S. hegemony continues in the postcolonial Philippines. In *Dogeaters*, a gang of Filipino military men rape an abdicated Philippine teen beauty queen. As in *América's Dream*, Hagedorn's rewrite of the literary narrative of rape depends on the physical rape being read in conjunction with colonialism's symbolic rape and points to the complicity of an elite, male-dominated Philippine government in continuing to oppress the Philippine people. Otherwise, the rape scene can be read simply as a representation of Philippine government corruption and violent suppression of opposition.

In her examination of literary representations of rape during British colonial rule in India, Jenny Sharpe argues that such representations were deployed at strategic moments to articulate political anxieties.[43] Daisy Avila's rape in Jessica Hagedorn's *Dogeaters* focuses on a particular moment of political trauma in Philippine history, the assassination of Senator Benigno Aquino Jr., the primary and most powerful figure opposing President Marcos's imposition of martial law. In revising the rape-as-colonialism metaphor to represent this particular historic moment, Daisy's body becomes a site where political antagonism and violence against Senator Aquino is carried out.

Hagedorn introduces us to Daisy's character after a mock newspaper article describing the latest demonstration against the Filipino government's disrespect for human rights by her father, Senator Domingo Avila. This introduction takes the form of a flashback, giving us a quick summary of the events leading to her father's death and her rape: "Before her twentieth birthday, before she marries a foreigner in haste and just as hastily leaves him, before she is given the name *Mutya* by her guerilla lover in the mountains, Daisy Consuelo Avila is crowned the most beautiful woman in the Philippines."[44] Marking Daisy's coronation as the beginning of her story, we receive no knowledge of her life prior to this event. Her body is only significant when identified with her father and through her coronation, when she becomes a symbol of Filipino national identity. Literary scholar Allan Isaac argues that this passage represents Daisy as a ghostly trace or a passive subject that has been disappeared by U.S. imperialism. He points to how Daisy is further eclipsed by a description of the Philippine natural and sociopolitical landscape that immediately follows her introduction[45] and mentions at length Senator Avila's concerns for the Philippines: "Senator Avila declares that our torrid green world is threatened by its legacy of colonialism and the desire for revenge. He foretells more suffering in his eloquent speeches, which fall on deaf ears. He is ridiculed and vilified in the government-run newspaper.... He describes us as a complex nation of cynics, descendants of warring tribes which were baptized and colonized to death by Spaniards and Americans."[46]

Hagedorn's careful choice of wording here relies on a vocabulary of religious apocalypse. Senator Avila is a prophet warning of an upcoming day of reckoning. The adjective "torrid" accurately describes the Philippines' tropical climate, but it also alludes subtly to hell's heat and to illicit passion. Avila speaks of colonialism's legacy and the desire for revenge as sins that must be atoned for through more suffering. The senator uses religious vocabulary to argue for social change that will finally free Filipinos from their colonial legacy. Ironically, the imagery and metaphors used here are only comprehensible to Filipinos precisely because Spanish colonialism imported and instituted Roman Catholicism to the Philippines. The prophetic language Hagedorn deploys in this passage foreshadows the social disorder surrounding the senator's assassination.

In Hagedorn's description of Senator Avila as an opposition leader to the dictator-managed Philippine government and as a politician who advocates further decolonization, she clearly references the late Senator Aquino. Like the character Senator Avila, Aquino traced present-day Filipino problems back to colonialism and saw Marcos's regime as another form of colonial rule. Aquino's popularity among the Filipino people made President Marcos and his supporters resort to accusing Aquino of being a communist sympathizer and a CIA spy to discredit him and cast doubt on his loyalty to the Philippines.[47] Hagedorn also constructs Senator Avila's character as a threat to the novel's Philippine dictator. As in the case of the Philippines during martial law, the dictator controls the media in *Dogeaters* and uses the media to link Senator Avila to communists. The newspaper article preceding Daisy's introduction reports that charges against "Avila and his leftist cohorts" are filed.[48]

The similarities between the official government account of Senator Avila's assassination in *Dogeaters* and that of Senator Aquino's further suggest that the novel's character is a fictional representation of Benigno Aquino. In an interview with the First Lady, a reporter names Orlando Rosales, another character in the novel, as Avila's accused assassin. His motive for killing Senator Avila is not clearly stated; his links to "a group of subversives in the Cordilleras" determines his guilt.[49] There is no way to refute the accusation because Rosales conveniently "was shot down in the middle of a busy intersection, in broad daylight."[50] Hagedorn makes it clear that Senator Avila's actual murderers work for the government. A witness to the murder, Joey Sands, watches Senator Avila die and notes that his murderer wears "regulation sunglasses," suggesting that the murderer is part of the Philippine military.[51] Given that the military is tightly controlled by the Philippine dictator, Hagedorn implies that the dictator was privy to, or ordered, the Avila assassination.

Aquino's assassination took place when he returned to the Philippines after a three-year exile in the United States. Shots rang out as he descended from the airplane. The Philippine military conveniently killed Rolando Galman, the man they deemed the main suspect in Aquino's murder, eliminating opportunities for questioning him. Galman was described as having communist ties, thus casting the guilt away from the government and toward Marcos's opposition. However, the government's official account of Aquino's assassination did not hold up. Inconsistencies in the story and investigations by Japanese newspapers eventually proved that the military assassinated Senator Aquino and convinced the populace of Marcos's involvement in the affair.[52] Although Hagedorn makes it clear that her character Senator Avila and the details of his assassination reference the circumstances of Senator Aqunio's assassination, *Dogeaters* does not simply reiterate Filipino history. Rather, Hagedorn actively rewrites Filipino history here, squarely pinning the responsibility for Senator Aquino's assassination on Marcos by imagining the individual stories that Marcos could have easily silenced in order to maintain his innocence. By representing myriad perspectives of the Avila assassination alongside the rape of Daisy-as-the-Philippines, Hagedorn also emphasizes that Marcos's violence affected not only high-profile figures like Senator Aquino but the Filipino people as a whole.

In her discussion of political cartoons during the American Revolution, Shirley Samuels argues that political threat and its violent suppression manifests in cultural representations as violence against the woman-as-nation.[53] Against a background of political turmoil, Daisy participates and claims victory in a national beauty pageant. Sarah Banet-Weiser discusses how the Miss America beauty pageants attempt to resolve national anxieties regarding gender and race through performances highlighting diversity and femininity. Therefore, the body of the beauty queen becomes a site where national crises or debates over what constitutes the national culture can be fought or resolved. National crises can be resolved only if the female body dutifully represents the accepted notion of femininity and national culture.[54] I extend Banet-Weiser's analysis of beauty pageants' reconciling potential to examine Daisy Avila's role as beauty queen in *Dogeaters*. Daisy's coronation offers a resolution to Avila's challenge of the dictator's power. The pageant, "a government-endorsed beauty contest run by the First Lady," encapsulates a Filipino national identity that the dictator endorses.[55] Being a Filipino beauty queen requires Daisy to perform and conform to the accepted ideas of Filipino femininity and national culture. Crowning Daisy a Filipino beauty queen works in the dictator's interests because Senator Avila's permission for Daisy to compete for and be the beauty queen can be interpreted as his acceptance of the dictator's rule.

The talent portion of the beauty pageant reveals government-endorsed notions of Filipino national identity. Beauty pageant contestants carefully select what talents to perform. The contestant's performance must illustrate a refined talent that falls within boundaries of national acceptability and conveys to the audience her independence—but not her outspoken feminism.[56] Daisy does not push the limits; she "recites two florid sonnets by Elizabeth Barrett Browning from memory, and also sings a tentative '*Dahil Sa Iyo.*'"[57] Her recitation of canonical English poetry illustrates her familiarity with supposed high, refined culture. The novel does not specify which sonnets Daisy chooses to recite, but characterizing the sonnets as "florid" indicates a degree of excess showiness. On Daisy's part, choosing these sonnets illustrate her desire to display her command of Western culture. In contrast, Senator Avila denounces the desire to identify with "refined" Western culture, claiming that "Pinoys suffer collectively from a cultural inferiority complex. We are doomed by our need for assimilation into the West."⁵⁸ Instead of struggling against this form of cultural imperialism, Daisy performs it as an indicator of national identity.

"Dahil Sa Iyo," the song Daisy chooses to sing, is a popular Tagalog love song and categorized as OPM (Original Pilipino Music). The creation of OPM in the 1970s grew out of the growing awareness that there was no original Filipino-made music. These songs may be original Filipino creations and contain Tagalog lyrics, but they strongly reflect Western influence on the Philippines in structure and style. Thus, in singing "Dahil Sa Iyo," Daisy further emphasizes the importance of Western culture to Filipino national identity. However, the song title "Dahil Sa Iyo" also refers to Filipino nationalism, as a phrase taken from the last line of the Filipino National Anthem: "Ang mamatay ng dahil sa iyo." This line, translated roughly into English, means "I would die because of you," with the addressed subject as the Philippines.⁵⁹ This line foreshadows Avila's eventual assassination. The "senator cringes during the talent competition" because his daughter performs an idea of Filipino national identity that privileges and imitates Western culture.⁶⁰ He opposes Filipino cultural self-degradation and the self-inflicted cultural imperialism celebrated in the beauty pageant.

Daisy performs a specified femininity and nationality for consumption and wins the title of Young Miss Philippines. Her duty as queen includes the continued performance of this role, undermining her father's efforts and resolving the political crisis between the dictator and his most outspoken opponent. However, Daisy's body does not offer an easy resolution to the political threat that Avila presents to the dictator. After her coronation, Daisy inexplicably refuses to perform the responsibilities accompanying her crown. Instead, she goes into hiding. Her irresolute loyalty to her crown erases any possibility of conflict resolution because the resolution to political instability depends on the presentation of a stable woman to represent the nation.⁶¹ Her sudden and prolonged disappearance from the public eye leaves the pageant's sponsors "furious" at her. "Her stubbornness has already cost them millions of pesos. A scheduled whirlwind tour of the provinces is indefinitely postponed, and Daisy's cameo role in the upcoming Tito Alvarez–Lolita Luna disco-dance drama *Loverboy* is cancelled."⁶² She is no longer an available national commodity. She does not possess the desired stability for portraying a unified, unchanging, and unchallenged national identity. Instead of playing a role, Daisy chooses to break out of it. In her first public appearance she "seizes the opportunity to publicly denounce the beauty pageant as a farce, a giant step backward for all women"⁶³ Rather than symbolically bridging the differences between her father and the dictator to represent a unified nation,

Daisy underscores the differences between the dictator and his opposition, revealing national divisions.

After rejecting her crown, Daisy quickly becomes involved with two different men. These men are metaphors for President Marcos's reactions to financial trouble in the early 1980s. During the 1960s and 1970s, the Marcos regime developed an economic strategy that relied heavily on supporting the United States in the Vietnam-American War. After the withdrawal of U.S. troops from Vietnam in 1975, Marcos needed to find alternate sources of financial support. Daisy's relations with men after refusing her pageant crown serves as an allegory for Marcos's struggle to keep his political power amid economic turmoil. Her first husband, a foreign banker named Malcolm Webb, represents Marcos's acquisition of international monetary aid in the early 1980s. International funding resulted in only a short-lived relief to the Philippine economy.[64] Her marriage, like the economic relief from international funding, is brief, and the blame falls on her shoulders when she and Malcolm separate. The weak Philippine economy agitated the urban poor and resulted in increased support for the CPP (Communist Party of the Philippines). Daisy's second suitor, Santos Tirador, embodies the Communist Party's political threat to Marcos, especially in his "involvement in the recent ambush on PC (Philippine Constabulary)."[65] Thus, Daisy and Tirador's relationship can be read as the fear of the Communist Party's seduction of the Philippines. Daisy strays too far from the acceptable boundaries of behavior. She and Malcom Webb never officially divorce, making her relations with Santos Tirador an extramarital affair. Beauty queens are expected to portray a modest sexuality to exhibit their respectability.[66] In a letter to Daisy, her cousin Clarita prophetically warns her to not "be shocked by how much you are going to suffer. After all, you're still a married woman in everyone's eyes."[67] For defying the accepted notions of Filipino femininity and culture, Daisy suffers dearly.

Daisy's rape symbolizes Marcos's moves to suppress his political opposition. Members of the Philippine military take turns raping her at a camp for political subversives: "Colonel Jesus de Jesus asks to be first. He assaults her for so long and with such force, Daisy prays silently to pass out. Her prayers go unanswered. The other men crack jokes, awaiting their turn. 'Lover boy *talaga*,' one of the officers grunts in admiration. When he is finished, the baby-faced Colonel licks Daisy's neck and face. 'My woman,' he announces, heaving himself off her. The room starts to stink of sperm and sweat. The President's aide is next."[68] The name, Colonel Jesus de Jesus, references Catholicism in the Philippines. Ironically, Jesus is not sent to save Daisy but to violently subdue her. In much the same way, Spain subdued the Philippines through the use of Catholicism. Catholic friars were charged with converting Filipinos and enjoyed a great deal of authority over them, especially in the rural areas. Toward the end of Spanish rule, the main charge laid against Spanish colonization by Filipino reformists and nationalists was the abuse of power by corrupt friars.[69] Though the Spanish believed they were saving Filipinos by converting them to Catholicism, in reality Catholicism subdued and maintained order in the Philippines. Through this religious reference, Hagedorn makes Spain and Catholicism complicit in the rape of Daisy-as-Philippines. The presence of the dictator's aid also clearly implicates the dictator's culpability in Daisy's violent punishment.

Daisy is repeatedly raped not only to punish her for refusing to play the role of a proper Philippine beauty queen and for her perceived marital infidelity but also to symbolize President Marcos's violent suppression of his political opposition. In fact, women imprisoned for participating in social movements opposing President Marcos were often gang raped by their captors. Such actions were justified by equating their disloyal political ideologies with sexual excess.[70] By freely entering into a relationship with a member of the political opposition, Daisy-as-Philippines represents the nation that no longer wants martial law. Only by rape can she be suppressed back into the role of "My woman," a possession. Just as Correa's violence stole América's independence so that she exists only in relation to Correa, as "Correa's woman," rape also takes away Daisy's individuality. Gang raping Daisy signifies Marcos and the ruling elite's desire to reclaim her body and thus regain control of the Philippines. Before her rape, she learns of Santos Tirador's murder. A general shows her photographs of Tirador's disfigured, dead body, pointing out "the young man's mashed testicles, the close-up of his gouged-out eyes."[71] In order to halt her sexual infidelity, it was necessary to murder him. His mutilated genitals clearly illustrate Santos's sexual threat and the anger resulting from the fear of sexual inadequacy. By elaborating on the violence against Santos Tirador, Hagedorn illustrates how official Philippine nationalism, in this case that which was sanctioned by Marcos, not only requires disciplining the woman-as-nation but also necessitates violence against social movements that threaten his position.

All interactions between the military and Daisy are bracketed, in bold print. These interactions are interwoven with a popular radio serial program called *Love Letters*. Hagedorn's structural style in this passage critiques Marcos's use of political theatrics to distract Filipinos from his involvement in Aquino's assassination. After evidence refuting Marcos's claim that Galman shot Aquino surfaced, he formed an investigative panel (that lacked credibility) in order to buy time, hoping that public discontent would die down.

A second panel reached a split decision after a lengthy investigation and discussion.[72] The inconclusive findings of these panels aggravated Filipinos further, and after Aquino's death the seeds of resistance bore fruit. Aquino's death led eventually to the first People Power Movement that removed Marcos from the presidential office and sent him into exile in Hawaii.

The rape scene does not explicitly implicate any character that might represent the United States. Specifically implicating Spanish imperialism and the dictator's corrupt government in this rape allows for the United States to escape explicit culpability here and maintains hegemonic narratives of U.S. exceptionalism and third-world corruption. However, the absence of explicit U.S. participation demonstrates how this rape scene serves as a metaphor for U.S. neocolonialism. The lack of official political ties allows for plausible deniability for its role in the economic and military subordination that maintains U.S. interests in the Philippines and Asia.

Our last glimpse of Daisy, hidden away in the mountains, foregrounds other forms of resistance to Marcos besides the official resistance of People Power that is recognized and legitimized by the media, by history, and by international world leaders. Despite the success of this movement and the end of Marcos's despotic rule, many problems in the Philippines have not been addressed. Economic disparities between the rich and the poor have not been bridged. There are few employment opportunities in the Philippines that offer a living wage.[73] Through Daisy's retreat to the mountain guerrillas, Hagedorn recognizes these guerilla fighters as enacting a legitimate resistance, directly contradicting how the Philippine government and international media negatively construct guerilla fighters.[74] After her excessively violent rape, Daisy does not seek a man to protect her as she did after her beauty pageant fiasco. Instead, Hagedorn authorizes Daisy-as-Philippines as an active participant in future struggles. Like América, Daisy refuses to be simply a national object used or abused to garner national resistance.

Daisy not only arms herself, she teaches others how to protect themselves. Among those she trains is Joey, who witnessed her father's assassination.[75] As a sex worker exploited by the postcolonial foreign tourist industry, Joey represents how Filipino lives are affected by U.S. neocolonialism. This act can be read as the woman-as-nation authorizing other marginalized groups to participate in fighting for and imagining a different Philippine future. Daisy and Joey's interaction also points to how the metaphor of colonialism as consensual romance or rape depends on heteronormativity. Hagedorn calls into question whose experiences of violence are erased through this metaphor. At the end of the novel Daisy no longer only symbolizes a nation, but she actively works for a better future with those whom national discourses have forgotten in order to correct historic inequities against the Filipino people.

Conclusion: Reinscribing the Revised Rape-as-Neocolonialsm Metaphor

Literary representations of rape use sexual violence as a metaphor for national crises. Although literary representations of rape in a colonial context often represented only the fear of foreign intrusion and the reality of conquest and colonialism, Santiago and Hagedorn rewrite this narrative to capture the complexity of neocolonialism in Puerto Rico and the Philippines. The original metaphor of colonialism as rape uses women's bodies to represent the nation in order to relay the message that the woman-as-nation needs the protection of its male citizens. This metaphor is particularly potent because it relies on constructions of "legitimate" rape. The colonial rapist invades the woman-as-nation's domestic space and violently invades. The rapist is a stranger to the victim, of a different race than the victim. These meet all the criteria of legitimate rapes according to pervasive rape myths in U.S. culture.

The rape in *América's Dream* represents U.S. imperialism as the subjugation of Puerto Rico made possible by an emphasis on Puerto Rican cultural nationalism that obscures Puerto Rico's economic dependence on the United States. Rape in *Dogeaters* represents the violent suppression of political opposition during martial law under President Marcos, who was supported by the U.S. government during his twenty-year dictatorship and afterward given safe haven in Hawaii. The novels portray Puerto Rican and Filipino men as the rapists to represent local complicity in the perpetuation of U.S. neocolonialism in Puerto Rico and the Philippines. Ironically, the revised metaphor articulates neocolonial power *too* well. Neocolonial power is less visible than traditional colonial power because it is less explicit. Corrupt postcolonial governments can easily be held completely responsible for persisting poverty and economic stagnation when Spanish and U.S. colonialism often created these problems and the conditions that allow these problems to persist. Similarly, when read through the lens of U.S. hegemonic culture, the rapes in these two novels are suspect because these women are understood as partially responsible for their rapes. América's long-term boyfriend, not a stranger, rapes her. The rape was not Correa's first abusive act against her either. For this reason, some would argue that América allowed the abuse. Rape victims' behavior is often dissected. If the victim was dressed provocatively, out alone at night, consuming alcohol, or otherwise deviating from acceptably safe practices, the victim is construed as having invited the rape to some degree. From the perspective of the Philippine government during martial law, *Dogeater*'s Daisy also acts inappropriately. These hegemonic understandings of legitimate rape in U.S. culture erase how the continuing subjugation of Filipinos and Puerto Ricans is enabled by U.S. imperialism. Correa represents the empowerment of Puerto Rican cultural nationalism that elides Puerto Rico's continuing political insubordination. The military figures who rape Daisy represent the United States' implicit sanctioning of President Marcos's political oppression in the Philippines. However, these more complex readings are easily reduced to metaphors for Puerto Ricans and Filipinos exploited by their own traditional patriarchies or corrupt governments.

Santiago and Hagedorn not only rewrite the metaphor of colonialism as rape to capture how global power has been rearticulated in the neocolonial era, but they also challenge the gendered assumption at the heart of this metaphor: women are the property of men. They can be violently taken by masculine aggressors and thus must be defended by its citizenry. In the metaphor of colonialism as rape, women are merely allegorical national symbols. Santiago and Hagedorn underscore how women are objectified for nationalist purposes by representing neither Daisy nor América as possessing a sense of agency at the outset of these novels. Instead of reinstating the masculine privileged perspective through representations of gender violence avenged by masculine rescuers, Santiago and Hagedorn revise literary representations of rape by having both América and Daisy claim their right to agency at the end of the novels. This represents the active participation of women in nationalist resistance that is not usually recognized and demonstrates the role Puerto Rican women and Filipino women play in actively imagining the nation's future. For example, Puerto Rican Creole women reconciled feminism with nationalism in the 1920s, transforming the image of feminists from culturally suspect traitors to protectors of Puerto Rican culture who provide guidance for men engaged in nation building. However, this transformation still relegated Puerto Rican women to supporting roles in the nationalist project, and this role would eventually place the burden of the reproduction of Puerto Rican culture on women.[76] In the Philippines, feminist organizations like Gabriela articulate a nationalist feminism and actively organize against the consequences of U.S. neocolonialism in the Philippines.[77] Feminist groups were active in protesting the outcome of the Subic rape case, where four members of the U.S. armed forces went to trial for the gang rape of Filipina Suzette Nicolas.[78] As this chapter illustrates, imperialism and neocolonial nationalisms are gendered processes that privilege masculine power; therefore, imagining a truly postcolonial world requires a feminist imagining.

Just as Santiago and Hagedorn have revised the metaphor of colonialism as rape to encapsulate neocolonialism, narratives of U.S. exceptionalism have likewise been revised to better suit the current nature of U.S. colonial projects in the Middle East. The current iteration of the metaphor of U.S. colonialism as a consensual, heterosexual romance is that of the United States as a champion of women's rights that rescues women in third-world countries from oppressive traditional cultures. Whereas a long-term, heterosexual romance implies a long-term commitment from the United States, the representation of the United States as a savior implies a short-term action. It is this revised narrative of U.S. exceptionalism that also further undermines Santiago's critique in *América's Dream*. The cover packaging of *América's Dream* frames this novel as a female empowerment story and liberation from domestic abuse. The review excerpt from the *Washington Post* on the front cover describes the novel as "lyrical" and "haunting." "América's liberating epiphany will have readers . . . on their feet and cheering." On the back cover, Terry McMillan, author of *How Stella Got Her Groove Back*, a popular novel of the empowerment of an African American woman (the book was adapted into an equally popular movie), compliments Santiago's writing. Another blurb hails Santiago as "one of the most powerful new voices in American fiction." Here Santiago is included in a minority-women writer's canon. Her narrative is framed to fit in with narratives that celebrate the liberation of minority women from oppressive, minority, patriarchal cultures. The summary blurb first describes América's awful home situation in Puerto Rico with her alcoholic mother and her physically abusive lover. Her opportunity to leave Puerto Rico for the United States is represented as her "door to escape," and América eventually "dare[s] to care for another man." American culture, represented as offering equal rights and opportunities for women that are not available in traditional Puerto Rican and other third-world cultures, offers a path for progress for third-world women. This racialized logic often serves as a justification for current U.S. interventions in the Middle East: the United States is saving veiled Muslim women from oppressive, fundamentalist Muslim men.[79] Thus, the marketing of *América's Dream* upholds narratives of U.S. exceptionalism that represent Western cultures as enlightened and progressive and obscures the novel's revision of the longstanding rape-as-colonialism metaphor to account for the complexity of neocolonial power.

3. Bastards of U.S. Imperialism

*Demanding Recognition
in the American Family*

> There was once an old 'Yank' who lives in a shoe
> covered all with red, white, and blue
> His family is large and still growing bigger
> The result of good work in snapping the trigger.
> —Eugene Zimmerman, "The Old Yank"

If heterosexual relations, whether consensual or nonconsensual, are a metaphor for the United States' relationships with the Philippines and Puerto Rico, then by extension the products of these relationships—the resulting governments, the hybrid cultures, the subsequent im/migrants to the United States, and so on—are these relationships' offspring. The United States' disavowal of empire further casts these populations, societies, and their cultures as bastards of U.S. imperialism—the illegitimate children of colonial relationships that have been willfully forgotten.

In the previous chapters the comprehensive critiques of neocolonialism in *Dogeaters* and *América's Dream* were undermined by packaging that incorporated the novels into hegemonic narratives of U.S. multiculturalism and exceptionalism. Furthermore, our understandings of the genre of novels as fiction, even historical novels, can delegitimize the very critiques that these two novels make. In this chapter, I examine cultural critique in the documentary film genre. In contrast to fictional novels, documentary films are often expected to represent reality—real history, real experience, real people. Particular conventions of this genre emphasize that the narrative presented is not fiction, that it is truth. The narrative authority of documentary films is often constructed through interviews with experts and incorporates archival film footage or photographic stills.[1] It is this expectation that documentary films represent the truth, however problematic that assumption is, that makes documentary films a fruitful site for challenging hegemonic narratives of U.S. exceptionalism.

I examine the possibilities and limitations for Filipino American and U.S. Puerto Rican cultural critique in two documentary films: Camilla Benilao Griggers's *Memories of a Forgotten War* (2001) and Rosie Perez's *Yo soy Boricua, pa'que tu lo Sepas!* (I'm Puerto Rican, Just So You Know!) (2006). Similar to how *Dogeaters* and *América's Dream* critiqued and revised the colonialism-as-rape metaphor, these two films resurrect a metaphor used to justify U.S. colonialism in the Philippines and Puerto Rico, one that imagined colonialism as paternal relationship, to discuss the notion of colonial illegitimacy. The narrators of both documentaries are products of relationships that are not institutionally recognized and are personally disavowed by a patriarchal figure, U.S. American men who went to the Philippines or Puerto Rico as a result of U.S. imperialism. Thus, the films represent colonial illegitimacy both literally and metaphorically, connecting their narrators' literal illegitimacy that results from the paternal disavowal to the metaphorical illegitimacy that manifests as illegitimate narratives that are disavowed by hegemonic narratives of U.S. benevolent assimilation and exceptionalism.

In the early twentieth century, representations of U.S. colonialism as a paternal relationship were more ubiquitous than representations of U.S. colonialism as a consensual, heterosexual romance. Political cartoons depicted a fatherly Uncle Sam generously taking in dark-skinned, orphaned children representing the United States' new colonial possessions.[2] The metaphor was used by anti-imperialists and imperialists alike. Political cartoons arguing against U.S. overseas expansion would depict Uncle Sam overwhelmed by too many colonial children and represent the colonial children as unruly and dangerous. Those advocating for U.S. expansion underscored Uncle Sam's efforts to civilize and educate his colonial children. Like the metaphor of U.S. imperialism as a heterosexual relationship, the paternal metaphor also naturalized the unequal relationship between the U.S. and its island colonies. Colonies are immature children requiring discipline and guidance from Uncle Sam, their guardian and authority figure. Unlike the heterosexual-relationship metaphor, this metaphor does not imply a mutual decision for both the colonized and colonizers. Representing the island colonies as children suggests that they are not yet capable of making good decisions and thus need an authority figure to decide what is in their best interest. This metaphor argues that consent is not required and the desires of island natives can be totally disregarded. Even better, the paternal metaphor encapsulates both benevolent assimilation and the white-man's burden by representing Uncle Sam as a selfless man willing to take on the burden of raising savage children.

Uncle Sam adopts orphan colonies. Joseph Keppler Jr. "A Trifle Embarrassed." *Puck*, August 3, 1898. Found in Abe Ignacio et al., *The Forbidden Book: The Philippine-American War in Political Cartoons* (San Francisco: T'boli, 2004).

I argue that *Memories of a Forgotten War* and *Yo soy Boricua, pa'que tu lo Sepas!* resurrect the metaphors of imperialism as heterosexual romance and paternal benevolence to question the narrative of U.S. colonial benevolence. These documentaries revive the familial metaphors used to justify U.S. imperialism given the widespread disavowal of the history of U.S. imperialism today. Privatizing U.S. imperial violence allows the films to demonstrate how U.S. imperialism affected and continues to affect the individual. Though both documentaries highlight how U.S. imperialism has rendered histories and their families illegitimate and insist on the recognition of these disavowed relationships, the narratives they strive to legitimize reflect the different neocolonial relationships the United States maintains with the Philippines and Puerto Rico. *Memories of a Forgotten War* explicitly holds the United States responsible for knowingly abusing the Philippines during the colonial period, completely abandoning the Philippines by granting it independence, and conveniently disavowing both the abuse and the relationship through historical amnesia. It demands that the abusive history of the Philippine-American war be legitimized by the United States to enable the healing of both Filipinos and Americans from the war's trauma. *Yo soy Boricua, pa'que tu lo Sepas!* critiques U.S. colonial oppression primarily to emphasize the resilience of the Puerto Rican community and assert its presence in the United States, not to hold the United States accountable for its actions. More specifically, the documentary demands the recognition of Puerto Rico's special relationship to the United States and how this relationship defines the Puerto Rican community. It strives to tell the unique story of the Puerto Ricans' experience so that their histories and contributions can be recognized within the United States' multicultural melting pot.

I begin my analysis with an examination of the Griggers family in *Memories of a Forgotten War*, how the film's explicit deployment of the family's history of marital abuse and illegitimacy that scars subsequent generations is a metaphor for U.S. colonialism in the Philippines. I will then analyze the contrasting representation in *Yo soy Boricua, pa'que tu lo Sepas!* of familial illegitimacy as an open family secret that is easily resolved through the reunion of legitimate and illegitimate family. This film does not explicitly correlate Rosie Perez's familial illegitimacy with Puerto Rico's relationship to the United States. The two documentary films' differing representations of familial illegitimacy not only reflect different individual responses to the knowledge of a family member's disavowal but also reflect the different relationships between the United States and the Philippines and Puerto Rico, respectively. The Philippines was violently forced into the United States at the turn of the twentieth century, and then its relationship to the United States was historically forgotten after being granted independence in 1946. As a U.S. commonwealth, Puerto Rico is officially part of the United States, though not often recognized as such.

In identifying the more explicit critique in *Memories of a Forgotten War* and the easier path to reconciliation implied in *Yo soy Boricua, pa'que tu lo Sepas!* I do not mean to suggest that the critique of U.S. imperialism articulated in the former is better than that articulated in the latter. Rather, I argue that the more a cultural narrative deviates from hegemonic narratives, the more likely it will be limited to a niche audience. Conversely, a cultural narrative that can be incorporated into hegemonic narratives can more easily be packaged for consumption by a mainstream audience. I end this chapter by considering the limitations of documentary film as a site for challenging hegemonic narratives of U.S. exceptionalism. By examining the different production processes and distribution of the two films in light of the representations of U.S. colonialism in the films, I argue that the mainstream market plays a significant role in popularizing documentaries whose narratives affirm, and thus reproduce, hegemonic narratives of U.S. exceptionalism. On the other hand, documentary films that are too critical of these hegemonic narratives are marginalized and reach only niche audiences.

Delegitimizing Benevolent Assimilation in *Memories of a Forgotten War*

Memories of a Forgotten War is an experimental documentary that takes narrator Camilla Benilao Griggers's family history as a metaphor for the history of Philippine and American relations. She explicitly parallels the U.S. colonial period in the Philippines to the failed relationship between her Filipina grandmother and her grandfather, a U.S. military serviceman. Identifying how the Filipinas in her family (her mother, her aunt, and her maternal grandmother) were all disrespected and abused by their American husbands, Griggers concludes that the dysfunctional dynamics of these couplings are manifestations of the United States mistreatment of the Philippines. She argues that the erasure of the Philippine-American war facilitates the reproduction of these dynamics generation after generation and that revealing her grandfather's and the United States' abusive history is the key to stopping the cycle. Such a revelation would legitimize her branch of the family tree and the violent history of U.S. colonialism in the Philippines. The documentary supports its historical narrative through montages of old photographs of Filipinos, colonial-era archival footage of the Philippines, footage of the contemporary Philippines, and reenactments of the violence of the Philippine-American war.[3] Whereas traditional documentaries usually reenact events that have been substantially documented as fact, the reenactments in this film speculate what the lives of Filipino victims of U.S. military violence might have been like. These speculative reenactments at times reference documented archival evidence or significant events but do not rely solely on them. Griggers takes poetic license to recreate "memories" of violence forgotten by the archives.

This documentary was produced by Griggers and Sari Dalena with support from various U.S. and Philippine arts advocacy groups: the Philippine National Commission of Culture, the Pennsylvania Council of the Arts, and the Women in Film Foundation.[4] The movie was not nationally broadcast on public or cable stations. No popular actors or artists were attached to the film. In the United States, the film was screened at several Asian-interest film festivals in 2001, including the New York Asian American Film Festival and the Hawaii International Film Festival. The film premiered in the Philippines at the University of the Philippines on January 8, 2002. Griggers has since screened the film at several universities in the United States. In later years the film was featured at special events like the Independence Day Kalayaan Fair held at Intramuros in the Philippines in June 2005 and as part of a 2010 Southeast Asian Cinema showcase at Australia's National Film and Sound

Archive. The audience this film ultimately reached was limited to Asian film enthusiasts and university professors and students with an active interest in the film's content.

Perhaps as a result of its limited release and distribution, *Memories of a Forgotten War* has not been the subject of much academic analysis. However, Griggers's documentary bears some similarities to Filipino American filmmaker Marlon Fuentes's experimental documentary *Bontoc Eulogy* (1995). *Bontoc Eulogy* centers on the filmmaker's search for the fate of his grandfather, one of the Igorot tribespeople on display at the 1904 St. Louis World's Fair. Though the film includes archival photographs and footage, the documentary's main narrative is fictional. Fuentes's grandfather was not on display at the World's Fair. Film scholars argue that Fuentes's use of documentary film conventions to tell this fictional story critiques how colonial and ethnographic documentary practices reify privileged perspectives as objective truth. Specifically, Fuentes critiques how indigenous Filipinos were put on display at the 1904 World's Fair to substantiate the claims of Filipinos as racially inferior savages and to thereby legitimize U.S. colonialism in the Philippines. Representing the fictional story of one of these natives on display emphasizes their objectification for an American audience but also calls attention to the colonial archives' bias. Whereas the archive records the stories of colonial officials, those who planned the 1904 World's Fair, and the fair's attendees, the archive has no record of the natives' lives. Lost to history, one can only imagine their stories, as Fuentes has done.[5] Similarly, *Memories of a Forgotten War* literally gives voice to colonial subjects by representing their possible stories and perspectives. Though some film critics criticize *Bontoc Eulogy* for being misleading, the film highlights how colonial archives render the colonized speechless. Creative reenactment is one method of recuperating their subaltern perspectives.

Memories of a Forgotten War frames its historical narrative within the Griggers's family biography. Though this is a true story, it is rendered illegitimate by the archive. When Camilla Benilao Griggers's American grandfather left the Philippines, he left behind her Filipina grandmother and never again acknowledged the family they created together. Framing the colonial relationship between the United States and the Philippines through her grandparents' failed marriage emphasizes the gendered discrepancy in narrative authority to legitimize family and national histories. Griggers's grandfather's perspective of family history is institutionally recognized, while her grandmother's is not. Histories of the U.S. colonial period in the Philippines privileging the narrative of benevolent assimilation are institutionally recognized, while U.S. colonial violence is not. In highlighting this discrepancy *Memories of a*

Forgotten War foregrounds the privileged perspective inherent in metaphors justifying U.S. imperialism that represent the United States as an adoptive father or the United States as a masculine savior of feminine colonies. This questions the legitimacy of the benevolent assimilation narrative and lays the foundation for legitimizing forgotten histories of colonial violence imagined in the creative reenactments. However, using her grandparents' failed marriage as a metaphor for U.S. colonialism in the Philippines leaves intact the notion that the colonial relationship is a consensual one, thus upholding a main tenet of the narrative of U.S. exceptionalism.

The film opens with Griggers narrating her personal genealogy in a voice-over while the camera pans across black and white photographs of Filipino women and children: "I am the granddaughter of a Filipina who married a U.S. cavalry soldier who abandoned her on the eve of World War II. . . . Like her motherland, my grandmother was a victim of betrayal and abandonment. . . . I recently tracked down my grandfather, found his grave in Portland, Oregon. His obituary named all his living descendants. My name was not there, nor the name of my mother. My grandmother's name was not mentioned."[6] Not only does this set up her grandparents' relationship as a metaphor for U.S. colonialism in the Philippines, it also frames her illegitimacy as a metaphor for the illegitimate histories of the Philippine-American war. Her contradictory wording points to the power that institutional archives have in defining what constitutes history. The obituary names "all" of her grandfather's living descendants and yet fails to account for her and her mother. Though not legitimized by the archives, Griggers still exists. Her existence in the absence of archival validation serves to validate the forgotten memories of the Philippine-American war represented in the film that contradicts hegemonic narratives of U.S. benevolent assimilation.[7] Institutional archives are neither all-inclusive nor objective, but they are nevertheless designed to perpetuate hegemonic narratives of nuclear families and countries.

Griggers elaborates on the parallels between the Philippines and her maternal grandmother by describing both as the victims of unmet responsibilities. Her grandmother fell victim to the "failure of the sanctity of the marriage contract in [a] biracial family" while the Philippines fell victim to the "failure of the sanctity of the social contract between the United States of America and the Philippine islands."[8] Using her abused, abandoned grandmother as a metaphor for the Philippines directly contradicts the metaphor of Uncle Sam as the masculine protector of a feminine Philippines. By explicitly referencing both relationships as contractually based, Griggers contends that the metaphor of U.S. imperialism as a heterosexual romance hinges on mutual consent to specified terms. Though she does not elaborate on the terms of her grandparents' marital contract, she represents the public promises made by the United States for the Philippines in a reconstruction of a speech given by President William McKinley. Black-and-white footage of President McKinley speaking on a platform in front of a large crowd accompanies scratchy audio of a voice stating that the United States will "educate the Filipinos, and uplift and civilize and Christianize them, and by God's grace do the very best we could by them."[9] These are the promises of benevolent assimilation, premised on the racist assumption that Filipinos are racially inferior and thus unfit to govern themselves.

The footage of McKinley's speech represented here as archival evidence of U.S. imperialism is doctored. Though the original footage shows McKinley giving a speech, there is no accompanying audio recording of that particular speech. In fact, this quote from McKinley is not attributed to a speech but instead to an interview given to *The Christian Advocate*.[10] Given that the quote is readily attributed to McKinley, what does giving the impression that there is audio-visual footage for this quote accomplish? Why alter the voice-over to mimic old, archival audio instead of presenting it as a modern reading of a quote? This scene knowingly exploits our assumption of documentary as representing truth. Here, Griggers relies on our assumptions about documentaries, that we will accept this audio-visual evidence of this quote. This scene demonstrates how easily archival evidence can be framed or manipulated in documentary film and still be unwittingly accepted as truth because that is what is expected of this genre.

While Griggers takes pains to create seemingly authentic audio-visual of McKinley's defense of benevolent assimilation, she represents the accepted memory of benevolent assimilation as an inauthentic, incomplete accounting of U.S. colonialism in the Philippines. Black-and-white photographs of Filipino youth with white American female schoolteachers and of well-dressed, professional Filipinos fade in and out while Griggers explains in a voice-over that what is remembered of U.S. colonialism in the Philippines is the "cultural work of empire." She describes how "groups of educators such as the Thomasites instituted an American-style education to carry out the work of benevolent assimilation, but the assimilation was not benevolent." At this point, the documentary cuts from the still shots of teachers and students to black-and-white footage of a storage facility for U.S. military ammunition followed by black-and-white photographic stills of injured Filipinos standing or lying in white tents. During this sequence, Griggers discusses the U.S. military's brutal tactics during the Philippine-American war, including the policies of slash and burn and the policies of executing any Filipino resisting U.S. rule. Whereas the photographs of American teachers and Filipino youth offer direct evidence of the educational aspect of benevolent assimilation, the footage of ammunition and photos of injured Filipinos do not substantiate her claims of the brutality of the U.S. military against Filipinos. Those injured in the photos have bandages around their heads or legs, but they are still well enough to pose for the photographer. The discrepancy between what is described and what the photos visually represent suggests how archival evidence can easily be manipulated, in this case by including only photographs of victims with minimal injuries, to provide evidence for benevolent assimilation but not the violence of the Philippine-American war. However, the discrepancy between the photographs and narration also suggests that the narrator is unreliable. We can read this as another critique of the authorial narrative voice in documentary films.

Griggers offers visual evidence of this violence in her creative reenactments of the Philippine-American war. Dispersed in between Griggers's narrations of family and Philippine history, these reenactments depict the senseless executions of Filipino women and children. Without archival evidence to substantiate these reenactments these scenes could be disregarded as nothing more than fiction. However, just like Griggers, her mother and grandmother exist despite her grandfather's disavowal and their archival exclusion; these fictional creative reenactments rehabilitate a Filipino perspective that may capture violence that U.S. colonial archives actively erased. Read this way, this documentary is a subaltern imagining of the Philippine-American war because it attempts to fill in the absences left by the archive, calling attention to the privileged, colonial bias of archival histories.[11] Hegemonic narratives of U.S. colonialism in the Philippines are written from the perspective of the American victors. Millions of those who resisted are dead and their stories forgotten.[12] These creative reenactments are ghost stories, as sociologist Avery Gordon defined them. Free from the disciplinary restrictions of the academy, fiction allows different histories to emerge.[13]

Two of *Memories of a Forgotten War*'s creative reenactments represent weddings. The first is a Christian wedding procession represented from the bride's perspective. The second sequence, which is longer, depicts a Muslim wedding ceremony from an omniscient point of view. Both weddings end in unprovoked violence and senseless murder. Given that the documentary likens U.S. colonialism in the Philippines to an abusive, failed marriage, I contend that these marriage sequences articulate more than just the forgotten American military brutality against Filipinos during the Philippine-American war.

In the first bridal scene, a young Filipina dressed in a simple white dress with a long veil covering her face walks through the rural countryside en route to a church with her bridal party. The colors in this scene are faded, conveying that this scene represents the distant past but also foreshadowing the bride's diminished future prospects. The bride's thoughts narrate the scene; the voice-over in Tagalog, accompanied by English subtitles, conveys the bride's thoughts on her new domestic responsibilities as a wife: choosing window dressings, preparing meals, tending to the garden. Her concerns with consumer goods seem to indicate her belonging to a relatively privileged class and convey concerns seemingly similar to newly married twenty-first-century American women. This similarity reveals a shortcoming of imagining history. Details used to fill in creative reenactments may be more indicative of the society and culture the writer inhabits. However, this limitation might also be understood as a strategic representational tool deployed by the writers to encourage audience members to identify with the bride by conveying that this woman is an everyday person with hopes and dreams similar to her current-day counterparts in the audience. Read as intentional or unintentional, the brides' musings on newlywed life demonstrate how subaltern histories often still represent a Western perspective because subaltern academics are trained in Western institutions.[14]

Establishing this link between the audience and the bride underscores the senseless nature of U.S. violence against Filipinos during the Philippine-American war, emphasizing the importance of remembering this war and holding those responsible for the violence to count. The scene cuts out as the voice-over ominously reveals that the bride has a tragic premonition. When we rejoin the marching wedding party, young girls dressed in white throw flower petals as the bride approaches the entrance of the church. The scene pans upward to an American soldier in a room looking out of a window. Slowly and with no emotion on his face, he takes his gun, points downward, and shoots. The scene returns to the bride, who turns toward the sound of the gun and then falls to the floor.[15] Here, Griggers represents how the U.S. military's subjugation of the Philippines did not only involve violence against those resisting U.S. rule but also against all Filipinos. This indiscriminate murder interrupted the normal lives of all Filipinos.

Griggers more dramatically represents the U.S. military's senseless violence against Filipino civilians in a second bridal scene. This creative reenactment is preceded by Griggers's describing in voice-over the Battle of Bud Dajo, also known as the Moro Crater massacre, where hundreds of Filipino Moros were murdered by the U.S. Army in 1906 for evading taxes.[16] The second bridal scene begins with the bride and groom processing to the ceremony site as Griggers states how the resisting Moros fortified themselves in Mount Dajo where "women fought alongside the men inside of simple fortifications and held their children before them, having sworn to die rather than yield."¹⁷ The bridal party's attire and the kulintang music (played on a set of small, horizontal gongs) reference Filipino Moro culture. Unlike the first bridal scene, this bride arrives safely at the ceremony. She and her husband complete the wedding rituals with a large number of guests in attendance. Celebration ensues but is cut short by the blast of large explosions that send debris flying through the air and people fleeing for safety. No place is safe. When the explosions stop, the camera pans over dozens of dead bodies, zooming in on bloodied feet and hands while a woman sings mournfully in a Filipino dialect that is not Tagalog. Finally, the camera focuses and then remains on the bride's lifeless body and slowly zooms out to reveal that the bride is in a pile of bodies. The color of the still shot fades into a widely circulated black-and-white photo of the Moro Crater massacre. Though this scene does not represent the historical narrative attached to this archival photo, transitioning from the creative redramatization to an actual photograph of U.S. soldiers posing with the bodies of hundreds of murdered Filipinos insinuates that this photograph is evidence of a wedding-day massacre. The seamless transition from creative reenactment to archival photograph seemingly legitimizes the reenactment's events and fills in the gaps in colonial historical archives, suggesting a subaltern history.

It can easily be argued that Griggers blatantly manipulates the audience by suggesting that the photo represents the senseless massacre of Filipinos gathered for a joyous celebration. However, by pairing this imagined history with a popular archival photograph, Griggers explicitly questions documented history. Given that the U.S. military did murder Filipino civilians with impunity, who can say with certainty that the documented reason for the massacre, that these Filipino Moros refused to pay colonial taxes, is the actual reason these people were massacred? What if the circulation of photographic evidence of a massacre in the Philippines necessitated an explanation, one conjured up after the fact? If that were the case, the difference between the story of tax evasion and the story of massacred wedding party would be institutional, archival legitimacy. In juxtaposing institutional fact with a fictional reenactment, Griggers casts doubt on colonial archival memory and the written histories that depend on it. The represented memories Griggers attributes to the forgotten, everyday Filipinos who lived through the violence of the Philippine-American war are meant to discredit the institutional memory of benevolent assimilation that the archives support.

The senseless murder she portrays violates the terms of the social contract she argues defined the relationship between the Philippines and United States, a contract she likens to a marriage contract: "My grandfather failed to uphold

Shot zooms out from murdered bride's face and transitions seamlessly into an archival photograph taken of Filipino bodies piled in a crater at Mount Bud Dajo.

the sanctity of his marriage, just as the U.S. failed to uphold the sanctity of its relationship to the Philippines. Proffering partnership, it took freely what it wanted from the heart of the Filipino people, from the wealth of its resources. It plundered and warred, then betrayed and abandoned and then lied, hiding the truth of what it had done."[18] Representing the relationship as one that is contractually bound enables Griggers to critique the violence of U.S. colonial occupation in the Philippines as a failure to meet contractual obligations. This implies that the rhetoric of benevolent assimilation represented promises made to the Philippines, promises that were disregarded and then covered up. However, in conceptualizing the colonial relationship as contractual Griggers also implies consent between two equal parties. That is, the Philippines consented to colonial subordination. Thus, in the end, her use of the metaphor of colonialism as consensual, contractual marriage adheres to the narrative of U.S. exceptionalism, that the United States is the selfless exception among otherwise greedy imperial powers. Whereas other empires conquer territories with no regard to the indigenous people, the United States first seeks the people's consent. Griggers leaves untouched the notion that the United States' intentions are initially honorable while questioning whether these intentions are carried out.

Camilla Griggers's biracial identity could easily be exploited to represent a harmonious racial intermingling resulting from the successful, consensual colonial relationship between the Philippines and the United States.[19] However, the representations of U.S. military violence in *Memories of a Forgotten War* refuse such an interpretation of Griggers's subjectivity by emphasizing the abusive nature of the colonial relationship. She also contradicts her implication of the Philippines' consent to colonial subjugation by the United States, emphasizing that "several million Filipinos resisted occupation . . . men, women, children, civilians resisted."[20] The violent marriage sequences provide some insight to the contradictory messages of a consensual relationship within the film's metaphoric frame and the representations of Filipino resistance. In the metaphor of colonialism as marriage the bride represents the Philippines. The act of marriage represents the bride's consent to be governed and subjugated. The groom represents the governing state. In the film's main narrative frame the groom is Griggers's grandfather. He represents a violently abusive United States. In the two marriage scenes, the grooms are not American. In the Christian marriage scene, a U.S. sniper murders the bride before she reaches the church and her groom. Though the groom is left unrepresented, we can assume that the groom is also Filipino, as the U.S. military would not likely murder a woman about to marry a fellow soldier or a colonial official. In the Moro marriage scene the groom is represented and the marriage ceremony is successfully completed before the U.S. military slaughters all those in attendance. Applying the metaphor of consent to government as consensual romance, these weddings can be read as Filipinos' desire for a local, native government. The U.S. military's violent destruction of these marriages represents the United States' military efforts to prevent the establishment of an independent Philippine nation by Filipino nationalists who fought successfully against Spain. Preventing these local marriages paves the way for the colonialism-as-marriage metaphor. Reading the violent marriage sequences in light of the colonialism-as-marriage metaphor raises the question of how consent was secured. It was not the allure of U.S. benevolent assimilation that led to the Philippines' consent to be governed, but military violence that finally secured Philippine consent to U.S. colonial rule.

Memories of a Forgotten War uses fiction in a documentary format to question how histories are legitimized. Griggers uses archival photographs and footage to seemingly legitimize the film's challenge to U.S. benevolent assimilation in the Philippines. She blurs the line between archival "fact" and hypothetical subaltern histories to demonstrate that the United States still maintains narrative authority of the representation of the U.S. colonial period in the Philippines. In actively disavowing its violent past, U.S. imperialism renders illegitimate the history of millions of Filipinos who died resisting U.S. occupation. She relates this to the way archival history, in the form of the newspaper obituary, grants narrative authority to her American grandfather who abandoned her grandmother and disavowed their offspring, thus rendering the narrator illegitimate and invisible. The film reveals colonial power's role in determining narrative power to question mainstream history of U.S. colonialism in the Philippines and to legitimize previously illegitimate voices, Griggers's included. In *Memories of a Forgotten War* legitimating illegitimate histories of the Philippine-American war depended on the de-legitimization of hegemonic narratives of U.S. exceptionalism. In the next section, I will examine how a documentary film legitimizes hitherto marginalized history by inserting that history into hegemonic cultural narratives.

Legitimizing Narratives of U.S. Multiculturalism

IFC (the Independent Film Channel) Films produced *Yo soy Boricua, pa'que tu lo Sepas!*, a documentary of Rosie Perez's personal history located within Puerto Rican history. Actor Jimmy Smits, who is half Puerto Rican, is the film's narrator.[21] The film's title is taken from a track by the popular Puerto Rican rap artist Taino, otherwise known as Joel Bosch. Such star power ensured widespread interest and provided ample marketing potential to a U.S. Puerto Rican audience. The documentary's IFC broadcast premiere was timed to coincide with the annual Puerto Rican Day Parade in 2006 and was marketed to the crowds in attendance. From a financial standpoint this film was a relatively safe investment.[22]

The documentary received a significant amount of attention in both U.S. Latino and mainstream media. It premiered at the 2006 Tribeca Film Festival and was subsequently screened at the 2006 Miami International Film Festival, the 2006 Tulipanes Latino Art and Film Festival in Holland, Michigan, and the 2008 Caribbean Cinematic Film Festival. The film was reviewed in widely read U.S. newspapers, including the *New York Times* and the *Washington Post*. Rosie Perez promoted the film in an interview with National Public Radio. Interest from the mainstream media indicates that the film was not only marketed to Puerto Ricans and Latinos specifically, but to a larger national audience as well.

Like *Memories of a Forgotten War*, the documentary *Yo soy Boricua, pa'que tu lo Sepas!* frames the marginalization of Puerto Rican history in the United States with the narrator's personal story of familial illegitimacy. Whereas the former alleges that her illegitimate histories are intentionally kept secret to preserve hegemonic familial or national narratives, *Yo soy Boricua, pa'que tu lo Sepas!* approaches illegitimacy as well-kept but unnecessary secrets. The documentary's protagonist, Rosie Perez, does not question what institutional powers rendered her illegitimate, nor does she question the role that U.S. colonial power plays in marginalizing Puerto Rican history. By representing illegitimacy as the result of unnecessary secrets, the film offers a simple solution to resolving issues of illegitimacy. To become legitimate, one must simply stop keeping secrets. Sharing secret family histories will bring the illegitimate and legitimate together, breaking down distinctions between the two. Thus the film itself is the solution for legitimizing both Perez's place in her grandfather's larger family and Puerto Rican history as part of U.S. multicultural history. Without the interrogation of why her family and Puerto Rican history are illegitimate *Yo soy Boricua, pa'que tu lo Sepas!* can be taken at face value as a straightforward cultural nationalist narrative. As an often-unrecognized part of the United States, Puerto Rico is itself an illegitimate part of the U.S. "family," but the film suggests that this can be remedied with enough publicity—that is, with enough displays of Puerto Rican cultural nationalism.

As discussed in chapter 2, Puerto Rican cultural nationalism is divorced from Puerto Rican calls for political sovereignty and thus do not threaten U.S. colonialism in Puerto Rico. Likewise, this film's narrative does not threaten U.S. colonialism in Puerto Rico. The film is a traditional documentary with a linear storyline and takes demonstrative displays of ethnic pride at the New

York Puerto Rican Day Parade as a springboard for exploring Puerto Rican history. The documentary follows actress Rosie Perez, her sister, and her cousin as they visit several family homes and Puerto Rican cultural institutions to answer the question, "Why are Puerto Ricans so damn proud?" The answer takes the form of a teleological narrative, beginning with a discussion of Puerto Rico's precolonial indigenous populations, briefly touching on Spanish colonialism, moving through the consequences of U.S. colonialism in Puerto Rico, and ending with Puerto Rican migrants' efforts to build community in the United States.[23]

The film's celebratory, multicultural representation of Puerto Rican history at once articulates Puerto Ricans as culturally Caribbean but also as a part of the United States, conforming to narratives of U.S. multiculturalism and U.S. exceptionalism. In his critique of romantic constructions of Filipino American identity, ethnic studies scholar Dylan Rodríguez argues that representations of Filipino Americans that emphasize and celebrate Filipino progress (from immigrant to U.S. citizen, from tradition to modernity, from colony to independence) all contribute to the teleological narrative of U.S. multiculturalism and of U.S. benevolent colonialism that renders racism and colonialism as past tense.[24] Such logic implies that continued calls for civil rights and decolonialization are unnecessary. Here, I will extend Rodríguez's analysis to demonstrate how expressions of Puerto Rican cultural nationalism likewise affirm historical narratives of U.S. multicultural and colonial progress and thus can be recognized as a legitimate part of those narratives. I argue that the film's representation of Perez's happy reunions with legitimate family members without a serious reconciliation of the past suggests Puerto Ricans can likewise be accepted into the U.S. family without an accounting of past wrongs.

Though the film's main narrative centers on a teleological representation of Puerto Rican history that actively attempts to conform to narratives of U.S. multiculturalism, it does present a critique of U.S. colonialism in Puerto Rico, articulated by the documentary's narrator, by some of its interviewees, in some segments taken from other documentaries, and in film footage of recent New York Puerto Rican events. However, Rosie Perez herself does not offer a critique. The double-voiced discourse of the film critiques U.S. imperialism as it simultaneously constructs Puerto Rican culture to conform to U.S. multiculturalist narratives. Philosopher Mikhail Bakhtin defines a double-voiced discourse as one that expresses authorial intent in a refracted way.[25] In this case, Perez explicitly affirms U.S. multiculturalism while the critiques of U.S. imperialism are refracted through the voices of others in the film. The double-voiced discourse is not a contradiction. Rather, it points to the way U.S. Puerto Rican culture is fundamentally at odds with narratives of

U.S. exceptionalism. Perez constructs her own familial narrative to conform to narratives of U.S. exceptionalism and performs the good, deserving migrant who belongs to a multicultural America. The slippage between Perez's careful construction and the documentary's critique of U.S. imperialism underscores that hegemonic narratives of U.S. imperialism need constant maintenance.

Yo soy Boricua, pa'que tu lo Sepas! opens with footage of the Puerto Rican Day Parade in New York City. Perez's cousin Sixto is wearing a Puerto Rican flag as a cape. Vendors sell all manner of Puerto Rican nationalist paraphernalia to willing consumers who are en route to the parade. In a voice-over, Perez poses the question, "Why are you Puerto Ricans so damn proud?" Her immediate response to this question is: "We have amazing history. We have amazing people that we have to be proud of.... We all come in so many different colors." The scene cuts to a discussion between Perez and other family members who elaborate on Puerto Ricans' mixed heritage. Perez begins by identifying the three populations recognized by popular narratives of Puerto Rican cultural nationalism: Tainos (the indigenous population), blacks (the descendants of imported African slaves), and Spaniards.[26] Her companions dispute her and insist that Puerto Ricans are mixed with "black, Spanish, French, Taino, Arawack, Irish, and German."[27]

Dylan Rodríguez identifies a similar pride in mixed racial heritage among Filipino Americans and argues that the ahistoricity of these malleable constructions of Filipino racial identity conform to celebratory multiculturalist narratives.[28] The multiracial construction of Filipinos and Puerto Ricans willfully forgets the physical and political violence that precipitated such mixed populations. During the early Spanish colonial period in Puerto Rico, the indigenous Taino population was basically enslaved to the conquistadors. The inhumane treatment of Tainos and the introduction of European diseases decimated the Taino population. By 1520 Tainos in Puerto Rico were virtually nonexistent.[29] No one in the group mentions American as an identity within the Puerto Rican mix, conveniently erasing cultural traces of U.S. imperialism.[30] In place of this history is a romanticized multiracial figure that projects an image of harmonious racial intermingling. In stark contrast to Griggers's insistence on explicitly connecting her racial and ethnic identity to the violent history of U.S. colonialism in the Philippines, Perez celebrates the mixed racial and ethnic heritage of Puerto Ricans that depends on the history of unequal power relations in Puerto Rico.

In Perez's interactions with her great-grandfather's legitimate family, past pains are likewise glossed over, implying that past indiscretions have no bearing on present relationships. Hence, there is no need to reconcile with the past, only to recognize it. In a scene with members of her great-grandfather's legitimate family, Perez explains that their great-grandfather decided whom to marry based on skin color. Her great-grandmother was darker skinned than the legitimate wife of her great grandfather. Sixto, Perez's cousin from the legitimate side of the family, comments on the irony of their great-grandfather's decision by holding his dark-skinned arm up to Perez's lighter skinned arm. The rest of the family erupts in laughter.[31] Despite the great-grandfather's conscious choice of wife to ensure his legitimate heirs to be lighter skinned, this was not the outcome. Though laughter can be complex, conveying multiple meanings depending on an individual's subject position, this scene visually frames the laughter to humorously imply that Perez's great-grandfather made the wrong choice.[32] There are no quick cutaways in this scene to individual expressions of anger, guilt, or discomfort to suggest unresolved tension among the family. Without explicitly critiquing the choice Perez's great-grandfather made, the documentary implicitly accepts the racist logic used in making the decision; he is not held accountable for the turmoil that Perez's great-grandmother might have felt or for any turmoil their children might have felt for being illegitimate. Any negative consequences that Perez's great-grandfather's actions may have caused her family are never represented. In representing the easy reconciliation of the family members without prior context—When did Perez first realize Sixto was her cousin? How did Sixto's family first regard Perez? Did the film production influence the outcome of this reconciliation? Could this reconciliation have taken place if Perez were not a successful Hollywood actress?—the film represents the past as irrelevant. The present reunion of the legitimate and illegitimate sides of the family resolves the problem of illegitimacy and absolves the American great-grandfather of any wrongdoing. The film implicitly dismisses racism as an individual (and incorrect) choice rather than as a symptom of a racist U.S. colonial hierarchy that affected the personal lives of Puerto Ricans.

Despite the film's overarching celebratory multicultural narrative, *Yo soy Boricua, pa'que tu lo Sepas!* does critique U.S. colonialism in Puerto Rico by representing colonial inequalities and violence, but not through Perez's familial narrative. These critiques are undercut by their incorporation into a narrative of U.S. racial progress that emphasizes the Puerto Rican fighting spirit, all of which is crafted through the representation of Perez's journey in the context of her family and Puerto Rican history. The documentary tackles head-on the issue of Puerto Rico's status vis-à-vis the United States. Against a black background, the definition of "commonwealth" is written in white text while the narrator reads the definition aloud: "A political unit having autonomy but *voluntarily* united with the U.S." Italicizing voluntarily visually insinuates that Puerto Rico's union to the U.S. is anything but. The narrator further delegitimizes the official definition of commonwealth by stating that

"Puerto Rico is more like a colony." In the next sentence, the narrator emphasizes Puerto Ricans' lack of power by contrasting Puerto Rican national responsibilities with their national disenfranchisement: Puerto Ricans "are U.S. citizens. They pay taxes, can be drafted, but cannot vote for the president." This emphasizes for an American audience that Puerto Ricans have the responsibilities of citizens but do not enjoy all of the same privileges that U.S. citizens residing in states enjoy. That is, not all citizens are equal. Continuing the documentary's direct challenge of the narrative of benevolent assimilation, the narrator explains that the U.S. colonial project in Puerto Rico "wasn't all about democracy and freedom. Between the United States government and American corporations the island was turned into one big military base and sugar plantation." While showing old black-and-white footage of sugar cane harvesting and both older and more recent footage of military wagons, naval ships, and planes, the narrator further describes how the United States militarized Puerto Rico to protect the entry of foreign ships into the Panama Canal and allowed large absentee U.S. corporations to establish sugar plantations, displacing Puerto Rican farmers. This restructuring of Puerto Rico's economy led to a high level of unemployment and poverty.[33]

The critique of how U.S. interests created poverty in Puerto Rico by transforming its agrarian economy is undermined by a sequence focusing on Perez's family. Against a slideshow of black-and-white photos of Puerto Rican slums, Perez confesses that her father's family lived in the slums when he was growing up. Her family's economic circumstances did not change until her father enlisted in the U.S. military.[34] The segment ends with an excerpt of a discussion between Perez and Dr. Felix Matos Rodriguez, the director of the City University of New York's Center for Puerto Rican Studies at Hunter College. He states that U.S. military recruitment practices take advantage of "the lack of opportunities and choices that *young* people have. They use that as a way to push them into the war. They were doing that in Puerto Rico, too, where you *also* had a lot of poverty. The military became a ticket out."[35] Critics of military recruitment practices argue that recruitment efforts focus on low-income neighborhoods, but this statement actually undermines their critique.[36] Instead of the film explicitly attributing a "lack of opportunities and choices" to poverty, it attributes these circumstances to youth in general. This implies that U.S. military recruitment efforts target the young and impressionable, not vulnerable, poor communities of color. In Puerto Rico, where there was "also . . . a lot of poverty," recruitment efforts targeting the youth would naturally result in the disproportionate recruitment of poor youth. Though the previous segment explicitly held the United States responsible for creating poverty in Puerto Rico, representing the U.S. military "as a ticket out" for displaced, unemployed Puerto Ricans also depicts the United States as providing opportunities in places where few other job opportunities exist. Instead of explicitly attributing to U.S. colonialism and militarization the fact that military service is one of the few employment opportunities available to poor Puerto Ricans, the film chooses to praise Puerto Ricans in the military who willingly fight and die for a president for whom they cannot vote. Put more simply, this part of the film praises Puerto Ricans for enthusiastically accepting their unequal status.

For its intended mainstream U.S. audience, the film's representation of military opportunity conforms neatly to U.S. historical narratives of how World War II pulled the U.S. economy out of the Great Depression and created widespread economic prosperity in the mid-twentieth century.[37] After all, Perez's father started off in Puerto Rican slums, picked himself up by his bootstraps, and joined the military, which allowed him economic mobility and opened up opportunities for his children—one of whom would go on to become a successful actress. However, whereas World War II was a ticket out of economic straits for the United States and military service was a ticket out of poverty for Perez's father, World War II was not a ticket out of economic subordination for Puerto Rico, as implied by an earlier scene in the film. Against a black background in white text is written "50% of Puerto Rico today lives in poverty."[38] This critique of U.S. colonialism is overshadowed by Perez's family narrative of economic mobility, a narrative that reinforces popular narratives of U.S. exceptionalism imagining the United States as the land of opportunity that attracts and welcomes immigrants.[39] Shifting the discussion from U.S. colonialism's production of inequality to the individual's determination to escape poverty also shifts the responsibility of poverty from the colonial power to the individual Puerto Rican. One can choose to escape poverty. This individual drive for success is a key component of the rags-to-riches stories at the heart of the American Dream: hard work and perseverance will lead to success.[40] Thus, the discussion of Puerto Rican resilience within the context of overcoming poverty becomes a quintessentially American story, one that can be recognized and related to by a mainstream American audience.

The narrative of the United States as a nation of immigrants celebrates a certain kind of immigrant: self-sufficient individuals who find success through hard work. For this reason, such a narrative serves as a disciplinary mechanism that constructs good and bad immigrants.[41] *Yo soy Boricua, pa'que tu lo Sepas!* is careful to represent Puerto Ricans as good migrants who deserve to be welcomed in the United States. This representation can be understood as challenging decades of anthropological constructions of Puerto Ricans as bad migrants unable to overcome their "culture of poverty."[42] While discussing Operation Bootstrap, the Puerto Rican commonwealth policy that resulted in the migration of a half-million Puerto Ricans to the United States in the 1950s, the documentary visually emphasizes their hard work and determination. Black-and-white film footage and photos of Puerto Ricans at ticket counters and boarding commercial and cargo planes underscore their willingness to travel long distances to find work. Perez locates her aunt and mother within this large wave of Puerto Rican migrants. She shares that her mother took work in a factory even though she was college educated.[43] Instead of using this example to discuss explicitly how racism limited job opportunities for people in the United States, or why the development of the Puerto Rican economy did not create jobs for Puerto Rican professionals, Perez cites her mother's experience to further affirm the determination of Puerto Ricans. Underscoring Puerto Rican perseverance, she explains that her aunt and mother were "determined for us to make it."[44] The first-generation migrants sacrificed for the well-being of their children, yet another key component of the immigrant narrative. Thus, the film constructs Puerto Ricans as the quintessential "good immigrants."

The film, in order to take the family experience as recounted by Perez and generalize it to Puerto Ricans of the Operation Bootstrap migration cohort, follows Perez's personal history with a montage of archival photographs and film footage of factory workers, commuter trains, slums, and Puerto Rican families, all set to a recitation of the famous poem "Puerto Rican Obituary," by the late Nuyorican poet Pedro Pietri. The poem's text scrolls along the bottom of the screen, allowing the audience to read along:

> They worked
> They were always on time
> They were never late
> They never spoke back
> when they were insulted
> They worked
> They never took days off
> that were not on the calendar
> They never went on strike
> without permission
> They worked
> ten days a week
> and were only paid for five
> They worked
> They worked
> They worked
> and they died.[45]

This excerpt represents the exploitative labor conditions that Puerto Ricans endure in the United States. Read in its entirety, the poem critiques the passiveness of Puerto Rican workers who unquestioningly accepted their exploitation—a larger critique that is obscured by the documentary's sequencing. Pietri's poem is the end of the DVD chapter titled "Facing Adversity." Having just emphasized the importance of Puerto Rican perseverance and Perez's family's sacrifice for the next generation, this excerpt and the accompanying montage are easily read as further evidence of the diligent workers who knowingly endured such exploitation and ultimately succeeded in obtaining their goal of creating opportunities for the next generation. After all, Perez's father grew up in the Puerto Rican slums, and her mother lived in the Brooklyn projects, but today Perez is a successful Hollywood star. The documentary leaves out Pietri's critique of a racialized hierarchy in the United States that is designed to keep Puerto Ricans from attaining the American Dream:

> These dreams
> These empty dreams . . .
> about the ideal white American family
> with black maids
> and latino janitors.[46]

This critique of racial power would have contextualized the discussion Perez had with her family about her great-grandfather's choice of wife. Elsewhere in the poem Peitri asserts that though Puerto Ricans worked hard, they were never adequately compensated for their work, morbidly declaring that these hard-working Puerto Ricans

> were born to weep
> to keep the morticians employed
> as long as they pledge allegiance
> to a flag that wants them destroyed.[47]

Here, Pietri explicitly links the exploitation of Puerto Rican workers to Puerto Rico's colonial subordination to the United States, challenging the notion of social mobility in the United States that *Yo soy Boricua, pa'que tu lo Sepas!* reproduces. Pietri instead argues that Puerto Ricans were born to be exploited and cannot escape the fate that U.S. imperialism preordained for them. However, these scathing critiques are conspicuously absent from the documentary. The part of the poem excerpted in the documentary, coupled with Perez's admiration for Puerto Ricans' willingness to sacrifice for their children, does not convey the poems' hopelessness and despair at the futility of simply being good workers who accept their lot in life in exchange for their children's future success.

Despite the way that the film's recurring motif that Puerto Ricans are resilient can be co-opted to reinforce narratives of U.S. exceptionalism, the documentary critiques the totalitarian nature of U.S. colonialism by representing Puerto Rican nationalist Pedro Albizu Campos and the Ponce Massacre. Perez characterizes Albizu Campos as Puerto Rico's greatest hero, the Harvard-educated leader of the Puerto Rican Nationalist Party in the 1930s who advocated for political independence.[48] In 1937 he was imprisoned for attempting to overthrow the colonial government. Puerto Rican nationalists organized a demonstration at the University of Puerto Rico's Ponce campus against Albizu Campos's imprisonment. The peaceful demonstration and parade ended in violence: the Insular Police shot twenty-one unarmed Puerto Ricans dead, and wounding two hundred others.[49] In the documentary, the massacre is represented with spliced scenes of Perez's visit to the Museo de la Masacre de Ponce (Ponce Massacre Museum) and archival photographs of the parade. Photographs of demonstrators congregating outside of (what is today) the museum fade into footage of Perez's visit, visually suggesting that Perez is not simply visiting the museum but is taking a trip to the Ponce Massacre. From the second-floor balcony of the museum, Fay Palmer, curator of the Museo de Arte de Ponce (Ponce Museum of Fine Art), points to street-level locations where the nationalists gathered. As the camera pans to where Palmer points, the present-day footage is replaced with archival photographs of uniformed men marching. This sequence visually immerses the audience within the history, giving the sense that we are witnessing the march from Perez's perspective on the balcony.[50] Thus, we witness U.S. colonial violence as the archival photograph montage segues from scenes of demonstrators in formation to scenes of uniformed Puerto Rican nationalists lying on the floor, covered in blood, while the narrator reports the wounded and casualty counts.

Representing the events of the Ponce Massacre through a museum visit lends historical credence to this event. The archival photographs are tangible evidence of the violent repression of Puerto Rican resistance to U.S. colonial rule. This representational strategy legitimizes the depiction of the Ponce Massacre in *Yo soy Boricua, pa'que tu lo Sepas!* as fact, in direct contrast to the creative reenactments of U.S. colonial violence in *Memories of a Forgotten War*. However, the archival legitimization of this depiction also comes at a cost. This representation of the Ponce Massacre strictly adheres to the institutional narrative of the event that justifies the use of violence by the Insular Police. The documentary's critique of the emphasis on excessive U.S.

Camera pans up from an archival photo of Puerto Rican nationalists gathering outside the building of what is today the Ponce Massacre Museum and transitions into a shot of Rosie Perez and Fay Palmer.

colonial violence is tempered by questioning who instigated the massacre. Before the montage of archival photographs switches focus to the aftermath of the attack, Palmer states, "No one knows who fired the first shot."⁵¹ The documentary leaves open the possibility that the U.S. Insular Police were provoked and thus justified in their use of violence. Making this declaration prior to the audience's witnessing of the use of colonial violence allows the audience to blame the violence on the victims instead of the perpetrators. In contrast to *Memories of a Forgotten War*, this documentary does not question the official investigations into the massacre that were unable to determine whether the Insular Police or the demonstrators fired the first shot, even though eyewitness reports claimed that the Puerto Rican nationalists were not armed, making it impossible for them to fire the first shot.⁵² Apparently, these eyewitness accounts could not be substantiated accordingly to be considered legitimate history or to be included in the film. The tradeoff for institutional, archival legitimization is that official accounts cannot be questioned.

In addition to its tempered critique of colonial violence, the documentary is also very critical of the treatment of Puerto Rican political prisoners, many of them incarcerated for advocating for Puerto Rican independence. The film focuses on political prisoner Albizu Campos particularly, the narrator describing how Albizu Campos spent much of the previous twenty-five years incarcerated. During his imprisonment Albizu Campos wrote letters describing how he was tortured. In the representation of Albizu Campos's imprisonment, the narrator reads excerpts from these letters while graphic black and white photos of Albizu Campos's injuries are shown on the screen. Part of the narration is highlighted as written and translated text on the screen: "para quemarme viva—to burn me alive."⁵³ The combination of the images of burns and cuts on Albizu Campos's frail body and his accounts of being subjected to repeated electrical shocks underscore the U.S. colonial regime's brutal efforts to suppress Puerto Rican independence. Imprisonment was not enough punishment; neither was starvation. The scene ends with a shift in narration from the unseen narrator to Perez, who comments "He just wanted his country to be free. He wasn't trying to overthrow the United States. He was just saying let us be free," and she goes on to compare Albizu Campos to both Martin Luther King Jr. and Che Guevara.⁵⁴ Her concluding sentiments are contradictory: she insists simultaneously that Albizu Campos wanted freedom for Puerto Rico but did not want to overthrow the United States. However, given the United States' use of force against Puerto Rican independence movements as represented in the documentary, it seems that Puerto Rican independence could only be achieved by overthrowing the U.S. colonial government. In fact, Albizu Campos strove to achieve Puerto Rican independence by any means necessary, including violence.⁵⁵ The historical comparisons Perez offers are telling. Choosing Martin Luther King Jr. and Che Guevara locates Puerto Rican resistance within the U.S. civil rights movement and within Latin American anticolonial movements. In the United States, Martin Luther King Jr. is most celebrated for his commitment to nonviolent protest as a means of achieving racial equality. His more radical critiques of inequality in the United States and of U.S. imperialism are conveniently overshadowed, just as Albizu Campos's more radical views are de-emphasized by Perez. Che Guevara was a guerrilla revolutionary who worked toward the overthrow of governments but who is now most readily recognized in the United States as a commodified icon symbolizing revolution.[56] Thus, in Perez's concluding statements on Albizu Campos she represents him in terms recognizable and palatable to a U.S. audience: as a nonviolent, revolutionary martyr who did not want independence. She appeals to American's commitment to freedom and equality while obscuring the Puerto Rican independence movement. In doing so, she evacuates the historical figure of Pedro Albizu Campos of his revolutionary resistance.

Referencing Martin Luther King Jr. not only tempers Albizu Campos's critique of U.S. colonial rule but also undermines the critiques of inequality that the film represents. In mainstream U.S. histories of the civil rights movement, Martin Luther King Jr. is most memorialized for his "I Have a Dream" speech, particularly the line, "I have a dream that my four little children will one day live in a nation where they will not be judged by the color of their skin but by the content of their character." Conservative U.S. politicians have misappropriated this quote to argue against the continuing need for government programs that aim to rectify centuries of racial inequality. Such arguments insist that the United States is a postracial society where everyone does have equal opportunity and where everyone should be judged by the content of his or her character.[57] In other words, they claim antidiscriminatory laws are discriminatory to white people. Thus, Martin Luther King Jr. as a civil rights icon signifies a narrative of racial progress in the United States. According to this narrative, the dream King dreamed is now a reality. This narrative dismisses present-day racism by comparing it to blatant racism in the United States' past: African American slavery, the genocide and displacement of Native Americans, segregation. It emphasizes how much worse life used to be for minorities and lauds the progress ushered in by the civil rights movement to discipline those who organize against present-day racism.

Perez's documentary does not explicitly declare racism defeated, but her representation of the strides made by Puerto Ricans in the United States reaffirms the narrative of racial progress. In particular, the narrator focuses on the work of the Young Lords, a group of U.S. Puerto Rican college students who organized for social change in the 1960s. The segment opens with the narrator declaring, "In the early years, maintaining our cultural ties was not half as difficult as establishing a political presence." Black-and-white footage of the Young Lords shows them marching and serving New York City communities as a voice-over recounts their accomplishments: securing a reliable garbage collection policy from the city, appropriating hospitals to provide healthcare services to the underprivileged, and taking over the First Spanish Methodist Church to provide a daycare center and breakfast program for underprivileged children in Harlem.[58] That is, the Young Lords brought services to the Puerto Rican community that the federal and local governments had failed to bring. Against the backdrop of footage of the arrest of the Young Lords for occupying the First Spanish Methodist Church, the narrator describes how these "polite revolutionaries" forced the city to recognize the needs of barrio residents. Like mainstream representations of Martin Luther King Jr., the film's representation of the Young Lords as "polite revolutionaries" conspicuously omits the party's critiques of U.S. power and inequality articulated. The Young Lords advocated for the independence of Puerto Rico and other colonies. They opposed capitalism and the U.S. military.[59] The film's representation of the Young Lords' community service, as it overlooks the group's "radical" politics, makes the organization palatable for a mainstream American audience. Likewise, the segments' emphasis on resilience and determination of the Young Lords providing for their own community can be interpreted as evidence that impoverished communities do not need government assistance, that these communities can and should take care of themselves with already available resources, affirming the construction of a postracial United States that need not allocate resources for marginalized communities of color.

The final segment of the documentary cements its affirmation of the narrative of racial progress in the United States. Returning to the New York City Puerto Rican Day Parade, the film represents the history behind the establishment of the parade through a series of interviews, conducted by Perez, of past and current parade organizers. The narrator adds that the impetus for organizers of the parade in the 1950s was to galvanize the dispersed Puerto Rican community, to challenge negative mainstream conceptions of Puerto Ricans, and to form a political voice. In particular the organizers wanted to challenge the negative mainstream image of Puerto Ricans as instigators of "pro-independence violence." Singling out pro-independence activists as the source of negative representations of Puerto Ricans as opposed to racial stereotypes of Puerto Ricans—constructed in part though U.S. colonial policies—demonstrates that though the film is critical of U.S. colonialism, it does not wish to advocate for independence from the United States. This is likewise articulated in the reconstruction of Albizu Campos as fighting for freedom of Puerto Rico but not the overthrow of U.S. colonialism.

The origin of this contradiction can be attributed to Muñoz-Marin's Operation Serenity, which constructed cultural nationalism separate from political nationalisms that articulate political sovereignty from the United States.[60] Perez attributes her understanding of her identity as Puerto Rican to the Puerto Rican parade, which serves as the basis for the documentary's narrative. The Puerto Rican commonwealth government has played a significant role in the organization of this parade since its inception and thus articulates Puerto Rico's cultural nationalism, a nationalism that constructs a Puerto Rican culture free from U.S. influence but does not challenge U.S. political control.[61] The film conflates cultural representation in the New York Puerto Rican parade with political empowerment. Footage of the 2005 parade highlights the attendance of influential U.S. politicians, including then–New York state senator Hilary Clinton, civil rights leader Al Sharpton, and then–New York Governor George Pataki.[62] The film interprets these politicians' appearances as evidence of Puerto Rican political empowerment. However, Puerto Rico's representative in the U.S. Congress still cannot vote along with other congressmen. There are no U.S. senators and only four voting U.S. congressmen of Puerto Rican descent. And yet the documentary ends with a celebratory, almost victorious note. Among the closing statements is the assertion that the parade demonstrates that Puerto Ricans "have arrived. We belong. We're just as good as anyone else."[63] This statement illustrates how neatly cultural nationalism supports narratives of U.S. multiculturalism. Despite the film's representation of cultural pride and distinctiveness, assimilation to the United States and adherence to the narrative of U.S. multiculturalism renders difference meaningless, or "just as good as anyone else." This film and the Puerto Rican Day parade itself are cultural representations that displace the violence of U.S. colonialism in Puerto Rico, much in the same fashion that Dylan Rodríquez argues that Filipino cultural nationalism displaces the violence of U.S. colonialism in the Philippines.[64]

Fittingly, the topic of Perez's illegitimacy is not revisited at the end of the film. The earlier representation of Perez's reunion with the legitimate side of her family conveys that, regardless of her illegitimacy, she belongs in the family. The past is swept away without mention of how being illegitimate affected the lives of Perez's great-grandmother, grandparents, or parents. All is forgotten in a public display of family unity. Likewise, *Yo soy Boricua, pa'que tu lo Sepas!* demonstrates that the price of Puerto Rican belonging to a multicultural United States is the willful obscuring of U.S. colonial violence in favor of public cultural demonstrations. The double-voiced discourse between the unseen narrator and Perez demonstrates how the erasure of U.S. colonial violence in Puerto Rico is never wholly complete because Puerto Ricans are constructed in relation to U.S. imperialism and thus are fundamentally at odds with narratives of U.S. exceptionalism. The documentary captures both Perez's active attempt to affirm narratives of U.S. exceptionalism and the way in which Puerto Rican history cannot fully conform to that narrative.

Reconciling the Past: Forget about It!

Both *Memories of a Forgotten War* and *Yo soy Boricua, pa'que tu lo Sepas!* critique U.S. colonialism. Both represent U.S. colonial violence against native resistance to varying degrees. Both explicitly demonstrate the inherent inequality in the relationships between these islands and the United States. Both also tell personal stories of familial illegitimacy. If we read the representations of illegitimacy in these documentaries as critically resurrecting the metaphor of colonialism as paternal benevolence, then what can we conclude from the very different representations of illegitimacy and possibilities for reconciliation? The different representations of legitimacy articulate the different ways that the Philippines and Puerto Rico are recognized and disavowed by the United States in the construction of a hegemonic narrative of U.S. exceptionalism. U.S. colonialism in the Philippines is recognized when necessary to provide an example of a successful democratization project. Thus, during the U.S. occupation of Iraq and Afghanistan, the United States took credit for the Philippines' current status as a democratic, politically sovereign nation. However, the United States did not acknowledge Philippine resistance to U.S. colonial rule or the violent military repression of this resistance, as it did not fit the hegemonic narrative of U.S. colonial benevolence as successful democratization that would now be implemented in the Middle East. *Memories of a Forgotten War* explicitly uses Griggers's experience of illegitimacy as a metaphor for the relationship between the United States and the Philippines to challenge hegemonic narratives of U.S. benevolent assimilation in the Philippines. Using the notion of illegitimacy as a frame for understanding U.S. neocolonial relations with the Philippines, the film demonstrates how narratives of U.S. exceptionalism render the violence of U.S. colonialism invisible. Griggers resurrects the metaphor of colonialism as paternal benevolence to thoroughly discredit it. Instead of a caring, attentive father, Griggers reveals the United States as a deadbeat dad shirking his responsibilities. The disavowal of that history, just like the disavowal of children, has enduring ramifications because the disavowed history is "incongruent[t] with our image of ourselves and dissonant with how the rest of the world sees us, sees the Philippines, and sees America."[65] The controlling narratives of U.S. exceptionalism encourage identification with a history of benevolent assimilation and a willful forgetting or misremembering of U.S. colonial violence. Dylan Rodríquez conceptualizes Filipino American identification with exceptionalist U.S. histories as a suspended apocalypse that prevents Filipino American resistance against current U.S. neocolonial projects.[66] Griggers argues that reconciliation and healing can begin only when the United States owns up to its violent history, legitimating the illegitimate memories of its forgotten war. Here we find another limit to using personal history as a metaphor for the colonial relationship between the Philippines and Puerto Rico. In the end, Griggers's prescription for healing privatizes inequality rather than addressing it. She does not demand recompense for past violence, merely a recognition of it.

On the other hand, *Yo soy Boricua, pa'que tu lo Sepas!* does not explicitly use Perez's personal experience of illegitimacy as a metaphor for the marginalization of Puerto Rican history within United States, nor is the narrative of illegitimacy threaded through the entire documentary. This separation between Perez's personal history and Puerto Rican history results in a double-voiced discourse. The documentary's representation of Puerto Rican history explores U.S. repression of pro-independence activism and the United States' exploitation of Puerto Ricans; Perez's family stories affirm hegemonic narratives of the United States as a land of opportunity that allows hardworking Puerto Ricans to succeed in the face of poverty. Similar to *Memories of a Forgotten War*, *Yo soy Boricua, pa'que tu lo Sepas!* does not suggest how the United States might make amends for its repression and exploitation of Puerto Rico. The representation of easy reconciliation between Perez with the legitimate side of her family suggests that the United States can easily reconcile with Puerto Rico. The documentary suggests that illegitimacy is an unnecessary family secret that need no longer be kept secret because it no longer makes a difference in the present day. The history of Perez's family can be researched, recorded, and shared in a way that reunites the entire family, both legitimate and illegitimate. Likewise, the history of Puerto Rico can be researched, recorded, and shared in a way that reunites Puerto Ricans within the multicultural American family. Thus Perez resurrects the metaphor of U.S. colonialism-as-paternal-benevolence as a reminder that Puerto Rico is indeed part of the United States. Puerto Rico's continuing status as a U.S. commonwealth is problematic for the United States' disavowal of empire. Even though U.S. imperialism manifests itself explicitly in the democratization projects in the Middle East today, the hegemonic narrative of U.S.

exceptionalism represents U.S. intervention as temporary, and clearly the United States is not in Puerto Rico temporarily. Thus, the documentary's focus on U.S. recognition without demands to reconcile the past reflects the United States' particular relationship with Puerto Rico and disavowal of said relationship. In focusing solely on recognition, the documentary does not hold the United States accountable for any of the continuing consequences of U.S. colonial rule, just as Perez does not hold her great-grandfather accountable for any of the consequences her family faced as a result of being illegitimate. The violent past can be recognized as simply *in the past*, with no bearing for current and future generations. The documentary's representation of the colonial violence as past tense legitimizes narratives of U.S. exceptionalism and in turn the affirmation of this mainstream narrative legitimizes the Puerto Rican story that the documentary tells.

The ability to reconcile a cultural narrative within hegemonic U.S. narratives has some bearing on its cultural and historical legitimacy. Such reconciliation determines how recognizable and acceptable these documentaries will be for a mainstream U.S. audience. In other words, it influences whether there are investors who will take the financial risk and provide resources to enable the widespread marketing and distribution of a documentary. *Memories of a Forgotten War* explicitly challenges U.S. hegemonic narratives of benevolent assimilation and exceptionalism. The documentary was funded primarily by nonprofit arts organizations and its distribution limited mainly to film festivals. Market logic dictates that documentaries with only marginal appeal are risky ventures or at best art house films. It is thus difficult to articulate alternative narratives because production companies are hesitant to produce cultural products with only a marginal appeal. When such cultural productions are produced, they secure only limited releases, reaching a small audience, and thus they cannot effectively change the discourse of popular U.S. narratives. Documentaries that attract enough funding and star power to reach a mainstream U.S. audience, including *Yo soy Boricua, pa'que tu lo Sepas!*, often reproduce narratives of U.S. exceptionalism. The power of the market, therefore, creates a vicious cycle that results in the continuing marginalization of violent histories of U.S. imperialism. Legitimate narratives of U.S. exceptionalism are continually reaffirmed; illegitimate narratives of U.S. colonial violence are continually disavowed or violently misappropriated within teleological narratives of progress. Or, using the metaphor of U.S. colonialism as a paternal relationship, this means Uncle Sam only recognizes his children when it benefits him.

Though resurrecting the metaphor of colonialism as a paternal relationship pointedly conveys how hegemonic narratives of U.S. exceptionalism have obscured U.S. colonial violence and exploitation in the Philippines and Puerto Rico, relying on this metaphor also privileges the heteronormative family while marginalizing nonfamilial violence. What claims to legitimacy do the offspring of one-night stands have? Or the offspring of rape? The resurrected metaphor implies that the United States needs to recognize publically its paternal relationships and fulfill its responsibilities to the Philippines and Puerto Rico. This obscures forms of U.S. neocolonial violence that are not accompanied by democratization projects, where the United States has made no public commitment of responsibilities.

4. Performing Genealogies
Poetic Pedagogies of Disidentification

> I went to school and I read their books and I learned about the rulers and the conquerors of the Earth. I learned about the rich man and how he tells his story but what about my story? What about the people's story? . . . Not a word about the injustice and certainly not a word about the heroes who selflessly fought for the rights and the welfare of their fellow man, woman, children. It's justice they demand and true freedom from oppression and poverty for true equal opportunity. This is our story. This is our people's story and that's why it's on us. It's on us. It's really on us to continue this story 'cause it's our people who are making history.
> —Aquilina Soriano, "What About My Story?"

The racist metaphor of turn-of-the-century colonies as unruly, orphaned children in need of a paternal figure not only justified the U.S. conquest of the Philippines, Puerto Rico, and other island territories, but it also reinforced the representation of U.S. imperialism at the turn of the century as a democratic pedagogical project. Many political cartoons at the time depicted U.S. territories as children in schoolrooms with Uncle Sam as their teacher. These cartoons echoed the rhetoric of benevolent assimilation that constructed the colonial project in the Philippines and Puerto Rico as political education.[1] As the exemplar of democracy, the United States would teach their island colonies how to become independent, democratic nations.

The institution of public education was vital to the U.S. colonial project in the Philippines and Puerto Rico because this would prepare Filipinos and Puerto Ricans to participate in and eventually maintain democratic institutions introduced by the United States.[2] An army of U.S. teachers was recruited and deployed to the Philippines and Puerto Rico to establish public schools.[3] By controlling the curriculum of colonial schools, the United States was able to construct Philippine and Puerto Rican history to legitimize their occupation of these islands. These institutionalized histories reproduced the ideology of benevolent assimilation, were disseminated by public schools to manufacture the consent of Filipinos and Puerto Ricans to U.S. colonial rule, and continue to influence the lives of Filipinos and Puerto Ricans a century later.[4]

In her poem "Our Story," in the epigraph above, Aquilina Soriano articulates how institutionalized histories, like those taught in public schools, erase histories of discrimination and resistance by privileging the perspective of the powerful. Soriano constructs two groups of people in binary opposition to one another. The powerful consist of rich, male rulers. The powerless consist of displaced, im/migrants of color who suffer from and fight against injustice. Notably, Soriano does not describe the powerful and powerless in the socially constructed terms of nationality, ethnicity, or race. Social theorist Homi Bhabba argues that the "linear equivalence of event and idea that historicism proposes, most commonly signifies a people, a nation, or a national culture as an empirical sociological category or a holistic cultural entity."[5] Events that are incorporated into institutionalized histories are narrated as part of a national history, closing off the possibility that different interpretations of the same event could support other historical narratives that do not privilege the nation.[6] Thus, we can read the absence of national, ethnic, or racial identifiers in Soriano's poem as a revision of history that decenters the nation to recognize how the transnational coalitions of the powerful work together to create the inequality that the powerless around the world experience.

This chapter examines how Filipino American and U.S. Puerto Rican performance-poet activists, including Soriano, understand the central role that education played in the colonial project and therefore deploy education as a tool in decolonizing activist projects. I argue that these performance-poet activists are organic intellectuals who teach their local communities how to disdenitfy with hegemonic narratives of U.S. exceptionalism and provide them with a repertoire of cultural tools to construct a genealogy of global power. Connecting disparate subjugated knowledge, they construct a history of oppression and resistance that they make available to their local communities. They reconstruct history outside a national framework to trace a genealogy of global power in their poetry. Foucault defines genealogy as a form of analysis that reactivates historically unrecognized local memories, dissenting opinions, and theories to explore how institutionalization of certain knowledge rendered other knowledge illegitimate.[7] These performance-poet activists reactivate subjugated knowledge not only by reproducing these projects for diverse audiences but by authorizing others to speak and articulate their own situated knowledge.[8] Soriano's direct address to the audience in her poem above, asking them "Can you tell me the real story?" exemplifies how performance-poet activists authorize others to speak and contribute to their genealogical project.

Filipino American and U.S. Puerto Rican performance-poet activists construct and reproduce a genealogy of global power to challenge institutionalized histories, especially hegemonic representations of U.S. exceptionalism. The cultural form their historical intervention takes is critical and sets them apart from novelists and filmmakers. These performance-poet activists approximate social theorist Antonio Gramsci's conception of organic intellectuals. In contrast to traditional intellectuals, organic intellectuals actively participate in "practical life, as a constructor, organiser, a permanent persuader, and not just a simple orator."[9] These poets are not full-time artists but full-time educators who consider performance poetry to be a tool for education. Performing poetry, instead of simply sharing the poem and its historical critique in its written form, enable these individuals to participate actively in the practical lives of their communities.

Performance studies scholars argue that performances, especially ritual performances, are a site of alternative history. In teaching ritual performances to subsequent generations, memories are likewise transmitted from one generation to the next.[10] For this reason, Diana Taylor theorizes that a repertoire of performances, gestures, rituals, and the like is much like an archive for embodied culture. In comparing the repertoire to an archive she does not suggest that performances can be read as texts. She argues that, unlike the archive, "[t]he repertoire requires presence: people participate in the production and reproduction of knowledge by being there," being part of the transmission."[11] Though the performance poetry I examine does not transmit alternate history through the teaching of rituals, Taylor's conceptualization of a repertoire still applies to the work of these performance-poet activists because, as educators, they teach cultural practices. Specifically, they provide their students and audiences with critical thinking skills to disidentify with narratives of U.S. exceptionalism and to create their own narratives. Thus, we can understand these performance-poet activists as using a repertoire to reproduce a genealogy of global power because they are teaching cultural skills and require the presence of others whom they hope to transform from passive listeners to active participants who will reproduce the knowledge they share. Performing live allows for the possibility of intimate interactions to take place between performer and audience member. It allows for authorization of the audience member to reproduce his or her own situated knowledge and thus reactivates those histories that institutions rendered illegitimate. In this case, performance is a vital component to the construction of a genealogy of global power at the heart of Filipino American and U.S. Puerto Rican decolonizing projects because their goal is the active participation of those present.

In this chapter, I focus on Los Angeles–based Filipino American and New York–based U.S. Puerto Rican performance-poet activists. My findings are based on personal interviews and qualitative research conducted from 2005 to 2006 and textual analyses of selected poems. The performance poets in this study are products of the colonial histories I outlined. The U.S. Puerto Rican performance poets and Filipino American poets I interviewed belong to different generational cohorts, reflecting the different im/migration patterns of Puerto Ricans and Filipinos to the United States. Of the performance poets I interviewed, most do not belong to the immigrant generation. The Filipino American performance poets are children of immigrants who entered the United States after the 1965 Immigration Act and belong either to the "one-and-a-half" generation or second generation. Due to the 1965 Immigration Acts' preferential quotas for highly skilled workers, most of these poets grew up in middle-class, suburban households, but a few grew up in low-income neighborhoods in the city of Los Angeles proper. The U.S. Puerto Rican poets are either part of the second or third generation, descended from Puerto Ricans who migrated to the United States in the 1950s as a result of Operation Bootstrap. Most of the New York Puerto Rican performance poets grew up in low-income neighborhoods in Spanish Harlem or the South Bronx, where most working-class Puerto Rican migrants made their homes.

Despite their varying class positions, most of the Filipino American and U.S. Puerto Rican performance poets I interviewed earned college degrees or had attended some college. At the time of the interviews, a majority of these poets worked either primarily as teachers, as writers, or as other cultural artists or community activists. They taught at the university, in elementary schools, in after-school arts programs, and in courses that teach English as a second language. Those focused on writing were not only poets but also playwrights, short-story writers, and print and electronic journalists. Others pursued careers as filmmakers, solo performance artists, members of rock and hip hop performance groups, or visual artists. They worked in local community arts organizations and those advocating for social change. Some of these jobs were stable, others were not. Some of the artists lived from paycheck to paycheck. At one of my interviews, I arranged to meet the interviewee at a doughnut shop near his home. He wanted me to call upon my arrival, which I did, only to find that his cell phone had been disconnected. When we finally met, he apologized, telling me that the gentrification and subsequent rising rents in his neighborhood made it difficult for him to pay his bills on time. The incongruence of their college education to the hand-to-mouth existence some of these poets live may suggest the declining value of a college degree, especially in the humanities. However, most of these poets see the work that they do in the community, for their art, and for social change as necessary, measuring their success not in financial currency but in the social contributions they believe they make.

These poets ethnically identify as Filipino American or Nuyorican, or a variation of either of these identities. My conversations with second-generation and 1.5-generation Filipino American performance poets indicate that the second generation's Filipino American identity forms largely during their college years, after Filipino American youth gain a certain amount of independence from their parents. In the home they were encouraged to assimilate to U.S. culture and thus looked outside the home to reclaim an identity and history they felt deprived of. These poets' identity formation in college was instrumental in their decisions to become involved in performance poetry and community organizations, confirming Yen Le Espiritu's assertions that second-generation Filipino Americans create their own distinct cultures in the United States that critique their place in U.S. society rather than moving from an essentialized Filipino identity toward a monolithic American identity.[12] The U.S. Puerto Rican performance poets I interviewed identified as Boricua, Nuyorican, or Puerto Rican. Boricua is the term given to the indigenous populations of Puerto Rico prior to Christopher Columbus's landing. Nuyorican is a term combining "New York" and "Puerto Rican" used to claim the particular history of Puerto Ricans in New York and the simultaneous sense of belonging and marginality they feel in both New York and Puerto Rico.[13] Their refusal to identify with the U.S. or as hyphenated Americans illustrates their insistence that the term "Puerto Rican American" is redundant because they are U.S. citizens and Puerto Rico is part of the United States.

All of the poets I interviewed had visited the Philippines or Puerto Rico. Most of the Filipino American performance poets had only been to the Philippines a couple of times; many visited for the first time as young adults. Witnessing the poverty of the Philippines often acts as an additional catalyst for the poets' involvement in U.S. organizations' advocating for social change in the Philippines. On the other hand, some of the U.S. Puerto Rican performance poets I interviewed visited Puerto Rico on a regular, sometimes annual basis. The circular migration between New York City and Puerto Rico facilitates the formation of a transnational Puerto Rican identity and enables

New York Puerto Rican performance poets to participate in transnational cultural and activist circuits.

I begin my analysis by examining several poems to demonstrate how these performance-poet activists construct genealogies of global power that challenge institutionalized narratives of U.S. exceptionalism. Foucault describes genealogical projects as reactivation of local knowledge deemed illegitimate by established institutional power.[14] Thus, the genealogies that Los Angeles Filipino Americans and New York Puerto Ricans construct are specific to their particular histories, social positions, and geographic locations. In that sense, though both groups construct a genealogy of global power, these genealogies are not comprehensive. After examining the genealogies of global power that these performance-poet activists construct, I discuss their pedagogical approach to disseminating and reproducing their genealogies. They educate inside and outside the classroom, targeting a socioeconomically diverse population. I end the chapter by conceptualizing their activist organizing not only as a call to action but also as the authorization of other speakers to contribute to their genealogies. Recognizing that institutionalized history depends on the exclusion of nonlegitimated perspectives and that their genealogical projects are always incomplete, never representing all perspectives, Filipino American and U.S. Puerto Rican performance poets train and encourage other people of color to speak in order to to reactivate the local knowledge or marginalized, aggrieved communities. The construction and reproduction of genealogies of global power make transparent and challenge institutional power that narratively excludes people of color to obscure global inequality.

The fact that these performance-poet genealogies of global power fundamentally critique and rewrite history means that their cultural narratives can neither be reconciled with hegemonic narratives of U.S. exceptionalism nor easily co-opted by celebratory narratives of U.S. multiculturalism. Therefore, their narratives are largely illegitimate and unrecognizable for a large, mainstream, U.S. audience. For the most part, the popularity of the performance poets I analyze is limited to their activist networks and their local communities. Part of this is intentional: these performance-poet activists wish to organize and galvanize their local communities to action, and this work is best done in more intimate performance settings. The downside to this strategy is that an intimate audience denotes a limited audience. A limited audience in turn means that though their historical critiques may be empowering within their local communities, the poets do not challenge the institutionalized narratives of U.S. exceptionalism in mainstream popular discourse.

Poetic Genealogies

U.S. multiculturalism produces additive histories that selectively incorporate histories of people of color to affirm hegemonic narratives of U.S. exceptionalism.[15] Representing the success of specific ethnic groups and individual people of color supports the narrative of the United States as an egalitarian land of opportunity in contrast to the lack of social mobility in other parts of the world. U.S. multiculturalism typifies what social theorist Martin Mastuśik defines as a "ludic multiculturalism" because it reduces minority histories into celebratory, essentialist, consumable commodities such as cuisine, costumes, and ritual performances.[16] The decontextualized performance of ethnic and racial difference enables the argument that the United States is postracial. That is, that the United States not only tolerates but celebrates difference in its inclusion and consumption of different cultures. This promise of inclusion in the United States, albeit a differential inclusion, encourages Filipino Americans and U.S. Puerto Ricans to identify with narratives of U.S. exceptionalism.[17] Instead of identifying with the hegemonic narratives of the United States as multicultural, postracial, and egalitarian and thereby performing their cultural heritage, Filipino American and U.S. Puerto Rican performance-poet activists disidentify with and critique the racist constructions produced by U.S. exceptionalist narratives. Performance studies scholar José Esteban Muñoz defines disidentification not as the simple act of rejecting a negatively constructed identity but as the rehabilitation of such an identity. He elaborates that "to disidentify is to read oneself and one's own life narrative in a moment, object, or subject that is not culturally coded to 'connect' with the disidentifying subject."[18] In reconstructing Philippine and Puerto Rican history, Filipino American and U.S. Puerto Rican performance-poet activists deploy an intersectional lens not only to disidentify with the negative constructions of other aggrieved minority groups around the world but also to disidentify with negative constructions of themselves.[19] By disidentifying, the performance-poet activists also imagine a world different from that constructed in hegemonic narratives of U.S. exceptionalism. They construct genealogies of global power according to their historic particularities and their specific social positions. Given their different situated knowledge the Los Angeles Filipino American performance-poet activists construct a genealogy of global power different from New York Puerto Rican performance-poet activists.

Los Angeles Filipino Americans use the Philippines' history of colonial subordination and Filipino American racial subordination in the United States as a point of departure in constructing their genealogy of global power.

They disidentify with negative constructions of other selfish colonizers, of other subordinate racial groups in the United States, and of others subjected to subsequent U.S. imperial projects by rejecting narratives of U.S. exceptionalism. These disidentifications allow Los Angeles Filipino Americans to create a genealogy of global power that connects their histories to those of other minority groups in the Los Angeles area in a substantial manner, as opposed to the superficial manner in which U.S. multicultural history incorporates groups through the evacuation of meaningful historical differences.

The hegemonic narrative of U.S. exceptionalism insists that the United States is a fundamentally different global power than other global powers. The reproduction and institutionalization of the construction of the United States as the selfless, benevolent global power encouraged Filipinos to consent to colonial rule not only by emphasizing the benefits of U.S. rule but also by emphasizing other empires' selfish designs. Given a choice of colonizers, the United States was the natural choice. Rejecting the notion that the United States is a better global power places the United States in a chronology of colonial powers in the Philippines and rehabilitates the resulting mixed-race populations deemed undesirable. In his poem "Conditions (an unrestricted list)" Napoleon Lustre challenges essentialist constructions of Filipino identity to reveal a history of the economic and political subordination of Filipinos: "You are Filipino if you descended from the children of the Spanish friars, priests or other unholy men. You are Filipino if your mother was an American base hostess and your eyes are green or any shade lighter than black really and your last name is Murphy, Sullivan or even Brown . . . You are Filipino if you are part Japanese even though your father was the fruit of betrayal, less than human they called them, and your grandmother killed herself after a lifetime as the local loca since the execution of her soldier invader lover."[20] Here Lustre explains the connection between colonialism and racial miscegenation in the Philippines. In particular, he underscores how the sexual exploitation of Filipinas was a common experience during all colonial occupations: Spain, the United States, and Japan. On the surface, the absence of the American colonial sexual predator counterpart to the "unholy" Spanish friars and the Japanese "soldier invader lover" seemingly reaffirms the exceptional nature of U.S. colonial occupation. However, the simple inclusion of the United States in this genealogy of foreign colonizers refuses the characterization of the United States as an exceptional empire. Instead, we can read this passage as an acknowledgement of but disidentification with the negative stigma attached to the Filipino descendants of "unholy" Spaniards and "less than human" Japanese that includes these mixed-race products of "bad" colonial occupations in the Filipino identity. This inclusion emphasizes that these populations are no different from Eurasian and Amerasian Filipinos who also are products of colonialism in the Philippines, despite the different ways these populations' histories are narrated. Lustre refuses the differentiation between "good" and "bad" colonists.

He shifts from a Filipino to a Filipino American perspective to portray interethnic and interracial coalitions wherein Filipino Americans disidentified with hegemonic, negative constructions of other ethnic minorities to successfully organize labor movements. These examples further contribute to a genealogy of global power, demonstrate the potential of coalitions enabled through disidentificaton to challenge global power hierarchies, and provide models for interracial activist coalitions. Lustre represents the experiences of Filipino migrant laborers to the United States in the early to mid-twentieth century to show how Filipino Americans are defined by their struggles against their exploitation: "You are Filipino if you are part Japanese ... [and] from Hawaii where your grandfather joined your grandmother against the white plantation owners.... You are Filipino if you are half Mexican, half Flip, that West Coast Catholic mix like the Irish Italians back East. My friend Tony's folks are both Mexipinos, got married in Oxnard. Tony always says he has two reasons to boycott grapes."[21] The phrase "you are Filipino if you are part Japanese" appears in both Lustre's historical explanation of miscegenation in the Phillipines and in the United States. The social and political context is important to understanding power hierarchies. Whereas the mixed-ethnic Japanese Filipino child signifies the sexual exploitation of Filipinas under Japanese occupation during World War II, the mixed-ethnic Japanese Filipino child in Hawaii signifies interethnic community formations as a way of surviving the racist exploitation of Asian laborers on plantations. Disassociating from the essentialist understandings of culture enables interethnic coalitions that distinguish individuals from the actions of their governments and recognizes that a victimizer in one context may be a victim in another context. This recognition of the complexity of identities is what makes disidentification particularly fruitful. According to Jose Esteban Muñoz, disidentification resists "an unproductive turn toward good dog/bad dog criticism and instead leads to an identification that is both mediated and immediate, a disidentification that enables politics."[22] Though the plantation strike that Lustre references takes place prior to the World War II in 1920, when ten thousand Japanese and Filipino sugar plantation workers went on strike on the Hawaiian island of Oahu, the representation of Japanese as both "soldier invader lover" and partner in the struggle encourages such coalitions in the future as needed, especially in the U.S. context where the poem is written. The second example of labor solidarity Lustre represents was the

1965 strike in Delano, California, organized by Mexican and Filipino grape workers fighting for better wages and working conditions. In this instance Filipino Americans disidentified with the already established stereotypes of Mexican laborers as undocumented immigrants undeserving of privileges enjoyed by other Americans in order to recognize their shared experiences of exploitation, of discrimination, and of limited economic opportunity and build interracial relationships and coalitions. Understanding history from this perspective emphasizes the intersections between Filipino, Japanese, and Mexican im/migrant history that reveal a genealogy of global power predicated on race. These histories do not conform to a multicultural narrative of assimilation but emphasize the United States' exploitation of racialized laborers. In deconstructing the diversity within the Filipino population, Lustre argues that relationships occur within historically specific hierarchies of power, and recognizing these historically specific hierarchies can provide common ground for a productive politics.

Narratives of U.S. exceptionalism are successfully used repeatedly to justify U.S. military intervention in no small part due to the identification of the colonized with this narrative. Identification with the narrative of the Philippines as a successful product of U.S. benevolent assimilation allows Filipinos to be recruited to contribute to other U.S. colonial projects. The Philippine government provided support to U.S. military efforts in Vietnam.[23] Recently, overseas Filipino contract workers were also sent to support U.S. bases in Iraq and Afghanistan.[24] During the Vietnam War, many Filipinos also enlisted in the U.S. military and were sent to fight in Vietnam. Identifying with U.S. exceptionalism prevents identification with subsequent targets of U.S. colonial projects. Filipino American performance poet Rebecca Baroma illustrates U.S. imperialism's ability to secure ideological power in the Philippines and to manufacture Philippine consent and cooperation in U.S. imperialist projects in her poem "Solving the Sweetest Science." Inspired by her father's service in the U.S. military during the Vietnam War, the poem describes her grandfather's "stomach aching fantasy" for his son to serve in the U.S. Navy, a fantasy born from her grandfather's participation in the Bataan death march during World War II.[25] The Vietnam War and the Bataan death march are usually represented to affirm narratives of U.S. exceptionalism. The United States intervened to rescue Filipinos from a brutal Japanese occupation and unsuccessfully intervened in Vietnam to rescue Vietnamese and the rest of Southeast Asia from the spread of communism. Though the United States cannot claim that it saved the Vietnamese nation itself, the exceptionalist narrative emphasizes the benevolence of U.S. policies that rescued Vietnamese refugees from their government. Here, Baroma disidentifies by delineating her family's problematic identification with U.S. exceptionalism and the resulting psychological consequences of this identification. Characterizing her grandfather's desire for his son to join the U.S. military as a "fantasy" suggests that the desire is somehow impractical or is otherwise an unrealizable goal. By citing her grandfather's experience of the Bataan death march as the rationale behind his fantasy, Baroma exposes colonial inequalities that U.S. institutionalized histories create. The prisoners of war the Japanese forced on the Bataan death march consisted of Filipino and U.S. soldiers alike. However, the Philippines was still a U.S. commonwealth during World War II, making Philippine soldiers still part of the U.S. military. After World War II ended, the U.S. granted the Philippines independence in 1946 and refused to recognize Philippine World War II veterans as U.S. World War II veterans, denying those Philippine soldiers the benefits guaranteed to their own military.[26] Representing the Philippine military and U.S. military as equal allies erases U.S. imperialism in the Philippines and erases Filipino veterans' claims to the privileges of serving in the U.S. imperial military. Within this context, Baroma's grandfather's desire for her father to join the U.S. military instead of the Philippine military points to his desire that his child be given the recognition that he himself never received as a Philippine solider. Joining the Philippine military does not guarantee the same benefits and rights as joining the U.S. military directly, yet, as Baroma demonstrates, the notion that Filipinos directly enlisted in the U.S. military as equal to their White American counterparts was fantasy.

Baroma's representation of her father's service during the Vietnam War and his duties in the U.S. military demonstrates the irony of Filipinos identifying with United States imperialism rather than with the Vietnamese. She characterizes his tour of duty in Vietnam as akin to "going back home to La Union," connecting the U.S. intervention in Vietnam to the history of U.S. colonialism in the Philippines.[27] She portrays the disrespectful treatment her father faced from his military superiors, to whom he was no more than hired domestic help:

> Houseboy? . . .
> make sure ya tell yer
> yella friends . . .
> ima cravin filet mignon

Furthermore, the representation of a military superior calling her father "yella" underscores how Vietnamese and Filipinos were similarly racialized as inferior. Though Filipinos in the U.S. military had more in common with the Vietnamese than with the U.S. soldiers they fought alongside, the United

States' ideological packaging of the Vietnam war as a Cold War intervention prevented Filipinos from identifying with the Vietnamese, despite the demeaning treatment they suffered in the U.S. military for being Asian. Baroma depicts how Filipinos were demeaned by racist treatment on duty and off.[28] By raising the similarities between the Vietnamese and Filipinos and depicting the racist treatment Filipinos endured in the military as Asians, Baroma illustrates how the reproduction of U.S. ideology emphasizing equality and global benevolence prevents the interpretation of U.S. "democratizing" projects as racist colonial projects, which also prevents Filipinos from recognizing their shared circumstances with the Vietnamese, and other U.S. colonials. She argues that Filipino identification with U.S. exceptionalism results in the acceptance of racist treatment and implies that identifying with the Vietnamese is more reasonable.

Lustre and Baroma disidentify with narratives of U.S. exceptionalism, allowing them to identify with others victimized by colonialism in the Philippines, others targeted by U.S. imperialism, and others subjected to racial discrimination. Seeing through the narratives that U.S. exceptionalism construct about themselves and others reveals common ground upon which Los Angeles Filipino Americans can build coalitions. This process allows them to counter narratives of U.S. exceptionalism with a genealogy of global power that takes Philippine and Filipino American history as a departure point. As genealogical projects are inherently local, their genealogy of global power specifically reflects the Los Angeles Filipino American community. Lustre's and Baroma's poems illustrate the similar histories of oppression that Filipinos share with other large Asian populations in California, specifically Japanese and Vietnamese. Lustre also illuminates the shared history that Filipinos and Mexicans share as im/migrant laborers in California. Sharing a space with Japanese Americans, Vietnamese Americans, and Mexican Americans in Los Angeles facilitates the recognition of shared histories and similar global forces that led them to the same place.

New York Puerto Ricans likewise disidentify with narratives of U.S. exceptionalism to construct a genealogy of global power that takes their subjugation as a colonized people, experiences resulting from their racialization, and the particular histories of their geographic location as a departure point for understanding the struggles of other aggrieved groups. In his poem "One Man's Fight for Love," Bonafide Rojas locates Puerto Rican history within the history of oppressed people around the globe. He claims authority to narrate history as a poet: "When I cradle the title poet/ I will be the voice of them."[29] Rojas's poem is dense with allusions to historic oppression and atrocities, leaders of resistance movements, and radical writers. There are three references to Puerto Rican historical figures or events: a rise in the incidence of cancer among those living on Vieques as a result of military bomb testing; nationalist figure Lolita Lebrón, who attempted an attack on the U.S. capitol; and nationalist leader Pedro Albizu Campos. None of these is explicitly identified as part of Puerto Rican history, demonstrating Rojas's privileging of a global historical perspective over nation-centric histories. This disidentification with the construction of discreet national histories enables Rojas to completely identify with others' experiences of oppression, evidenced in his claiming of the Armenian genocide as "our genocide." His authority to articulate these other histories derives from the history and experiences of Puerto Rico. Though he does not identify himself as Puerto Rican in the written text of the poem, he performs the poem as a New York Puerto Rican male. In her study of cultural memory and performances in the Americas, Diana Taylor argues that "it is impossible to think about cultural memory and identity as disembodied. The bodies participating in the transmission of knowledge and memory are themselves a product of certain taxonomic, disciplinary, and mnemonic systems."[30] Rojas's tanned complexion and full-bodied curly hair (often worn as an Afro) racialize him generally as Latino or a light-skinned African American, but in New York City and other cities with large Puerto Rican populations he is readily read as a U.S. Puerto Rican. As a Puerto Rican, he can relate to "survivors of Hiroshima" and Palestinian children because of the history of U.S. bomb testing in Vieques. He can articulate the police brutality that killed African American Amadou Diallo because police brutality also led to New York Puerto Rican Anthony Baez's death. He understands Augusto Sandino's resistance against the U.S. military presence in Nicaragua in the late 1920s and Gandhi's resistance to British rule because of Pedro Albizu Campos's fight for Puerto Rican independence. He can connect Lolita Lebrón's imprisonment for her political resistance to U.S. colonial rule to the imprisonment of Assata Shakur for her involvement with the Black Panthers and Emma Goldman's imprisonment for her anarchist views and political activism. As a New York Puerto Rican poet, he knows what it means to articulate resistance in creative writing and locates himself within a poetic tradition of resistance that includes the African American, Jewish, Russian, and Latin American poets he cites.

Rojas illustrates the coalitions that are possible for New York Puerto Ricans in constructing a genealogy of global power that enables identification with other aggrieved groups. Complementing Rojas's efforts, New York Puerto Rican performance poet Shaggy Flores portrays the danger of identifying with popular constructions of Puerto Rico that delegitimate narratives of Puerto Rican resistance and oppression. In his poem "Oye Lo Boricua"

Flores represents the construction of Puerto Rico that elides its history of colonialism and paints Puerto Rico as a paradise of coconut trees, quaint sugar plantations, picturesque beaches, and exotic cocktails. He dubs this depiction of Puerto Rico "a perverted yanqui fantasy" that imagines Puerto Rico as an anonymous, tropical-island getaway, promising year-round warm weather and relaxation and imagines Puerto Ricans as carefree reproducers of traditional culture.[31] Describing Puerto Rico's beaches as "Caribbean Playas" paired with the catchy, capitalized phrase "Cold Piña Coladas" underscores the commodification of Puerto Rico as an exotic tourist destination.[32] Flores limns this idyllic imagining of Puerto Rico as unrealistic. Identifying with this construction of Puerto Rico perpetuates the erasure of Puerto Rico's history of violent occupation and displacement. Instead, Flores disidentifies with the multiculturalist construction of Puerto Rican culture as a harmonious blending of European, African, and Taino traditions engineered by Luis Muñoz Marin in the mid-twentieth century.[33] Disidentifying with this narrative makes visible the violence of conquest, the decimation of the Tainos, and the forced immigration of African slaves to fulfill the European colonizer's greed for gold. It likewise discredits accepted histories of Puerto Rico that characterize Christopher Columbus as its discoverer and explains the decline of the Taino population as largely the result of disease. Disidentifying with history from the perspective of power reconfigures Christopher Columbus as a "butcher" and squarely places blame on Spanish conquistadors for actively slaughtering Tainos.[34]

Identification with narratives of U.S. exceptionalism leads Puerto Ricans to migrate to the U.S. mainland, where the reality of racial inequality presents obstacles to their realization of social mobility and the American Dream. Flores shows how global power structures do not adhere to national boundaries but limit economic opportunities for an exploited working class the world over. He tells a narrative of Puerto Rican migrants

> Seeking streets
> paved of gold and a new start
> Finds you
>   Broken dreams
>   futility
> and Broken hearts.
>
> Subjected
> to racist Amerikan
> Stereotypes and
> Inferiority complexes . . .

Moms and dads
Perservering
from Slum to Slum.
Puerto Ricans, Not
Welfare slaves
Remembering
that Jibaros
were never bums![35]

Flores's representation of Puerto Rican migration to the United States in search of a better life differs significantly from Rosie Perez's story of her father's migration and Esmerlda Santiago's account of her title character's migration to New York City. For Perez's father and for América in *América's Dream* the United States seemingly delivers on its promises of economic prosperity. The difference in these representations indicates how identification with the United States as the egalitarian land of opportunity obscures experiences refuting that narrative. *Yo soy Boricua, pa'que tu lo Sepas!* describes the racist treatment that Puerto Ricans in the U.S. military faced, implying that Perez's father had to endure such treatment; and *América's Dream* describes how América was unable to find work except as a hotel maid in New York City. Yet in the end, both the film and novel adhere to a celebratory narrative of the United States as offering an escape from oppression back home in Puerto Rico. Flores disidentifies with this narrative to underscore the false promise inherent in the construction of the U.S. as a land of im/migrant opportunity. His repetition and capitalization of the word "Broken" emphasizes the emptiness of narratives of U.S. exceptionalism for working-class Puerto Rican migrants who find themselves living in poverty in the United States. Replacing the "c" in American with a "k" to reference white supremacist groups like the Ku Klux Klan, Flores underscores the virulent nature of the racism that Puerto Ricans face due to their racialization as black in the United States. He attributes negative stereotypes about Puerto Rican migrants to racism to debunk the stereotype of Puerto Ricans as lazy dependents of welfare. He also counters the stereotype of Puerto Ricans as welfare dependents with the stereotype of the quintessential Puerto Rican icon, the *jíbaro*, the hardworking fieldworkers of the Puerto Rican countryside. Contrasting the stereotype of Puerto Ricans in the United States as an opportunistic drain on U.S. government resources with the seemingly contradictory, nostalgic, colonial representation of Puerto Ricans as industrious agricultural workers demonstrates how these images are constructed for complementary purposes. The former justifies racist social hierarchies in the United States, whereas the latter contributes to the nostalgic construction of an untouched Puerto

Rican countryside and Puerto Rican culture that enables the easy disavowal of any negative effects of U.S. imperialism on the island. In this poem, Flores disidentifies with narratives of U.S. exceptionalism to reveal how these narratives produce knowledge about Puerto Rico and Puerto Ricans to secure its own interests and reproduce racial hierarchies.

Studies on the formation and popularization of hip hop illustrate how Puerto Ricans in New York participate in a Black Atlantic culture, one that follows the historical routes of the slave trade and the current routes of migration from former colonies to former imperial metropoles.[36] Likewise, Filipinos in Los Angeles can be located within an Asian Pacific Culture, one that follows U.S. imperial and economic expansion across the pacific and that traces the migrations that followed such expansion.[37] These transnational cultures can be understood as a result of and as a response to global power inequalities. In their local communities Los Angeles Filipino American and New York Puerto Rican performance-poet activists disidentify with hegemonic narratives of U.S. exceptionalism, creating transnational genealogies based on shared histories and experiences with other people of color to build interracial coalitions and work toward social change together. Despite this similar organizing tactic, the coalitions that these poets work to forge differ according to their location and their racialization. New York Puerto Rican performance-poet activists reconstruct Puerto Rican history by locating it within a genealogy of global power by disidentifying with narratives of U.S. exceptionalism and connecting the history and experiences of Puerto Ricans to other Caribbean im/migrants, U.S. Latina/os, African Americans, and Jews. This genealogy reflects their racialization in the United States and the communities of color with whom they share space in New York City, just as the communities of color in Los Angeles and the racialization of Filipino Americans as Asian American influences the construction of a genealogy of global power by Los Angeles Filipino American performance-poet activists. At all times, these poets use their experiences and understanding of the Philippines or Puerto Rico as a lens to understand and connect to other anti-imperialist struggles and to the struggles of other people of color in the United States.

Reproducing Genealogies

Los Angeles Filipino American and New York Puerto Rican performance-poet activists recognize education as an important tool for decolonizing minds. That is, they aim to teach their local communities to disidentify with narratives of U.S. exceptionalism and multiculturalism in order to recognize global power hierarchies that reproduce racial and class inequality. If public education was used to manufacture consent to U.S. imperialism in the Philippines and Puerto Rico, it can also be used to challenge it. However, these performance-poet activists do not have the same resources as the U.S. colonial government did to reproduce their genealogies of global power on a national or transnational scale. Just as establishing a career as a successful, popular novelist or filmmaker often requires economic resources and/or the right professional network, participating in the politics of cultural representation at the national level requires access to economic and/or political resources. Without access to these resources, Los Angeles Filipino American and New York Puerto Rican performance-poet activists engage institutionalized history at the local level. In their own communities they have access to local resources they can avail themselves of to represent Philippine and Puerto Rican history within a genealogy of global power to the communities that matter to them.

Social theorist Antonio Gramsci states that organic intellectuals' active participation in everyday life distinguishes them from traditional intellectuals.[38] Whereas traditional intellectuals are disconnected from local communities and are isolated within an ivory tower, organic intellectuals work within their local communities to challenge hegemony. Gramsci elaborates that one strategy organic intellectuals deploy in mounting their challenge is "to work incessantly to raise the intellectual level of ever-growing strata of the populace, in other words, to give a personality to the amorphous mass element. This means working to produce elites of intellectuals of the new type which arise directly out of the masses, but remain in contact with them to become, as it were, the whalebone of the corset."[39]

The performance-poet activists I interviewed and observed embodied these qualities of organic intellectuals. Many of these poets were also educators by trade but committed themselves to educating also through performance in their local communities. Even those who were not educators viewed performance as a pedagogical tool to reach more students, or rather a different demographic of students—those who may not otherwise have access to the critical histories they represent. Recent literature on educational pedagogy argues that conceptualizing teaching as performance can help to improve effectiveness in the classroom.[40] Los Angeles Filipino American and New York Puerto Rican performance-poet activists realize that teaching and performance skills inform one another. One quality of a good performance is to engage the audience and get them to identify or disidentify with certain characters or actions on stage. The performance-poet activists do not approach teaching as the simple delivery of content; they engage their students to encourage disidentification with narratives of U.S. exceptionalism. In their performances they are also teachers, revealing their genealogies of global power to reach a larger and more diverse audience of students. I will examine the pedagogical and performative practices of performance-poet activists in the classroom and beyond.

Within the Classroom

The effectiveness of public education in manufacturing consent to U.S. colonization of the Philippines and Puerto Rico indicates the power of public education in disseminating ideas. Thus, public schools and universities are one crucial site where Filipino American and Puerto Rican performance-poet activists challenge narratives of U.S. exceptionalism. Their ability to make interventions in scholarship at the university was made possible by the establishment of ethnic studies programs in the late 1960s during the civil rights era. The rigidity of public-school curriculum at the primary and secondary levels makes interventions possible only at charter schools that can independently create their own curriculum.

Performance-poet activists do not teach Philippine and Puerto Rican history in isolation. Rather, they construct a genealogy of global power by teaching Philippine and Puerto Rican history in relation to the histories of other people of color and demonstrate how these histories are relevant to their students' lives. Understanding how aggrieved groups are constructed in relation to one another and in relation to power encourages students to disidentify with hegemonic U.S. racial narratives and identify with one another's struggles. They teach this not only through the content of their curriculum but also through their embodiment of disidentification. As educators of color they perform how to disidentify with U.S. hegemonic power, providing their students of color with an example to emulate and with the possibilities that such disidentification allows. Though performance-poet activists take advantage of the power hierarchies of the classroom to teach their genealogies of power, they attempt to break down the hierarchy of the classroom to become accessible to their students. This facilitates their students' identification with them as other members of aggrieved groups and encourages students to realize that their own perspectives are also valid, regardless of what hegemonic U.S. culture has told them.

Alan Aquino's experience of the inaccessibility of Filipino history and the lack of Filipino American studies specialists in his Asian American Studies Department led him to become a professor who offers courses in the Filipino American Experience and Asian American History at California State

University, Northridge (CSUN) to make Filipino and Filipino American history available, particularly to Filipino American students. He is particularly invested in teaching about the Philippine-American War for the same reason that Camilla Benilao Griggers created *Memories of a Forgotten War*. In Aquino's experience, institutionalized U.S. histories have so effectively erased this war from popular memory that many of his Filipino American students "are unaware of the war and its potential influence upon their lives."[41] Aquino wants his Filipino American students not only to learn about Philippine history but also to realize the relevance of this history in the present, just as Napoleon Lustre's poem insisted on understanding colonialism as present tense carried in one's blood, not simply in the past. To foster discussion on the present-day legacies of the Philippine-American war, Aquino screens Griggers's *Memories of a Forgotten War*. In leading discussions about the film, he takes students through a process of disidentifying with a perspective of U.S. imperialism. He encourages students to consider the long-term consequences of the Philippine-American War for Filipino history and in their lives. After challenging narratives of U.S. exceptionalism, he asks students to apply what they learn about U.S. colonialism in the Philippines to their understanding of the U.S. War on Terrorism in the Middle East and its possible consequences. To facilitate other ethnic studies and Asian American studies professors to implement similar discussions in their classrooms Aquino contributed his lesson plan to an edited anthology on planning Asian American studies courses.[42] This is a reasonable attempt at reaching a wider student population in the absence of significant resources to implement widespread curriculum changes that would ensure the incorporation of his syllabus.

Whereas Aquino's exercise connects Philippine history to the present, other performance poets reproduce their genealogy of global power connecting Philippine history to the histories of other people of color to give their students the tools to theorize groups relationally, to disidentify with racial stereotypes produced by U.S. racial hierarchies so that they realize how their histories are connected to one another. Aquino's former CSUN colleague Rebecca Baroma taught Developmental Writing and Introduction to Asian American Studies, and occasional literature classes. Regardless of what course she taught, she used her courses to approach socially constructed identities critically. Instead of organizing her Introduction to Asian American Studies classes by teaching the experiences of individual ethnic groups separately, she asks her students to examine different Asian American groups relationally through the social constructions of race, class, gender, and sexuality. She specifically teaches her students the specificities of Philippine history by exposing her students to scholarship by E. San Juan Jr., who writes prolifically about the widespread effects of U.S. colonialism on Filipinos, and introduces her students to orientalism and postcolonial theory to enable them to apply these theories to novels by different ethnic and racial groups.[43] These theoretical tools allow her students to understand the shared histories and experiences of people of color and how these are shaped by colonial institutions and racism.

Like Baroma, New York Puerto Rican Nancy Mercado teaches her students to disidentify with racist constructions of other groups and understand minority histories in the United States relationally. Mercado teaches at Boricua College, established in 1974 to address the high attrition rate of Puerto Rican and other Latino students in New York City through nontraditional curriculum. One of Boricua College's core classes is Affective Development, a class limited to twelve students. Students in the course discuss issues that they feel are relevant to their lives; instructors facilitate the discussion. Mercado teaches her students, who are predominantly students of color, how to recognize their social positions, to understand the social, economic, and political conditions that affect their lives. She then asks them to consider how these conditions connect them to others around the world. For instance, by framing the Israeli-Palestinian conflict through the lens of racialized settler colonialism, she makes these events relevant to her students and asks them to consider how they might take action.[44] By illustrating the students' interconnectedness to international events Mercado emphasizes that students have the agency to make a difference in these situations. She encourages them to take action by discussing "what can they do."

Teaching at the college level gives instructors the freedom to develop their own courses and choose which texts to use and how, thus making it easier to make curricular interventions to include histories of Filipinos, Puerto Ricans, and other people of color. The standardized textbooks and curriculum for public elementary schools and high schools make it more difficult to include these histories in public primary- and secondary-school curriculums. Introducing younger students to alternate histories becomes possible only at charter schools that are allowed to develop their own curriculum or more often through creative arts courses both during and outside of class. One example of a public elementary school that can independently determine its curriculum is El Puente Academy for Peace and Justice in Brooklyn. The academy was established in 1993 as part of New York City's Board of Educations' New Visions for Public Schools initiative. As part of a larger organization that works toward social justice through community involvement, the school's curriculum centers on issues of human rights and social justice. Like their counterparts at Boricua College, faculty members at El Puente are called facilitators. New York Puerto Rican Anthony Morales is one of El Puente's humanities facilitators. Instead of teaching a traditional humanities curriculum that centers on classical and modern European thinkers, he introduces his students to the shared histories and experiences of Puerto Ricans, Latinos, and African Americans in the United States through their writing.[45] Like Aquino, Baroma, and Mercado, he teaches his students to think about minority groups relationally so that they may identify with groups across racial and ethnic boundaries. Building a humanities curriculum centered on writers of color instead of the traditional canon actively challenges multicultural education and underscores the racism inherent in that educational model. Focusing on writers of color insists that their work is of equal value to work in the traditional canon for the purposes of teaching a liberal-arts education. Students can learn the same critical-thinking skills from analyzing these texts as they would by analyzing the classical canon. This approach fundamentally questions the multicultural model of education that simply adds on minority writers to diversify a curriculum and teaches students of color that writers of color are not merely the most talented writers of a racialized group, but talented writers in general.

These performance-poet activists' dedication to teaching Philippine and Puerto Rican history drives them to teach a genealogy of global power in courses that are not explicitly history classes. While teaching adult English as a Second Language (ESL) class at South Bay Adult School in Redondo Beach, Filipino American performance poet Dorian Merina discussed Spanish colonial history. In particular, he taught his students about the Spanish galleon trade route between Manila and Acapulco, which stopped in what is now Long Beach. Merina taught this history to challenge institutional histories centered on the experiences of white European immigrants that marginalize his students, mostly Spanish-speaking immigrants from Latin America. Histories of Mexicans and Filipinos in Los Angeles predating U.S. westward expansion, such as those of the galleon trade, showed his students that "their culture has been here for longer than the present culture" and affirmed that they belong in Los Angeles and in the United States.[46] Merina delegitimized institutionalized U.S. history and in so doing enabled his students to disidentify with narratives of U.S. exceptionalism that rely on racism. Demonstrating the Spanish colonial connection between Mexicans and Filipinos also emphasizes their shared history of colonial oppression, revealing their centuries-long, continuous subordination within a genealogy of global power.

As classroom teachers, Los Angeles Filipino American and New York Puerto Rican performance-poet activists teach Philippine and Puerto Rican history in relation to histories of other people of color, providing their students with the tools to disidentify with narratives of U.S. exceptionalism and understand the genealogies of global power they construct in their poetry. That they apply the teaching of these genealogies to a variety of courses spanning different educational levels indicates that they aim to reach as large and diverse a population as possible. Despite the institutional intervention that these poets can make in a classroom, the audiences that performance poets encounter in classrooms are limited to those who have the resources to attend college or who are lucky enough to be enrolled in public charter schools. In order to fully understand the scope of these performance-poet activists as organic intellectuals, I turn now to an analysis of their performances as pedagogical projects.

Without Classrooms

Los Angeles Filipino American and New York Puerto Rican performance poets realize the pedagogical potential of their community performances. Teaching in community spaces through performance provides complete freedom from any institutional constraints of an educational setting and gives performance-poet activists a diverse student body.[47] In her study of African American poetry communities, Maisha Fischer argues that poetry communities "created [their] own institutions for holding forums and exchanging ideas; cafes have been transformed into literary saloons and bookstores into educational centers."[48] Theater scholar Jill Dolan suggests that performance poetry is pedagogical because it "demonstrate[s] how to be active citizens to audiences who might not regularly see themselves as agents in their own lives, let alone in their political systems . . . [and] invite[s] citizen-spectators into a critical conversation about politics and oppression."[49] Los Angeles Filipino American and New York Puerto Rican performance poets likewise form their own poetic communities, spaces, and collaboratives with the explicit goal of empowering their local communities. U.S. Puerto Rican José Angel Figueroa likens poets to Cuban orators who read literature to factory workers as they worked "because [the workers] couldn't afford to go to school."[50] However, these performance-poet activists are more than mere orators: they are performing a repertoire, one that demonstrates how to think critically and disidentify with hegemonic narratives of race and U.S. exceptionalism. This demonstration encourages their audiences to do the same and to narrate their own experiences independent from hegemonic narratives. Community formation is heavily influenced by public space and the reproduction of social relations in that space. Here, I will discuss the New York Puerto Rican and Los Angeles Filipino American poetry communities, their pedagogical goals, and the challenges they face based on the different public spaces of New York City and Los Angeles.[51]

In *Methodologies of the Oppressed*, cultural theorist Chela Sandoval charts the different forms that minority movements in the U.S. assumed in the past and argues that the most effective social movements are ones that deploy a differential form of consciousness—that is, "a consciousness that perceives itself at the center of myriad possibilities all cross-working," one that produces strategically shifting subjectivities.[52] Lisa Lowe similarly argues in her analysis of Asian American writers that a coalitional politics based on the specificities of ethnicity is more productive than a cultural politics based on a homogenous construction of panethnic identity.[53] The ability to shift subjectivities allows social movements to build temporary coalitions with other movements as necessary to adapt to the shifting processes of hegemony.[54] New York Puerto Rican and Los Angeles Filipino American performance-poet activists enact differential forms of consciousness to build coalitions with other people of color based on their shared experiences of oppression by global power inequalities.

The New York Puerto Rican poetry community has a history spanning three decades. Established in 1974, the Nuyorican Poets Cafe provides a space for poetry, music, and theater for U.S. Puerto Ricans and other people of color. The hybrid identity, Nuyorican, combining New York and Puerto Rican, underscores the importance that New York City plays in the experiences and histories of New York Puerto Ricans. Such an identity allows New York Puerto Ricans to lay claim to New York City but differentiate their experience from that of other New Yorkers. Today, as in the beginning, the Nuyorican Poets Cafe offers a space where poets can articulate histories excluded from institutional history. On any given late Friday night, one can hear about the distortions of the U.S. media, the effects of colonialism on Africa, the oppression of Middle Eastern women, and economic imperialism. However, the Nuyorican Poets Cafe is not the only space available to New York Puerto Rican performance poets. The active poetry scene in New York City offers a multitude of spaces and weekly open mic opportunities for these poets to perform: the Bowery Poetry Club, Carlito's Cafe in East Harlem, Bar 13 near NYU, Ascentos in the South Bronx, and Bronx Bohemia at El Maestro Community Center. The gentrification of the Lower East Side and the increasing gentrification of Spanish Harlem resulted in the establishment of Ascentos and Bronx Bohemia open mic events in the South Bronx to ensure continued access to communities of color, particularly Latinos, to poetry spaces where they live. Their commitment to ensuring accessibility to communities of color underscores their commitment to making Puerto Rican history and the genealogies they locate this history in easily available to people of color.

In their local organizing New York Puerto Rican performance-poet activists use the history of U.S. imperialism in Puerto Rico as a platform for building coalitions with other people of color in New York, particularly African Americans, Afro-Caribbeans, and other U.S. Latinos. The dynamic nature of performance poetry makes it an especially useful tool for bridging communities because regardless of how a poem is written on the page, the poem can be modified during a performance to reach the audience more effectively. For this reason, the genealogies they teach through their performance are best understood as contributing to Diana Taylor's conceptualization of a performative repertoire of history instead of a written archive.[55] In a published collection of his poems, Shaggy Flores ends *Oye Lo Borica* with a centered, italicized list of activists who have worked to improve the lives of Puerto Ricans on the island and in the diaspora. In the printed version of the poem this list consists mostly of Puerto Ricans, with the notable exception of Asian American activist Yuri Kochiyama.[56] However, in other versions of this poem, he adds more names to the list, including African American figures like the Black Panthers, Malcolm X, Latino revolutionaries like Che Guevara, Chicano figures like Cesar Chavez, and even Filipino American labor activist Philip Vera Cruz. In the printed version, the line following this list reads "And all the Puerto Rican political prisoners that kept it real." When he adds names to this list, he also changes the following line to "And all the Puerto Rican, Black, Latino, Diaspora political prisoners that kept it real." On the stage, Flores strategically tailors the poem to the audience or to the event at which he is performing. By including other people of color and other third-world revolutionaries in a poem that focuses on the history of Puerto Ricans, Flores connects Puerto Rican experience to the experiences of other Latinos and African Americans for the audience and encourages interracial coalition building. The explicit inclusion of Latinos and African Americans reflects the population of color in the Northeast and Mid-Atlantic region of the United States, where Flores does most of his performance, activist, and academic work. However, the emphasis of the shared experiences of Puerto Ricans with other Latinos and African Americans also underscores how Puerto Ricans are understood or racialized as Latino, black, or both.

The strategy of using Puerto Rican history as a lens for understanding the experiences of other people of color is particularly effective because the United States often tests policies on the Puerto Rican population before implementing the policies in communities of color in the United States, as they did with the sterilization of Puerto Rican women and women of color in

New York City. Similarly, racial ideologies, like the culture of poverty thesis and the myth of the underclass, were developed in Puerto Rico prior to its use to describe people of color in the United States.[57] For example, in his poem "Drop the Bomb," poet Ray Ramirez equates life in New York City barrios with a military occupation that encompasses police brutality against people of color in the United States and their disproportionate imprisonment. He begins the poem by describing the poor health conditions resulting from U.S. military bomb testing on the Puerto Rican island of Vieques: "I'm going to drop the bomb about Vieques how the Navy harms Viequenses. Simple living is cancerous. The U.S. government is a scientist dumping toxic pollutants on this island."[58] The phrase "drop the bomb" is a double entendre that signifies the slang definition of imparting important, often unexpected, knowledge, but also likens his performance of the poem to a weapon in the fight to end U.S. military bomb testing. To explain how conditions in Puerto Rico and New York are connected, Ramirez likens the United States' scant regard for Puerto Rican living conditions to its scarce attention to the living conditions of people of color in New York City: "Vieques is likes Hunts Point. Our children are wheezing, most are Puerto Rican, Dominicans, Africanos, poor people in the ghetto. Wherever we're from, you know we're having problems from the police, the army, the navy, the marines."[59] Harlem and the South Bronx, home to a large population of underprivileged Latinos and African Americans, houses multiple bus depot stations and waste transfer stations. The rates of asthma among residents here, Ramirez says, are the highest in the United States and are often attributed to these stations and air pollution caused by automobile traffic crossing the bridge between Harlem and the South Bronx. The highest concentration of asthma cases is in Hunt's Point, a South Bronx neighborhood that is predominantly Puerto Rican.[60] By juxtaposing the cancer rates in Vieques to the asthma rates in Hunt's Point, Ramirez illustrates how Puerto Ricans, whether in Puerto Rico or in New York City, fall victim to environmental racism. Furthermore, in grouping the police with branches of the U.S. military, Ramirez argues that poor Puerto Ricans and other people of color reside under conditions similar to a military occupation regardless of where they live. The shared conditions of occupation are underscored at the end of the poem, when Ramirez exclaims, "The Navy, they've got to go from Vieques and the barrio."[61]

In New York City, establishing permanent poetry spaces for the reproduction of Puerto Rican history makes the most sense, given the accessibility of public transportation and how underprivileged people of color depend on it. The established poetry scene also allows the sustainability of such spaces through nominal cover charges and the sale of food and drinks at sponsoring restaurants. Thus, most New York Puerto Ricans performance poets put their efforts toward establishing poetry spaces where they and other poets can teach through performance. Exceptions to this trend are New York Puerto Ricans Ray Ramirez and Hector Lavoe, who established the Welfare Poets, a pan-Latino poetry collective with an explicit pedagogical mission to teach Puerto Rican history. However, their collective was not established in New York City but Ithaca, a small college town in upstate New York. They founded the Welfare Poets in 1990 while they were students at Cornell University. Both Ramirez and Lavoe were members of Simba Wachanga, a campus support group for men of color, and they contributed their poems to the organization's newsletter. The newsletter began to circulate at other college campuses in New York, and students of color at Union College in Albany, impressed with Ramirez and Lavoe's writing, asked them to perform on their campus. Through this performance, the poets realized the pedagogical potential of poetry for reproducing the Puerto Rican history they were learning in their own independent research. Soon after, Ramirez and Lavoe formed the Welfare Poets as a poetry collective with an explicit pedagogical mission.[62]

Today the Welfare Poets is a group of Latino activists, educators, and artists based in New York City. Their mission is to "bring information and inspiration to those facing oppression and to those fighting for liberation" by teaching workshops, grassroots activism, and through musical performances that combine hip hop with Latin beats and rhythms.[63] Not only do they offer creative writing workshops for elementary and high school students, but they also offer workshops on the poetry of resistance and community organizing. In keeping with their mission statement, the Welfare Poets always schedule performances in African American and Latino communities. When the group is invited to perform at the University of Illinois—Chicago, they make the time to perform also for the Puerto Rican community. When they perform in Los Angeles, they perform also in Compton and East Los Angeles. By doing so, Ramirez hopes that their art can make "positive change and [be] accessible to the community, to the people that we work with."[64]

Establishing poetry collectives instead of permanent poetry spaces allows poets to travel to reach diverse audiences. This pedagogical strategy is most effective if the poets' desired audiences/students are dispersed. Ramirez and Lavoe's decision to form a poetry collective instead of establishing a permanent poetry space reflects their desire to reach scattered Puerto Rican, African American, and Latino communities. Similarly, the suburban sprawl of Los Angeles and the multiple Filipino American communities spread across the Greater Los Angeles area make the establishment of poetry collectives instead of permanent poetry spaces more effective for reaching as many of their target audiences/students as possible. Filipino American poetry collectives travel between different Filipino American community spaces, university events, museum exhibitions, and open mics, and they organize annual events to teach through their performances.

Los Angeles–based Balagtasan Collective, a now-defunct Filipino American performance poetry group, has a mission similar to that of the Welfare Poets: "Cultivating community and art for social justice." However, whereas the Welfare Poets membership is panethnic, the Balagtasan Collective's members are of Filipino ancestry, to emphasize the specificities of Philippine history. Balagtasan's Collective's founding members, Faith Santilla, Kiwi, and Terry Valen, were all poets who were also part of the League of Filipino Students (LFS), the largest youth and student political organization in the Philippines, with chapters both inside and outside the Philippines. LFS advocates for social change in the Philippines: nationalization of industries in the Philippines, and rights for the indigenous minorities in the Philippines who are faced with open-pit mining on their land and logging by foreign companies, for example. As both artists and members of LFS, Santilla, Valen, and Kiwi were often asked to perform at local political events. However, they questioned their effectiveness when performing solely at political events to audiences already sympathetic to their message. They felt that performing at these events was tantamount to "preaching to the choir."[65] They also questioned whether the rhetoric used to speak about social change by organizations like LFS was accessible to those outside the university.

To address their concerns about effectiveness and accessibility, Santilla, Kiwi, and Valen formed the Balagtasan Collective in November 1998. Through their performance poetry they discuss the issues brought up by LFS and issues of local significance but use different rhetoric to reach the local Filipino community and other local communities of color. Thus, the Balagtasan Collective has an explicit pedagogical goal: to open up for discussion issues like U.S. imperialism to other community members outside the university. As artists, they realized art is a medium that people can understand and thus decided to use performance poetry to teach the community about U.S. imperialism in the Philippines. One of the Balagtasan Collective's annual events, the "Bus Stop," was designed to educate Filipino high school students. So they chose to hold the event in Echo Park, a Los Angeles neighborhood with a large Filipino population.

LA Enkanto Kollective, another defunct Filipino American poetry collective that included some members of the Balagtasan Collective, formed specifically in December 2001 to produce a spoken-word CD, "In Our Blood: Filipina/o American Poetry and Spoken Word From Los Angeles." Inspired by CDs produced in Filipino American poetry communities in Seattle and San Francisco, their goal was to articulate the Los Angeles experience from a Filipino American perspective.[66] In doing so, they claim their stories as part of an unrecognized history of Los Angeles. In their CD and in their collective's name, Los Angeles Filipino American history is framed as haunting mainstream constructions of Los Angeles. They chose to include the term "enkanto" in their name because it means "spirit" in Tagalog, but also because it sounds similar to the word "song" in Tagalog (kanta) and Spanish (canción). Thus, for them, their name translates to Los Angeles Spirit or Los Angeles Song.[67] The opening track of the CD features multiple voices repeatedly naming different suburbs and neighborhoods of Los Angeles with large Filipino populations. The voices begin softly at first with each location articulated clearly and independently. The voices become louder and the utterances of place names overlap, before fading into a chant of the phrase "song of Los Angeles." The increasing, overlapping voices produce a haunting effect, suggesting the presence of a large population of Filipino Americans marginalized at the edges of Los Angeles. As the voices switch from naming a specific suburb or neighborhood to chanting "song of Los Angeles" the poets lay claim to Los Angeles and to their place within Los Angeles history.[68] Through the distribution of the CD and several performances in the years following the release, the LA Enkanto Kollective reproduced the specificities of a Los Angeles Filipino American experience that challenge mainstream constructions of Los Angeles that marginalize their presence and history.

In their organizing, Los Angeles Filipino American performance poets likewise relate the history of and current situation in the Philippines to their own experiences in the United States as well as to the history of and current situations of other third-world countries to build interracial coalitions. Balagtasan Collective's Faith Santilla performed at a January 2005 event for the nonprofit organization Strategic Actions for a Just Economy. Dedicated to economic justice and popular education, the event raised money and awareness for the low-income tenants of the Morrison Hotel in downtown Los Angeles. At the time, the Morrison Hotel was in danger of being closed down for the creation of a new development. The event drew a young crowd that consisted of local artists invited to perform, academics from local universities, local activists, Morrison Hotel tenants, and some hip hop enthusiasts there to see KRS-One, an influential, progressive MC. The program began with guest speakers who spoke about the Morrison Hotel dilemma and the plight of people of color in cities and ended with a series of featured performers, including Santilla.

During the evening, a Native American woman spoke of her experiences as one of Morrison Hotel's residents. She spoke of what little respect she received as a low-income person and appealed to the crowd at the event to help prevent the closure of her home. At that event, Faith performed a piece called "Mirror Images," which she dedicated to that woman. To emphasize women's shared experiences of struggle and the need for solidarity, this poem illustrates the continuity between 1898 and present United States foreign policy: "So now where are the warriors that we once were? Where is Gabriela who fought alongside Diego? Where is Malinche? All of whom drove out the Spaniards while Uncle Sam was on his way to hand you NAFTA and to me APEC cuz both president Estrada and Zedillo have American dog collars around their necks trained to sit, heel and stay."[69] Here she references resistance to Spanish colonialism in the Philippines and Mexico. Gabriela Silang is the wife of Diego Silang, who led a revolt against the Spanish in 1792. After Diego's assassination, Gabriela took control of the revolt and was later captured and executed. Faith also references Malinche, a female figure often blamed for the downfall of the Aztecs but who has recently been reclaimed by feminists as a revolutionary figure.[70] She represents how women like Gabriela and Malinche fought to free themselves from Spanish control to encourage women of color to resist United States control together. By linking the North American Free Trade Agreement (NAFTA) and the Asian Pacific Economic Cooperation forum (APEC), Santilla demonstrates how both Mexico and the Philippines are influenced by U.S. neocolonialism. Both NAFTA and APEC promote open trade that ultimately exploits third-world labor to the benefit of U.S. corporations. Santilla emphasizes how economic trade agreements reproduce global power inequalities by representing former Mexican president Ernesto Zedillo Ponce de Leon and former Philippine president Joseph Estrada, whose governments agreed to these trade agreements, as the U.S.-trained, domestic pets. Santilla provides concrete examples of how the United States maintains its economic control of both Mexico and the Philippines. In this example, Santilla links colonial struggles to contemporary neocolonial struggles. Though she did not explicitly modify her poem to relate U.S settler colonialism's subjugation of Native Americans to U.S. overseas colonialism's subjugation of Filipinos, dedicating her performance to the Native American woman invokes the history of resistance to colonial violence and underscores shared struggles of people of color in Los Angeles.

As an organizing tool used in Los Angeles, "Mirror Images" strategically relates the past and present experiences of the Philippines and Mexico to enable Filipinos and Mexicans in Los Angeles to disidentify with negative racial stereotypes of one another and rally around their long history of related struggles. In 2002, Santilla performed "Mirror Images" alongside the other women of the Balagtasan Collective at the annual Mujeres de Maiz live art show commemorating International Women's Day. Mujeres de Maiz is a Los Angeles–based organization of Chicana and Latina artists. The set performed by the women of the Balagtasan Collective began with a projected screen that read "Makibaka! Luche!" These are the command forms for struggle in Tagalog and Spanish, respectively, already setting the stage for translating their struggles as one they share. The first screen was replaced by a projection of a woman and a map of the Philippines. Alison de la Cruz performed a poem allegorizing the Philippines as seven thousand daughters of the sea and sky, making clear to the audience the specific social positions from which they speak. Santilla's performance of "Mirror Images" followed De La Cruz's performance, making explicit the histories they, as Filipinas, share with the members of Mujeres de Maiz and with the largely Chicano/Latino audience. In addition to Santilla's performance of "Mirror Images," the other women of the Balagtasan Collective performed poems representing World War II in the Philippines, Filipinas as a global labor force, and the Filipina American experience. The performance ended with all of the women singing "Bayan Ko," a patriotic Filipino song, in front of a screen projecting the words "International Women's Day." After establishing their common histories and experiences, the women of the Balagtasan Collective share their specific histories and struggles to teach and find other people of color who will join and support their activist pursuits.

Los Angeles Filipino American performance-poet activists also participate in local Asian American activist events. In November 2005, mETHODOLOGY, "a monthly jam of community, consciousness, and culture" in L.A.'s Chinatown featured Balagtasan Collective founder and Native Gun member Kiwi. This particular mETHODOLOGY served as a fundraiser for an L.A. delegation to protest at the December 2005 World Trade Organization (WTO) Conference in Hong Kong. mETHODOLOGY took place at Chow Fun, a Chinatown restaurant that was transformed into a late-night dance and lounge space one Saturday every month. On this particular night, Kiwi's performance attracted a large crowd consisting mostly of young Asian Americans. Once he took the stage, everyone packed the dance floor facing him, transforming the dance space into a mini concert space. His high-energy set kept the audience dancing and waving their arms in the air when he did. One poem he performed that night, "Work It," dealt specifically with the labor conditions that globalization creates for workers in the third world, one issue that the L.A. delegation wished to highlight by protesting at the

WTO conference. The poem links exploited labor conditions in Africa, Latin America, and Asia:

> I keep my wrists ice cold with the shiny stone fresh picked by some workers in Sierra Leone, or some Filipino kids that have their futures postponed, 12 years old looking like they could be one of my own, that made my phat kicks on my cellular phone, or the way the cap fitted on top of my dome, blood stain right beneath where the stitches were sewn, hidden from the crowd when I'm reading my poem. . . . What Guatemalan family picked them coffee beans, broke their back for my broccoli and artichoke.[71]

He references diamond miners in Sierra Leone, Filipino factory workers, and Guatemalan farmers who are all exploited to produce commodities for a typical American lifestyle. In doing so, he argues that the average American is complicit in creating the poor working conditions these workers suffer under. At the end of his performance he encouraged the crowd of revelers to take action by buying t-shirts in support of the L.A. delegation and to learn more about the WTO and other ways they could contribute to the protests from the delegation's information desk. Santilla's and Kiwi's choice of events to perform at and the poems they choose illustrate their efforts to build Asian panethnic and interracial coalitions that reflect the population of color in Los Angeles.

New York Puerto Rican and Los Angeles Filipino American performance poets reproduce the genealogies of global power they construct both inside and outside the classroom in order to reach and teach as wide and diverse an audience as possible. In challenging hegemonic narratives of race and colonial history, they demonstrate how to disidentify with power and its accompanying negative constructions of racialized groups and of themselves. Through this disidentification they invite students to voice their own experiences free form the hegemonic narratives that have defined, silenced, and marginalized them.

Authorizing Other Speakers

Foucault identifies the "activation of local knowledges" as an important component of a genealogical project.[72] The emphasis that New York Puerto Rican and Los Angeles Filipino Americans place on the local in defining their identities and the significant role that the local plays in their construction of genealogies of global power illustrate their investment in articulating a genealogy that is specific and relevant to their own local experiences. This specificity points to the incomplete nature of these genealogical projects. However, the goal of a genealogical project is not to replace one comprehensive historical narrative with another but rather to produce an "insurrection of knowledges" by authorizing everyone to speak regardless of their social position.[73] The established poetry scene and the institutionalization of poetry programs in New York City public schools facilitate the production of new generations of New York Puerto Rican poets. On the other hand, cuts to funding for arts programs under former California governor Arnold Schwarzenegger and the short history of Los Angeles Filipino American poets prevented the production of a cohesive new generation of Filipino American poets.

At poetry events in New York City, New York Puerto Rican performance poets teach by doing. Regularly occurring poetry events in New York City consist of, in varying order, one or more featured poets, an open mic, and often a poetry slam. This format enables New York Puerto Rican performance poets to not only teach through the content of their poems but also to teach others how to become poets. As featured poets or participants in poetry slams, New York Puerto Rican performance poets demonstrate how to use poetry to articulate subjugated knowledges and one's own experiences. The open mics following the featured poets' performances allow the audience to practice their own poetry and become part of the poetry community.[74] At some open mics, poets are not only encouraged to keep performing but also are given comments on how to improve. At one sparsely attended Ascentos open mic night on a snowy Valentine's evening, the seven poets gathered around a table instead of the performance space. Everyone with a poem read one and received feedback. Thus, open mics offer the opportunity for performance poets to perform and can teach others to perform and thus authorize other speakers.

Fostering a new generation of poets also occurs through established poetry organizations that work in conjunction with the New York City public school system. The Teachers and Writers Collaborative and Urban Word NYC are two popular organizations among several that provide New York Public schools with poets either to teach individual workshops or to serve as a poet or writer in residence teaching a series of ten to fifteen workshops. The older of the two organizations, the Teachers and Writers Collaborative, was founded in 1967 on the belief that professional writers would be best qualified to introduce elementary and high school students to creative writing. Established in 1999 in partnership with the Teachers and Writers Collaborative, Urban Word NYC believes that "teenagers can and must speak for themselves."[75] In addition to providing creative workshops for schools, both organizations also have their own spaces in New York City where they host their own writing related events and programs. Many of the New York performance poets I interviewed worked or had worked for these types of organizations before and had done so with the specific goal of producing and authorizing a new generation of poets.

Bonafide Rojas represents the difficult but rewarding experience of teaching poetry to students that "society has deemed derelicts and hoodlums" for Urban Word NYC in his poem, "At the Head of the Class."[76] The poem's narrator identifies with these students, stating:

> I am them eight years ahead
> with poetry being the left turn I made at 17
> I tell them that road is approaching
> all they have to do it take that road
> and run down it so fast that their past
> will never catch up to them[77]

By identifying the narrator with the students, Rojas implies that those whom society has constructed as "derelicts and hoodlums" are not necessarily fated to the future that U.S. society imagines for them. He asks the students to dis-identify with this stereotype that has defined them; he serves as an example of someone who has done so successfully. Rojas posits that writing poetry can be that life-altering choice for these students. That is, he tells these students that their voices, which have been disregarded by society, are important. Although his rhetoric here echoes the rhetoric of the American Dream and that of personal responsibility, Rojas does not necessarily argue that these students are responsible for their own circumstances. Instead, Rojas argues that the act of writing poetry is an empowering act. Further in the poem, the narrator urges the students to

> tell them who you are
> tell them they're wrong for labeling you
> tell them fuck you for giving up on them
> tell them your life may not be worth shit now
> but tomorrow gives you hope
> so you won't take your life today or the next day
> tell them you will be here forever[78]

Here, Rojas explicitly departs from the rhetoric of personal responsibility. Whereas the rhetoric of personal responsibility emphasizes uplift through action and hard work, the narrator does not encourage the students to reform themselves and make a decent living. Rather, the narrator urges the students to break their silence, to speak back to "them," a society that abandons underprivileged urban youth. Rojas argues that students such as these are entitled to and should claim space by having the narrator encourage the students to "tell them you will be here forever." Finally, by representing a teacher committed to empowering underprivileged students, Rojas illustrates the importance of providing underprivileged students with teachers who understand their circumstances and can also keep the faith in students society deems worthless. This poem encapsulates the importance of teaching for New York Puerto Rican performance poets.

Part of what drives New York Puerto Rican performance poets to mentor a new generation of poets is to ensure the continuity of a poetic tradition that was passed on to them. By teaching his students creative writing, Anthony Morales fulfills a promise he made to his mentor, Willie Perdomo, who told him that "the most important thing for us to do is . . . to pass this on because truthfully it's not ours. I mean, this poetry, these words, I mean yeah, we can do it, but how much better for us to pass that love and the knowledge and the consciousness and the ability on to other people, on to kids who really need it, really need it, especially in this world where they're trying to be silenced, so much, every single day, every single day, every single moment."[79] Morales considers it his responsibility to teach his students to articulate their own experiences and subjugated knowledges. In the face of institutions and a society that attempts to silence students of color, Morales gives them the tools, opportunity, and encouragement necessary to authorize them as speakers who have stories worth sharing.

However, building students' self-confidence so they feel entitled to speak and claim space can be difficult, especially for those who cannot speak U.S. English fluently. Campaigns for English-only laws serve to demonize other languages, particularly Spanish.[80] Ana Celia Zentella argues that, in particular, "dialects like lower-working-class Puerto Rican English and Spanish" are considered to be "deformed linguistic models that frustrate children's acquisition and make logical thinking impossible."[81] English fluency becomes conflated with one's intelligence. When Puerto Rican performance poet Jesus Papoleto Meléndez leads writing workshops in New York City, he pays particular attention to the grammar errors that his students make. Melendez explains that the grammar errors made by his bilingual Latino students follow a particular logic because they think in Spanish and write in English:

> 'Think' is tink . . . and 'just' is always spelled youst. You youst sit down. And see, I can see it . . . She never puts 'I' in front of am . . . [she writes] 'am studying,' as opposed to . . . 'I am studying' . . . Every time she means 'and,' she spells it a-n . . . because she pronounces it 'an,' and not 'and' . . . With the Latino kids I try to solve it for them because I tell them . . . you don't have to think that

you're dumb. You're not. You're trying to deal with another language that isn't yours. You never mastered it and once you get a handle on it, you'll be able to express yourself in that language.[82]

Melendez shows his students that their grammar mistakes make sense for those who are fluent in Spanish and have yet to master the logic of the English language. In doing so, he demonstrates to his students that their grammar errors are not a reflection of their intelligence or their worth. Taking the time to understand his students' errors enables Melendez to build his students' self-confidence so that they feel authorized to write and express themselves.

While the history of the Nuyorican poetry community goes back decades, the Los Angeles Filipino American poetry community is not as established. This, coupled with the lack of established poetry spaces and the lack of poetry-teaching organizations, accounts for the limited success among Los Angeles Filipino Americans to systematically produce a significant population of new poets. Former California governor Arnold Schwarzenegger's repeated reductions to arts funding led many Los Angeles grassroots activist poetry spaces to close and caused the discontinuation of annual poetry festivals featuring the work of local activist poets.[83] Though new poetry venues do open, the lack of continuous space prevents the establishment of a regular poetry scene that consists of regular participants. Few regular open mics that Filipino American performance poets frequent remain. One example of such an open mic is the "Tuesday Nights Project," an event established in 1999 and held every first and third Tuesday during selected months in Little Tokyo's Aratani Courtyard. Similar in format to New York City poetry events, the "Tuesday Nights Project" consists of featured performers and an open mic, though it is not strictly a poetry event but a showcase for a variety of Asian American cultural productions. In this sense the "Tuesday Nights Project" does offer Filipino American performance poets the opportunity to teach poetry by performing, but the opportunities to do so are limited, since this is only one event that does not regularly occur during the year.

Likewise, the absence of established programs like the Teachers and Writers Collective and Urban Word NYC in Los Angeles limit opportunities for Filipino American performance poets to teach poetry to students in public schools and produce new poets. Some of these poets teach the arts to elementary and high school students at the Association for the Advancement of Filipino American Arts and Culture's (Fil-Am Arts) afterschool program, Eskwela Kultura, but as a single program in a single location, this does not have the widespread reach that the New York City–based organizations have. For these reasons Los Angeles Filipino American performance poets' genealogical project does not systematically produce new poets due to the short history of the Los Angeles Filipino American poetry community and the lack of resources for teaching poetry even though construct a genealogy of global power in their poetry and reproduce this genealogy by teaching in classrooms and teaching through performances.

Conclusion

Los Angeles Filipino American and New York Puerto Rican performance poets are committed to decolonizing genealogical projects that rely on their mutually constituitive pedagogical and performance skills. They are organic intellectuals who promote disidentifcation as a repertory strategy to construct genealogies of global power. Inside and outside the classroom, the genealogies of global power delineated in their poetry challenge institutionalized histories that privilege narratives of U.S. exceptionalism and marginalize alternative narratives. In their poetry and teaching they model how to disidentify with hegemonic narratives of U.S. exceptionalism and encourage others to create and share their own stories. Teaching inside and outside the classroom demonstrates how they embody Gramci's concept of organic intellectuals because they are committed to reaching and teaching those who do not have access to traditional education. They complete their genealogical project by arguing, in fact, that their genealogical projects are never finished and thereby authorizing a diverse public to contribute their perspectives. They urge those who have been taught that their perspectives are unimportant to believe that their views are significant. All told, these poets construct a genealogy of global power in their poetry and in their educational and performative practices to actively challenge hegemonic narratives of U.S. exceptionalism. Their genealogies are specific to their racialization as Asian American, African American, or Latino and to the populations of color in Los Angeles and New York City, reflecting their situated knowledges. The well-established New York City poetry community allows New York Puerto Rican performance poets to mentor new generations of poets and authorize them to contribute to their genealogy of global power. Similar poetry resources are not available in Los Angeles, resulting in a lack of systematic process for training new generations of Filipino American poets to contribute to their genealogy of global power. However, as the poem that I began this chapter with illustrates, Los Angeles Filipino American performance poets do authorize audiences to speak in their performances by directly addressing and asking questions of the audience.

These performance-poet activists' genealogies are a radical departure from and a critical challenge to hegemonic narratives of U.S. exceptionalism. In spite of their hard work to dismantle hegemonic narratives and their destructive influence on communities of color in Los Angeles and New York, their interventions are often limited to their immediate locales due to their lack of resources. They do not have access to national distribution as do popular novelists, such as Jessica Hagedorn and Esmeralda Santiago, or famous film producers, such as Rosie Perez. They do not have the resources to produce films articulating narratives of their genealogies of power and release them across the nation to a mainstream audience. Thus, they cannot challenge hegemonic narratives of U.S. exceptionalism for a popular, mainstream audience. Perhaps this is not their intent. As many of the poems and interview excerpts in this chapter illustrate, Filipino American and U.S. Puerto Rican performance-poet activists teach genealogies of power in their local communities to provide the critical thinking skills necessary to disidentify with narratives of U.S. exceptionalism and work toward social change. Genealogical projects are not primarily interested with replacing an existing hegemonic narrative with their own but are concerned with empowering others to disidentify with stereotypes created by hegemonic U.S. narratives and enabling them to tell their own stories. As educators, Los Angeles Filipino American and U.S. Puerto Rican performance-poet activists utilize cultural assets that are effective pedagogical and organizing tools as they hope to begin an organic movement that starts in their own neighborhoods and grows from there.

Conclusion

Imagining the End of Empire

So I ask of you, you can ask me, too, in what direction we're headed
for a world that's brand new?
—Johneric Concordia, "Do You Want to Know?"

The institutionalized history of U.S. imperialism in the Philippines and Puerto Rico tells a story of benevolent assimilation. In this narrative the United States reluctantly and selflessly developed the Philippine and Puerto Rican economies, offered these islands military protection, established "sovereign" democratic governments, and provided public education to civilize racially inferior Filipinos and Puerto Ricans. The United States recognized when its good work on these islands was completed and left Filipinos and Puerto Ricans to manage their own affairs. Any subsequent problems after the end of the colonial relationship are the responsibility of the islands and not of the United States. The Philippines and Puerto Rico have been constructed in U.S. hegemonic culture for the express purpose of justifying U.S. imperialism through a narrative of U.S. exceptionalism. For this reason, Filipino Americans and U.S. Puerto Ricans only become visibly legible for a mainstream audience when they can affirm narratives of U.S. exceptionalism as former colonial subjects or when they affirm narratives of U.S. multiculturalism as ethnic Americans.

Pop singer Bruno Mars's biography potentially embodies the intersection of multiple histories of U.S. colonialism. He was born in Hawaii to an ethnically Puerto Rican father and ethnically Filipino mother. Locating Bruno Mars within a history of U.S. imperialism, we might guess that his father and mother descend from Puerto Rican and Filipino migrants who were recruited to work on Hawaiian plantations in the early twentieth century.[1] Or perhaps his family more recently arrived in Hawaii, having been stationed there by the U.S. military. Or maybe it is a combination of the two. These explanations of his diverse heritage make historical sense, but the mainstream media do not try to offer historical explanations for his heritage. Rather, Mars's diverse heritage is deployed to reproduce lucid U.S. multiculturalism.[2] In 2014 Mars headlined the Super Bowl halftime show, evidence of his commercial success and mainstream popularity. The Super Bowl is among the most-watched live television events. Companies pay the highest premiums to advertise during the game. Mars's performance demonstrates how the products of U.S. imperialism can be hypervisible while the history of U.S. imperialism that should accompany those products is completely obscured. What is foregrounded is the celebration of the United States as multicultural and postracial. After all, how could the dark-skinned Bruno Mars be so successful and popular if the United States is a racist society?

In the preceding chapters I have demonstrated how Filipino American culture and U.S. Puerto Rican culture across various genres critique narratives of U.S. exceptionalism that justify U.S. colonial projects. However, these critiques are obscured either by hegemonic culture's incorporation or marginalization of the cultural productions. I return now to cultural theorist Raymond Williams's conceptualization of selective traditions. As quoted in the introduction to this book, Williams argues that "where a version of the past is used to ratify the present and to indicate directions for the future, . . . a selective tradition is at once powerful and vulnerable. Powerful because it is so skilled in making active selective connections, dismissing those it does not want as 'out of date' or 'nostalgic,' attacking those it cannot incorporate as 'unprecedented' or 'alien.'"[3] Hegemonic narratives of U.S. multiculturalism, U.S. exceptionalism, and the good immigrant all function to define and discipline Filipino Americans and U.S. Puerto Ricans. These narratives are all selective traditions that have privileged narratives of Filipino and Puerto Rican history that affirm a story that the United States tells about itself: a story of a reluctant, benevolent, global power and of a progressive, egalitarian, democratic society. Through the capitalist cultural industry, Filipino American and U.S. Puerto Rican cultural productions that are popular for a mainstream American audience are carefully marketed to affirm hegemonic U.S. narratives. Novels like *Dogeaters* and *América's Dream*—cultural critiques of U.S. imperialism—are marketed as cultural representations of corrupt national governments and oppressive, traditional, patriarchal cultures that serve as a contrast for an equitable and progressive United States and seem to invite U.S. intervention to fix such problems. Films such as *Yo soy Boricua, pa'que tu lo Sepas!* that demonstrate that continuity of U.S. imperialism from at least 1898 to the present are marketed as works celebrating vibrant minority cultures that showcase U.S. diversity and inclusion. Hegemonic U.S. narratives imagine the end of empire as the reproduction of U.S. liberal, democratic, and capitalist values around the world and selects Filipino American and U.S. Puerto Rican cultural productions that can be interpreted to support such an end.

However, Filipino American and U.S. Puerto Rican cultural productions that explicitly imagine a different end to empire and cannot easily be packaged to support narratives of U.S. exceptionalism, like *Memories of a Forgotten War* and activist performance poetry, are marginalized. Recognizing the popularity of performance poetry but unable to incorporate the radical critiques it produced, hegemonic U.S. culture instead neutralized those critiques through commodifying the cultural form. In February 2007, Volkswagen ran a television advertisement in the United States featuring a dark-skinned Asian American performance poet. The poet performs in an urban cafe patio at night. His rhythm, seriousness, and intensity are characteristic of hip hop sensibility, of spoken word poetry. He performs to a multiracial audience who drinks coffee as they nod in agreement to the poet's statements: "Conflict boils over like an angry sludge. Politicians lie to us like they've got a grudge. We're in a decaying spiral of fevered ferocity...." The poet is interrupted mid-performance by a white male gleefully driving a white Volkswagen sedan. The driver honks his horn as he drives past the café and shouts "Three V-dubs for under $17,000. Woo-hoo!" The poet pauses. A smile forms on his previously serious face. No longer reading from his poem, he resumes speaking and states "hope springs." This scene abruptly ends, cutting to a shot of the three Volkswagen sedans referenced earlier.[4]

Unlike the poems produced by the performance-poet activists earlier discussed, the poem read by the poet in this advertisement has no substantive critique. The phrase "politicians lie to us like they've got a grudge" indicates to the viewer that this poet distrusts the politicians that represent him, but he gives no specific reason for his distrust. The advertisement suggests that the poet's unhappiness has nothing to do with the failures of his government representatives, because his unhappiness is so easily remedied by the mere mention of affordable German import cars. The key to happiness, it seems, is not to hold the politicians accountable to the public but to consume luxury goods, because the source of unhappiness is not institutional inequality. Individuals are personally unhappy because they have yet to buy the right product. This particular advertisement was one in a series of hope-themed Volkswagen advertisements for their three sedans. Another advertisement in this series represented a white male about to commit suicide by jumping off a billboard; he changes his mind upon hearing the same driver spread the word about the sedans' pricing. Equating the performance-poet activist critical of the political system with a suicidal man underscores that the figure of the critical performance poet is to be understood as irrational.

In her study on Hispanic marketing in the United States, Arlene Dávila argues that "ethnic marketing... responds to and reflects the fears and anxieties of mainstream U.S. society about its 'others,' thus reiterating the demands for an idealized, good, all-American citizenship in their constructed commercial images and discourses."[5] Given how hip hop has historically been considered an African American form in the U.S. cultural imagination, featuring an Asian American as the performance-poet activist in this advertisement could be understood as recognizing the real diversity of American hip hop, yet I would like to argue that this is not the case. In representing an Asian American performance-poet activist verbalizing critiques, however inarticulate, of the U.S. government, this advertisement references the binary narratives of the undeserving and model minority. Asian Americans were constructed as model minorities to simultaneously construct those in the civil rights movement as undeserving minorities who wasted their time protesting government inequality when they needed only to work hard to succeed.[6] Thus, this advertisement functions as a disciplinary mechanism of performance-poet activists of color, in general, and Asian Americans, in particular, providing a model of what not to be and a model for reformation. A performance-poet activist can become a good, patriotic citizen through consumption.[7]

This Volkswagen advertisement demonstrates how hegemonic U.S. culture dismissed and delegitimized critiques emerging from performance poetry as a cultural form. Since then, performance poetry has been used by other major transnational corporations, including McDonalds. The use of performance poetry in corporate television advertisement shows how U.S. hegemonic culture co-opts emergent cultural forms through incorporation. Raymond Williams describes oppositional emergent forms as reflecting the formation of a new class that challenges hegemonic culture.[8] At the turn of the twenty-first century, performance poetry genres known as spoken-word and slam poetry surged in popularity. At open mic events and slam poetry competitions across the United States, poetry critical of U.S. culture, politics, and history emerged. This is not to suggest all spoken-word and slam poetry produced is oppositional. However, as I elaborated earlier, the few barriers to participating in this cultural form and the active efforts of performance-poet activists to cultivate new poets allowed for poetry that challenges U.S. hegemonic narratives to emerge. Threatened, U.S. hegemonic culture worked to incorporate this emergent cultural form, as evidenced by the Volkswagen commercials and others. Williams states, "Incorporation looks like recognition, acknowledgement, and thus a form of acceptance. . . . Elements of emergence may indeed be incorporated, but just as often the incorporated forms are merely facsimiles of the genuinely emergent cultural practice."[9] The Volkswagen commercial is a facsimile of spoken word that incorporates style but not substance. In fact, it actively attacks the critical substance of spoken word.

Arguably, the popularity of spoken word peaked sometime between 2005 and 2010. The establishment of a performance-poetry community that predated the popularity of spoken word facilitated the continued use of performance poetry for Nuyorican performance poet's decolonial genealogical work. For this reason, while many of the Nuyorican performance poets I interviewed still identify as poets, most of the Los Angeles Filipino American performance poets I interviewed have since moved on to other cultural forms for their decolonial genealogical work because they question poetry's pedagogical potential due to the commodification of spoken word and the popularity of slam poetry. Alfie Ebojo contrasts the spaces that Los Angeles Filipino American performance poets once frequented with slam poetry venues to underscore how slam poetry does not value the sharing of histories. Whereas she characterizes spoken-word open-mic events as creating a space for people of diverse backgrounds and experiences to share their stories, she describes slam poetry's competitive nature as discouraging people from understanding one another's experiences. The perceived increasing predominance of slam poetry venues that encourage competition instead of collaboration does not foster the formation of safe community spaces for sharing one's ideas through poetry or the authorization of other speakers. Ebojo cites this shift away from more collaborative performance poetry as a major reason that she has switched her artistic focus from poetry to graphic art.[10] Dorian Merina is now a reporter for Free Speech Radio News. Faith Santilla now works organizing healthcare workers in San Francisco. Cheryl Samson works for a Los Angeles-based nonprofit organization that provides music education to at-risk youth to foster better communities. Though many still write poetry and are part of writing collectives, they do not perform their poetry with the same regularity as in the past. In spite of this, those I interviewed continue to advocate for change, whether through programs targeting local communities or through cultural representation involving other cultural forms.

Their transition away from performance poetry can be attributed to several factors. First, these individuals have transitioned to adulthood. Unable to fully support themselves or their families as artists, they secure more stable employment and no longer have the time to perform poetry.[11] The defunding of arts programs, including the National Endowment of the Arts, beginning in the 1980s has made it incredibly difficult for independent artists to survive solely on their craft. Conservatives used explicitly sexist and homophobic arguments to cut funding to arts programs that they believed were incubators of radical social change.[12] They advocated that the cultural market would produce diverse artistic productions, free from government intervention, and that consumer-citizens should determine what art gets produced.[13] This assault on public arts funding coupled with the deregulation of telecommunications companies has led to the near impossibility of surviving as an independent artist.[14] As I have demonstrated in this book, the result of a consumer-driven cultural market is the reproduction of hegemonic cultural narratives.

Though I point to ways that spoken-word and slam poetry have been commodified in certain instances, I do not mean to suggest that performance poetry does not continue to be an empowering site where oppositional narratives can emerge. One example where this occurs is through Youth Speaks, a nonprofit organization based in San Francisco that seeks to empower young people to articulate their life stories through the arts. Among their programs is the annual Brave New Voices competition.[15] Such organizations seek to establish and/or continue poetry communities like as those in New York City. The fact that many of the Nuyorican performance-poet activists still actively identify as poets—whereas Los Angeles-based Filipino American performance-poet activists I interviewed have moved on from performing poetry—points to the different nature of the poetry communities in New York City and Los Angeles. As I previously discussed the Nuyorican poetry community is an establishment with decades-old roots. Los Angeles does not offer similarly robust resources, though the fact that Tuesday Nights Project has managed to provide a continuous open mic may indicate that one has now been established for Asian Americans. However, I understand also the transition of the Filipino American performance poets I interviewed as another indicator of their roles as organic intellectuals in their communities. Gramsci describes organic intellectuals as "never [tiring] of repeating [their] own arguments (though offering literary variation of form)."[16] Whereas some performance poets have used the cultural capital they accumulated to become educators in order to support themselves financially, other performance poets have chosen alternative employment where they can similarly make use of their cultural capital. In their continued cultural production, their community organizing, their teaching, their journalism, and their providing community services, these former Los Angeles Filipino American performance poets still articulate their genealogies of global power and work to address social consequences of these genealogies. The difference is that they have found new tools that they find more effective in working toward an end to empire and its consequences.

Filipino American and U.S. Puerto Rican culture contend that empire has not ended. Global capitalism and supranational organizations enable the continued subordination and exploitation of the postcolonial developing world. Though the colonial period in the Philippines and Puerto Rico officially ended shortly after World War II, neither U.S. empire nor the United States' will to global power has ended. Literary theorist Victor Bascara argues that imperialism today depends on the converging ideas of multiculturalism and globalization because these are "the leading antidotes to an accumulation of historical forces and conditions antagonistic to peace and progress, such as war and underdevelopment."[17] Mainstream U.S. ethnic cultural productions can be used to support U.S.-led globalization and U.S. multicultural narratives. They represent dire problems in the developing world that require humanitarian solutions and provide a prescription for such problems. Novels such as Hagedorn's *Dogeaters* and Afghan American Khaled Hosseini's *The Kite Runner* (2003) are representative of popular ethnic novels and films in the United States that represent government corruption and human despair in developing countries. I am in no way suggesting that these cultural productions are completely uncritical of the United States, imperialism, or globalization. However, taken on face value these cultural representations can be used to justify U.S. humanitarian or military intervention. One other hegemonic narrative reproduced in U.S. ethnic cultural productions is the narrative of immigrant assimilation that depicts determined individuals who leave their impoverished homelands and find success in the United States through hard work. Their American-born children culturally assimilate and build on their parents' success. Examples of the immigration and assimilation narrative in American popular culture include the films *The Namesake* (2007) and *Joy Luck Club* (1993). Ironically, the success and popularity of these assimilation narratives are used to celebrate U.S. acceptance of minority cultures. That is, assimilation narratives are used to affirm a narrative of U.S. multiculturalism. Though both globalization and multiculturalism seemingly celebrate difference, both actually advocate for *assimilation to* Western cultures. The former recommends developing nations to replicate U.S. democracy and capitalist system to facilitate their own national success. The latter recommends ethnic minorities to assimilate to U.S. culture in order to facilitate personal economic success. For the United States the end of empire is assimilation:

nations assimilating to a democratic, capitalist, global order and individuals assimilating to a progressive U.S. culture. Bruno Mars's appropriation by the mainstream cultural market for lucid multiculturalism and U.S. postraciality represents one imagining of the end of empire.

Filipino American and U.S. Puerto Rican culture imagine a different end to empire, an end that entails the empowerment of those who have been exploited by imperialism and subsequently by globalization. Hagedorn and Santiago argue nationalist movements need to meaningfully incorporate feminist nationalism in order to construct a truly decolonial nationalism. Griggers demands that the United States recognize the excessive violence during the Philippine-American war to allow for a more honest and equitable relationship to form between the two countries and between Filipinos and Americans. Perez argues that Puerto Ricans need and deserve political representation, implicitly advocating that Puerto Rico needs to be given either more political sovereignty or voting representation in Washington, D.C. Filipino American and Nuyorican performance-poet activists construct genealogies of global power that encourage disidentifcation with power and work toward empowering people of color in their own communities. Put simply, Filipino American and U.S. Puerto Rican culture imagine "a world that's brand new."

While Filipino American and U.S. Puerto Rican novels and films contribute to imagining a world that's brand new, performance-poet activists actively work toward that world. May 3–5, 2002, more than one hundred Puerto Rican, U.S. Puerto Ricans, and other artists against the U.S. military bomb testing gathered in Vieques to participate in "Viequethon 2002: Poetry and Concert for Peace." The international group of artists joined the local community in protesting and demanding an end to U.S. military bomb testing on the Puerto Rican island of Vieques. Despite former President Clinton's agreement to put an end to U.S. military testing in Vieques by 2003, President George W. Bush deemed more testing necessary after the September 11, 2001, attacks on New York City and Washington, D.C. The Viequethon was an organized response protesting the renewed bomb testing, regardless of the use of unarmed test dummies, and demanding the U.S. Navy withdrawal from Vieques promised in 2003. The event was organized by two New York Puerto Ricans: poet Pedro Pietri and photographer Adal Maldonado. In addition to poetry readings and performances, they also held seminars, told stories, and read poetry to children at a local public school.[18] The ability of New York Puerto Ricans to organize and participate in an event in Vieques points to the collaborations between Puerto Rican activists in New York and those in Puerto Rico enabled by Puerto Ricans' U.S. citizenship.

In 1999, City University of New York (CUNY) students organized a strike against tuition increases and the end of open admissions. Lenina Nadal describes how students from Puerto Rico with experience organizing hundreds of thousands workers in Puerto Rico during the 1998 general strike against the privatization of the Puerto Rican Telephone Company came to New York to help the CUNY students' organizing efforts and to enlist the support of the local Healthcare Workers Union (SEIU 1199) and the transit workers' union. The relationships established during the CUNY strike led to more activist collaborations between CUNY students and University of Puerto Rico (UPR) students. After the CUNY strike, Nadal returned the favor by participating in student activist struggles at the UPR while visiting the island, helping students organize for smaller class sizes and more parking spaces.[19] Such collaborations and sustained relationships of students of the same generation in Puerto Rico and the U.S. confirm Georges E. Fouron and Nina Glick-Schiller's assertion that transnational social fields simultaneously shape the identities of immigrants and their children in the U.S. as well as their counterparts in the homeland.[20] These particular transnational practices that Nadal describes are remarkable because they provide examples of a circular "long-distance nationalism." Fouron and Glick-Schiller define "long-distance nationalism" as "ideas about belonging that link people living in various geographic locations and motivate or justify their taking action in relationship to an ancestral territory and its government."[21] The transnational activist coalitions between CUNY and UPR not only show U.S. Puerto Ricans taking action in their home islands but also Puerto Ricans taking action to aid Puerto Ricans in the diaspora.

In contrast to the circular cultural and activist exchanges between Puerto Ricans in New York and in Puerto Rico, such exchanges between Filipinos and Filipino Americans are less feasible. As Philippine citizens, Filipinos cannot come to the United States without a visa. Obtaining a tourist visa is especially difficult for young Filipinos who are assumed likely to become undocumented immigrants. These conditions make the circulation of activists and artists less possible. Filipino Americans can travel to and from the Philippines as they please, but the expense of a round-trip ticket and the length of the transpacific flight to the Philippines also limit the number of trips that many Filipino Americans in Los Angeles can make.

The cultural exchanges that occur between Filipinos in Los Angeles and Filipinos in the Philippines depend largely on Filipino American travel to the Philippines. Filipino American performance poets perform in the Philippines to introduce their work to Filipinos. To introduce Philippine performance poetry to Filipino Americans, poets returning from the Philippines either recount their experiences or bring back examples of Philippine performance poetry to share. This is precisely what Filipino American performance poet and chair of Kabataang Maka-Bayan (KmB) USA (also known as Pro-People Youth) Johneric Concordia did. He spent four months in the Philippines in 2004 to experience firsthand the conditions that people living in Mindanao face as a result of joint U.S.-Philippine military operations there. While he was there, he performed a poem titled "Do You Want to Know?" The poem debunks the American Dream often packaged for Filipinos who long to immigrate to the United States. Johneric begins his poem by asking the audience, "Do you want to know what's happening in my town?" In his answer, he paints an image of misunderstanding, distrust, and violence in an inner city: "This kid was shot with a glock by another kid who would not appreciate the statement the other kid wouldn't talk. The bullet lodged in his heart and bloodless died on the spot. No second chance to advance for a future. All that it got: sixteen buried and wasted, lifer incarcerated. The concrete conditions we live in rarely debated. Up in congress, I guess our life is worthless, feel no justice, peace, solace."[22] Whereas Filipinos in the Philippines often hear stories about higher wages and economic success from their Filipino American counterparts, Concordia represents the life that low-skilled immigrants and their families face in the United States. The desire to secure a better future for their children often motivates Filipinos to immigrate to the United States. By representing two youngsters whose futures are cut short by violence, Concordia argues that the United States does not always offer a better future for immigrant children. Likewise, he insinuates that the conditions that foster such violence are unlikely to change because the U.S. lawmakers do not value the youngsters' lives. The image he paints for Philippine audiences contrasts starkly to immigrant success stories that reproduce the U.S. as a land of opportunity for anyone.

To complete the Philippine—Filipino American cultural exchange, Concordia wrote a second verse to this poem representing the struggles of the indigenous minority in the southern Philippines. Upon returning to the United States, he embarked on a twelve-city tour to perform the new version of "Do You Want to Know?" and then report back on what he observed during his time in the Philippines. He intended to perform his poem for Filipino American audiences, so he chose venues in major U.S. and Canadian cities with large Filipino populations. The second verse of his poem begins with the question, "Do you want to know what's happening back home?" To respond to this question, Concordia depicts how one man's family was murdered by the Armed Forces of the Philippines (AFP): "Here's the story of one father.

His child ripped from the womb. The mother died pretty soon, an example to anyone who would dare to assume, challenge AFP goons will bring about your own doom. They'll destroy all you love and keep whatever they can, too. Mother, daughter were buried. The rotten smells carried, found by the husband. They were just recently married. It's a nightmare he swears he can never wake from, so he hikes up the hills with a pack and a gun."[23] By uncovering the circumstances that compel Filipinos to join guerilla resistance movements in the mountains, Concordia illustrates that guerilla fighters have legitimate reasons for opposing the Philippine government. This representation challenges the construction of guerilla resistance in Mindanao as terrorists by the Philippine and U.S. governments and the international media.

Toward the end of both verses of "Do You Want to Know?" Johneric Concordia states, "So I ask of you, you can ask me, too. In what direction we're headed for a world that's brand new?"[24] With this question he encourages the audience to become actively involved in finding solutions to problems facing people of color in the United States and peasants in the Philippines. Ray Ramirez also asks his audience to take action by stating, "It's war. Which side you joining?" in his poem "Drop the Bomb."[25] Directly addressing or questioning the audience in their performances is a tactic New York Puerto Rican and Los Angeles Filipino American performance poets often use to organize their communities. They perform their poetry to build interracial, interethnic, transnational coalitions that bring together local concerns around the globe. They build coalitions that hegemonic constructions of race, immigration, and U.S. exceptionalism actively discourage and therefore work toward a different end of empire.

All of the cultural productions I analyzed in this book critique U.S. imperialism in its covert and overt forms. The novelists, filmmakers, and performance poets challenge the eventual outcomes of benevolent assimilation, thus questioning the initial sincerity of the promises of U.S. imperialism as exceptional. They illustrate the continuing social inequalities that are consequences of U.S. global power. Such critiques are telling in a moment wherein the United States attempts to construct an end to its interventions in Iraq and Afghanistan. The United States may celebrate the success of the democratic institutions it established and the gains that the Iraqi and Afghani people have made toward sustaining their own democratic nations, but the cultural narratives discussed in this book indicate that what we are witnessing is not the end of U.S. imperialism in the Middle East but a transition to a new beginning. A new beginning of political sovereignty given with strings attached, where political corruption is blamed entirely on power-hungry local leaders, not on the process of establishing democratic institutions under military occupation. The United States will take credit for the new beginning it has given to Iraq and Afghanistan but not take responsibility for the consequences of insisting on that new beginning.

Notes

Introduction

1. Lowe, *Immigrant Acts*, 6.
2. I use the term U.S. Puerto Rican in recognition of the poets' refusal of the "Puerto Rican American" label. By U.S. Puerto Rican I mean a Puerto Rican living in the U.S.
3. Espiritu, *Home Bound*, argues that a critical transnational perspective that examines the lives of immigrants both before and after the point of immigration makes visible the role that U.S. imperialism plays in the production of immigration to the United States.
4. Kim, *Bitter Fruit*, argues that Asian Americans and African Americans are racially triangulated to prevent recognition of racial hierarchy that marginalizes both groups and maintains white privilege.
5. Espiritu, *Body Counts*, coins the term "critical juxtaposition" to describe the important work of putting seemingly disparate narratives in conversation with one another.
6. Isaac, *American Tropics*, 182.
7. Williams, *Marxism and Literature*.
8. Go, *American Empire*, describes the similar initial colonial projects in the Philippines and Puerto Rico and how colonial policies changed over the first decade of the twentieth century. For a more detailed account of benevolent assimilation, see Miller, "*Benevolent Assimilation*."
9. These metaphors were often articulated in political cartoons in the late nineteenth and early twentieth centuries. A collection of these cartoons can be found in Ignacio, *Forbidden Book*.
10. Foucault et al., *Society Must Be Defended*.
11. Jones, "Specificity of U.S. Imperialism."
12. Cabranes, *Citizenship*. To this day, U.S. citizens in the U.S. territories of Puerto Rico and Guam do not enjoy the full rights of U.S. citizenship. Though they are part of the nominating process for presidential candidates, they cannot vote for president.
13. Kim in "Rethinking Colonialism" argues that in colonies where an economy is already established, like in the Philippines when the United States took control of it from

Spain, those economies are reproduced. Baver, *Political Economy of Colonialism*, demonstrates how the Puerto Rican economy becomes increasingly tied to the U.S. economy in the mid-twentieth century.

14. Sparrow, *Insular Cases*.
15. For more on the ethnic studies movement see Salomon, "Movement History"; Maeda, *Chains of Babylon*.
16. Love, *Race over Empire*, does a good job of discussing the debates between anti-imperialists and annexationists in the late twentieth century. However, his faulty conclusion that race does not matter because both sides were racist does not hold. Rather, it demonstrates the extent to which racism was accepted at the time instead of discounting it. Hoganson, *Fighting for American Manhood*, argues that the various justifications made for overseas imperialism can all be better understood through an analysis of contemporary gender roles.
17. For analyses of debates for and against U.S. overseas expansion see Miller, *"Benevolent Assimilation"*; Hilfrich, *Debating American Exceptionalism*; and Love, *Race over Empire*.
18. Hilfrich, *Debating American Exceptionalism*.
19. Lee, *Orientals*.
20. Kim, *Ends of Empire*.
21. Schirmer and Shalom, *Philippines Reader*.
22. Briggs, *Reproducing Empire*.
23. For differences in political and economic policies applied to the Philippines and Puerto Rico during the U.S. colonial period see Go, "Chains of Empire"; and Go, *American Empire*. For an analysis of why Puerto Ricans were granted U.S. citizenship while Filipinos were not, see Cabranes, *Citizenship*.
24. Bradley, *Imagining Vietnam and America*.
25. Sanger, "Bush Cites Philippines."
26. Johnson, *Blowback*.
27. Grosfoguel, *Colonial Subjects*.
28. A great photo book featuring these veterans is Rocamora and Ciria-Cruz, *Filipino World War II Soldiers*. A good documentary on the issue is Izon, *Untold Triumph*.
29. Gordon, *Ghostly Matters*, 25.
30. Foucault et al., *Society Must Be Defended*.
31. Truettner et al., *West as America*.
32. Yoneyama, *Hiroshima Traces*.
33. Williams, *Marxism and Literature*.
34. Lee, *Orientals*; Espiritu, *Asian American Women and Men*.
35. Okamura and Agbayani, "Pamantasan."
36. Ocampo, "Second-Generation Filipinos."
37. Ngai, *Impossible Subjects*.
38. Nill, "Latinos and SB 1070."
39. For in-depth analyses on laughter see Morreall, *Taking Laughter Seriously*; Gantar, *Pleasure of Fools*; Parvulescu, *Laughter*.
40. Lee, *Orientals*.

41. Though undocumented immigrants are constructed as a drain on social services, their contributions to the U.S. economy and the fact that they pay taxes is not widely recognized. See Nadadur, "Illegal Immigration."

42. Koshy, "Fiction of Asian American Literature," 327.

43. Espiritu, *Home Bound*.

44. Espiritu, *Home Bound*. This is not to say that the simplistic immigrant narrative that the United States offers economic success to hardworking immigrants from impoverished countries adequately explains Asian immigration to the United States. The hegemonic narrative of the United States as a land of opportunity for immigrants upholds the myth of U.S. exceptionalism. Espiritu argues that a transnational perspective on immigration is needed in order to prevent immigration experience from supporting such narratives.

45. Flores, *Divided Borders*, 143.

46. Kim, *Ends of Empire*.

47. Lowe, *Immigrant Acts*.

48. Bhatia in *American Karma* argues that Indian immigrants strategically identify with the model-minority myth because they believe it allows them protection from racism and access to white privilege. Park in "Continuing Significance of the Model Minority Myth" demonstrates how Asian American professionals and their children perform the model minority in order to assimilate into U.S. society.

49. Chuh, *Imagine Otherwise*.

50. Isaac, *American Tropics*.

51. Escobar, *Encountering Development*.

52. Ngai, *Impossible Subjects*, 99.

53. Williams, *Marxism and Literature*, 116.

Chapter 1. Consuming (Post)Colonial Culture

An earlier version of this chapter originally appeared in *Philippine Studies* 53:1 (2006).

1. Palumbo-Liu, "Introduction."

2. Jennings and Smith, "Examining."

3. Ween, "This Is Your Book," demonstrates how novels are packaged to emphasize the authenticity of the ethnic author and how it is problematic to do so.

4. Palumbo-Liu in *The Deliverance of Others* argues that the pedagogical practices of teaching ethnic literature often involves delivering the other to the American college student. Such a pedagogy often flattens differences between the other and the reader by having the reader identify with the represented other. This is possible only when the novels that are taught reproduce recognizable narratives of the other, such as the narrative of the hard-working immigrant. He recommends teaching a different way of reading ethnic novels that centers how our notions of difference and sameness are constructed.

5. Ngai, *Impossible Subjects*, 99.

6. Olivares, *Our Islands and Their People*.

7. Merrill's "Negotiating Cold War Paradise" describes how Puerto Rico reconstructed its national identity in order to attract U.S. tourists in the middle of the twentieth century.

8. Neumann, "Tourism Promotion and Prostitution."

9. World Travel and Tourism Council, "Travel and Tourism Economic Impact 2014: Philippines"; World Travel and Tourism Council, "Travel and Tourism Economic Impact 2014: Puerto Rico." This percentage reflects the total estimated contribution of tourism to economies of the Philippines and Puerto Rico, including the wider effects of tourism. The direct contributions of tourism, which does not take into account the consequent benefits of tourism, are 4.2 percent of the Philippines' GDP and 2.3 percent of Puerto Rico's GDP.

10. Sheth, "BBC to Acquire 75% Stake in Publisher Lonely Planet."
11. Peffer, *Puerto Rico*; Rowthorn et al., *Philippines*.
12. Olivares, *Our Islands and Their People*, 5 (emphasis added).
13. Ibid., 691.
14. Rowthorn, *Philippines*, 11.
15. Olivares, *Our Islands and Their People*, 285.
16. Peffer, *Puerto Rico*, 148.
17. Olivares, *Our Islands and Their People*, 559.
18. Rowthorn, *Philippines*, 62.
19. Ibid.
20. Ibid., 61.
21. For one such travel narrative, see Makow, *A Long Way to Go for a Date*.
22. Olivares, *Our Islands and Their People*, 287.
23. Cabranes, *Citizenship*.
24. Peffer, *Puerto Rico*, 9.
25. Peffer, *Puerto Rico*, 54.
26. Briggs, *Reproducing Empire*.
27. Findlay, *Imposing Decency*.
28. Dery, *From Ibalon to Sorsogon*. Such red-light districts exist around U.S. military bases in Asia. For more, see chapter 1 of Yuh, *Beyond the Shadow of Camptown*; Sturdevant, *Let the Good Times Roll*.
29. Eviota, *Political Economy of Gender*.
30. Richter, "After Political Turmoil."
31. Tadiar, *Things Fall Away*.
32. "Tourism."
33. Gilligan, "Puerto Rico Succeeds."
34. Pratt, *Imperial Eyes*, 53.
35. Santiago, *América's Dream*, 1.
36. McCaffrey, *Military Power*.
37. For more on U.S. support of the Marcos regime and martial law, see chapter 8 of Schirmer and Shalom, *Philippines Reader*, and Kessler, "Marcos and the Americans."
38. Hagedorn, *Dogeaters*, 73.
39. Gonzalez, "Military Bases."
40. Santiago, *América's Dream*, 31.
41. Harrison, "Tourism."
42. A similar phenomenon is occurring in the Philippines, where former U.S. military bases are being converted into casinos and hotels. See Goodno, "Casino."
43. Pratt, *Imperial Eyes*.

44. Santiago, *América's Dream*, 77.
45. Hagedorn, *Dogeaters*, 42.
46. Ibid., 72–73.
47. "Statistical Yearbook."
48. Santiago, *América's Dream*, 12.
49. Hagedorn, *Dogeaters*, 130.
50. Ibid.
51. de la Cruz, *Filipinas for Sale*.
52. Richter, "After Political Turmoil."
53. Escobar, *Encountering Development*.
54. Santiago, *América's Dream*, 30.
55. bell hooks in "Representing Whiteness in the Black Imagination" argues that centuries of oppressing blacks taught whites to deny black subjectivity by rendering their bodies invisible.
56. Fanon, *Toward the African Revolution*.
57. Santiago, *América's Dream*, 1.
58. Ibid., 37.
59. Ibid., 17.
60. Hagedorn, *Dogeaters*, 149.
61. Ibid., 13.
62. Santiago, *América's Dream*, 79.
63. Bunten, "Sharing Culture."
64. Hagedorn, *Dogeaters*, 77.
65. Ibid., 78.
66. Ibid., 132.
67. Vergara, *Displaying Filipinos*.
68. Isaac, *American Tropics*.
69. Richter, "After Political Turmoil."
70. Hagedorn, *Dogeaters*, 130.
71. Richter, "After Political Turmoil."
72. Hagedorn, *Dogeaters*, 40.
73. Lowe, *Immigrant Acts*.
74. Ween, "This Is Your Book."
75. Hagedorn, *Dogeaters*.
76. Ibid.
77. Ibid.

Chapter 2. Revising the Colonialism-as-Romance Metaphor

1. McClintock, *Imperial Leather*.
2. Hoganson, *Fighting for American Manhood*, demonstrates how the possibility of actual rape was used by both anti- and pro-imperialists. Pro-imperialists argued that the United States needed to protect Philippine women from becoming victims of rape; anti-imperialists argued that the Philippines would degrade the morality of American military, reducing them to rapists.

3. Santiago-Valles, "Sexual Appeal."

4. See Ignacio, *Forbidden Book*, 49, for one such example.

5. Sharpe, *Allegories of Empire*, illustrates how literary representations of rape by British writers during their colonial rule of India reflected British anxieties about race and gender. Some contemporary novels also deploy representations of rape to foreground continuing cultural imperialism in former colonies, and others also use rape to encapsulate foreign domination and penetration. See Emecheta, *Rape of Shavi*.

6. Anthias and Yuval-Davis, "Women and the Nation-State," 315.

7. For an analysis on how the Subic Bay rape case became a flashpoint for protests against the U.S.–Philippines Visiting Forces Agreement, see Winter, "Guns, Money, and Justice." Several rapes in South Korea by U.S. military personnel have been tried and convicted by the South Korean government in the recent past. After a U.S. military tribunal acquitted military personnel responsible for killing two South Korean schoolgirls in a traffic accident, protestors successfully demanded that such cases not be turned over to the U.S. military. These rapes have led to calls for the revision of the Status of Forces Agreement between South Korea and the United States. See Rowland, "Korea-Based U.S. Soldier"; Rowland and Chang, "SOFA."

8. McClintock, *Imperial Leather*.

9. Clay-Warner and McMahon-Howard, "Rape Reporting."

10. George and Martinez, "Victim Blaming."

11. McClintock, *Imperial Leather*.

12. Hagedorn, *Dogeaters*, 14.

13. Ibid., 74.

14. Santiago, *América's Dream*, 16.

15. Despite local protests, Vieques was a U.S. Navy testing site for more than sixty years. Uranium released from the bombs resulted in a higher cancer rate in Vieques and destroyed the island's ecosystem. After a bomb missed its target and killed a Puerto Rican security guard, opposition to naval testing gained momentum, attracting the support of the Catholic Church and prominent public figures. President George W. Bush finally agreed to stop bomb testing on Vieques. The navy pulled out of Vieques on May 1, 2003, but the land transferred to the U.S. Department of the Interior. For more, see Muñiz, "Goliath against David"; "U.S. Closes Vieques Test Range."

16. Santiago, *América's Dream*, 91.

17. Hagedorn, *Dogeaters*, 31.

18. Ibid., 47.

19. Ibid., 3–4.

20. Ibid., 22.

21. Walker, *Battered Woman Syndrome*.

22. Hagedorn, *Dogeaters*, 234.

23. Santiago, *América's Dream*, 6.

24. Ibid., 7.

25. Ibid., 11.

26. Duany, *Puerto Rican Nation*, takes an in-depth look at Operation Serenity (see chapter 5).

27. Santiago, *América's Dream*, 25

28. Benson-Arias, "Puerto Rico," and Baver, *Political Economy*, demonstrate the integral role of Operation Bootstrap in making Puerto Rico an industrialized island.

29. Santiago-Valles, "Sexual Appeal," argues, "The grammar of colonization was thus inseparable from the iconography of captured exotic women waiting to be ravaged and to be subjected to the carnal knowledge of Western science and government" (130).

30. Santiago, *América's Dream*, 118.

31. McClintock, *Imperial Leather*, discusses how women are constructed as embodying national tradition. Anthias and Yuval-Davis, "Women and the Nation-State," also make this point in discussing the contradictions between women in the nation-state as both subjects and objects of national interest.

32. Acosta-Belen, *Puerto Rican Woman*, analyzes representations of the liberated culturally tainted woman/humble culturally faithful woman binary.

33. Santiago, *América's Dream*, 109.

34. Ibid.

35. Until the passage of the Violence against Women Act in 2006, many states distinguished spousal rape as a lesser crime than other rapes. These laws are a reflection of hegemonic rape myths in the United States. See Ferro, Cermele, and Saltzman, "Current Perceptions."

36. Walker, *Battered Woman Syndrome*.

37. Santiago, *América's Dream*, 229–30.

38. Ibid., 231.

39. Ibid., 287.

40. Ibid., 318.

41. Ibid., 325.

42. Goodno, *The Philippines*.

43. Sharpe, *Allegories of Empire*.

44. Hagedorn, *Dogeaters*, 100.

45. Isaac, *American Tropics*.

46. Hagedron, *Dogeaters*, 100–101.

47. Goodno, *The Philippines*, 73.

48. Hagedorn, *Dogeaters*, 99.

49. Ibid., 219.

50. Ibid.

51. Ibid., 195.

52. Goodno, *The Philippines*, 79.

53. Samuels, *Romances of the Republic*, discusses numerous political cartoons in Great Britain and its American colonies from the sixteenth century to the eighteenth century. These political cartoons depicted situations that suggested imminent sexual violence to a defenseless America, reflecting the anxieties of both Great Britain and the colonial resistance over their threatened political situations in the "New World."

54. Banet-Weiser, *Most Beautiful Girl*.

55. Hagedorn, *Dogeaters*, 101.

56. Banet-Weiser, *Most Beautiful Girl*, 90.

57. Hagedorn, *Dogeaters*, 102.

58. Ibid., 101.

59. My translation.
60. Hagedorn, *Dogeaters*, 102.
61. Banet-Weiser, *Most Beautiful Girl*, 201.
62. Hagedorn, *Dogeaters*, 106.
63. Ibid., 109.
64. Goodno, *The Philippines*, 78.
65. Hagedorn, *Dogeaters*, 233.
66. Banet-Weiser, *Most Beautiful Girl*, discusses in depth Vanessa William's coronation as Miss America and how she lost her crown when it was discovered that she posed nude (142).
67. Hagedorn, *Dogeaters*, 116.
68. Ibid., 216.
69. Rizal, Lacson-Locsin, and Locsin, *Noli Me Tangere*, and Rizal and Augenbraum, *El Filibusterismo*, are popular cultural representations of the abuses of friars in the Philippines.
70. Hilsdon, *Madonnas and Martyrs*.
71. Hagedorn, *Dogeaters*, 215.
72. Goodno, *The Philippines*, 79.
73. Rodriguez, *Migrants for Export*, and Rhacel Salazar Parreñas, *Children of Global Migration*, both explain the lack of economic development in the Philippines that creates the Philippine export labor market.
74. Frake, "Abu Sayyaf," includes a discussion of how Muslims in the southern Philippines are negatively constructed.
75. Hagedorn, *Dogeaters*, 233.
76. Janer, "Creating a National Womanhood." See also Aguilar, *Toward a Nationalist Feminism*. Though Janer explores the contributions of the labor movement in Puerto Rico to the nationalist project, she does not delve into the intersections of the labor and feminist movements, or if there existed a women's labor's movement.
77. Aguilar, "Gender, Nation, Colonialism."
78. Mydans, "4 Marines." One example of a press release from Gabriela on this matter: Redonidez, "Rapist's Transferral."
79. Macdonald, "Demonizing Islam."

Chapter 3. Bastards of U.S. Imperialism

1. Spence and Navarro, *Crafting Truth*; Cowie, *Recording Reality*.
2. Ignacio (*Forbidden Book*) describes how the representation of colonies as infants of color often represented the "White Man's Burden" to take control of colonies and teach them how to be civilized.
3. Griggers et al., *Memories of a Forgotten War*.
4. Ibid.
5. Homiak, "Body in the Archives"; Blumentritt, "*Bontoc Eulogy*."
6. Griggers et al., *Memories of a Forgotten War*.
7. Ibid.
8. Ibid.

9. Ibid.
10. Rusing, "Interview."
11. Spivak, "Can the Subaltern Speak?"
12. Francisco, "First Vietnam." Rodriguez, *Suspended Apocalypse*.
13. Gordon, *Ghostly Matters*.
14. Spivak, "Can the Subaltern Speak?"
15. Ibid.
16. Bacevich, "What Happened at Bud Dajo."
17. Griggers et al., *Memories of a Forgotten War*.
18. Ibid.
19. Critiques of the celebration of the growing number of mixed race people as a evidence of a post-racial United States can be found in Goldberg, Racial Subjects. and Sexton, Amalgamation Schemes.
20. Griggers et al., *Memories of a Forgotten War*.
21. Aurthur, "Budgets."
22. Dominguez, "Smits."
23. Perez, *Yo soy Boricua, pa'que tu lo Sepas!*
24. Rodriguez, *Suspended Apocalypse*.
25. Bakhtin and Holquist, *Dialogic Imagination*.
26. Duany, *Puerto Rican Nation*.
27. Perez, *Yo soy Boricua, pa'que tu lo Sepas!*
28. Rodriguez, *Suspended Apocalypse*.
29. Tinker and Freeland, "Thief."
30. Duany, *Puerto Rican Nation*, demonstrates how the founding of the Puerto Rican commonwealth depended on constructions of Puerto Rican cultural nationalism that asserted cultural independence from the United States. Puerto Rican cultural nationalism separated nationalist rhetoric from calls for political independence. Thus, cultural nationalism perpetuates the ambiguous relationship of Puerto Rico and the United States.
31. Perez, *Yo soy Boricua, pa'que tu lo Sepas!*
32. Reincke, "Antidote to Dominance," examines the different possibilities of laughter for counteracting dominance: women laughing at men or women knowingly laughing with other women. For a more general discussion on the multiple interpretations of laughter, see Morreall, *Taking Laughter Seriously*; Gantar, *Pleasure of Fools*.
33. Perez, *Yo soy Boricua, pa'que tu lo Sepas!*
34. The U.S. military transitioned from relying on the draft to a volunteer force partially in response to critiques that the draft favored poor people of color. Evidence suggests that military recruitment of volunteers still targets these same economically vulnerable groups. For community responses to economically targeted recruitment see Tannock, "'Opting Out.'"
35. Perez, *Yo soy Boricua, pa'que tu lo Sepas!*, emphasis added.
36. Tannock, "'Opting Out.'" Critics of the military draft argued that lower-income individuals and people of color were overrepresented in war, on the front lines, and among those killed in action. The move to an all-volunteer force was meant to address this inequality, but critics contend that these same populations are now targeted disproportionately for recruitment.

37. Interestingly enough, this claim has recently come under partisan attack. These challenges affirm that this is a commonly held view among the public, historians, and economists and insinuate it is a liberal myth meant to justify the creation of a large government. In defense of laissez-faire capitalism, U.S. conservatives argue that the Great Depression did not end until after World War II, when government economic restrictions were lifted. See Horwitz and McPhillips, "Wartime Economy."

38. Perez, *Yo soy Boricua, pa'que tu lo Sepas!*

39. The myth of equal opportunity for all in the United States is captured in the poem "The New Colossus," by Emma Lawrence and engraved on the Statue of Liberty in New York City. The Statue of Liberty itself is constructed as a beacon of hope attracting unfortunate immigrants to the United States.

40. Cullen, *American Dream*, analyzes the shifting meaning of the American dream over the lifespan of the nation's history. Chapter 4 in *American Dream* looks specifically at the American dream as upward mobility.

41. Honig, "Immigrant America?" demonstrates that the figures of the good immigrant and the bad immigrant are two sides of the same coin. Good immigrants are praised for their commitment to family and community at the same time that their culture and communities are demonized for being too backward and insular. Good immigrants are praised for their resourcefulness in material acquisition, but if that resourcefulness is used to acquire or work for political rights, they become bad immigrants.

42. The "culture of poverty" thesis was first applied to Puerto Ricans in Lewis, *La Vida*. Since then Puerto Rican studies scholars have sought to shift the blame for Puerto Rican poverty from Puerto Rican culture to structural racial inequality. For one recent example, see Dávila, *Barrio Dreams*.

43. Perez, *Yo soy Boricua, pa'que tu lo Sepas!*

44. Ibid.

45. Ibid.

46. Pietri, *Puerto Rican Obituary*.

47. Ibid.

48. Perez, *Yo soy Boricua, pa'que tu lo Sepas!*

49. Corretier, "Albizu Campos."

50. Perez, *Yo soy Boricua, pa'que tu lo Sepas!*

51. Ibid.

52. Corretier, "Albizu Campos"; Rodriguez-Perez, "Reports."

53. Perez, *Yo soy Boricua, pa'que tu lo Sepas!*

54. Ibid.

55. Rodríguez-Fraticelli, "Albizu Campos," is a historiography of the characterization of Pedro Albizu Campos as violent. He argues that Albizu Campos practiced civil disobedience, which included armed confrontation as a strategy, among others, to be used if the circumstances necessitated.

56. For a discussion on what Che signifies among youth in London and Cuba, see Raman, "Signifying Something."

57. Turner, "Dangers of Misappropriation."

58. Perez, *Yo soy Boricua, pa'que tu lo Sepas!*

59. These points were part of the Young Lords Party 13-Point Program and Platform.
60. Duany, *Puerto Rican Nation*.
61. Ibid.
62. Perez, *Yo soy Boricua, pa'que tu lo Sepas!*
63. Ibid.
64. Rodriguez, *Suspended Apocalypse*.
65. Griggers, *Memories of a Forgotten War*.
66. Rodriguez, *Suspended Apocalypse*.

Chapter 4. Performing Genealogies

Portions of this chapter originally appeared in *Transnational Crossroads: Remapping the Americas and the Pacific*, edited by Camilla Fojas and Rudy P. Guevarra Jr., and is used by permission of the University of Nebraska Press. Copyright 2012 by the Board of Regents of the University of Nebraska.

1. Go, "Chains of Empire"
2. Justice, "Education at the End of a Gun," describes how public education and U.S. expansion were interlinked even before the United States became an overseas empire with aims of benevolent assimilation.
3. For more on colonial education in the Philippines and Puerto Rico, see the education section of McCoy and Scarano, *Colonial Crucible*.
4. Caronan, "Memories of U.S. Imperialism."
5. Bhabha, *Location of Culture*, 201.
6. Duara, *Rescuing History*.
7. Foucault et al., *Society Must Be Defended*.
8. Harraway, "Situated Knowledges."
9. Gramsci, Hoare, and Nowell-Smith, *Prison Notebooks*, 10.
10. Roach, *Cities of the Dead*.
11. Taylor, *Archive*, 20.
12. Espiritu, "Multiple Identities."
13. Algarín and Holman, *Aloud* (p. 5), provides a definition: "Nuyorican (nü yor´ē kan) (New York + Puerto Rican) 1. Originally Puerto Rican epithet for those of Puerto Rican heritage born in New York: their Spanish was different (Spanglish), their dress and look were different. They were a stateless people (like most U.S. poets) until the Cafe became their homeland. 2. After Algarín and Piñero, a proud poet speaking New York Puerto Rican. 3. A denizen of the Nuyorican Poets Cafe. 4. New York's riches."
14. Foucault et al., *Society Must be Defended*.
15. Education scholars have long discussed how to move from the additive, tokenistic model of incorporating multicultural education into public school curriculum. For more, see Nieto and Bode, *Affirming Diversity*; Schoorman and Bogotch, "Moving Beyond."
16. Matuštík, *Specters of Liberation*.
17. The term "differential inclusion," coined by Espiritu (*Home Bound*), describes how minority groups are selectively included into U.S. culture, history, and society.
18. Muñoz, *Disidentifications*, 13.

19. I am using a term from Crenshaw, "Mapping the Margins."
20. Lustre, *Conditions*.
21. Ibid.
22. Muñoz, *Disidentifications*, 9.
23. Noor, "Uncle Sam."
24. Javellana-Santos, "2,000 OFWs."
25. Baroma, "Solving."
26. The dwindling numbers of Filipino World War II veterans residing in the United States are still demanding equal benefits. For more on their struggles, see Gonzalves, "Neatly Folded Hope."
27. Francisco, "The First Vietnam," demonstrates the parallels between the Philippine-American War and the Vietnam War.
28. Filipinos in the U.S. Navy could only be stewards until 1973, when they were allowed to enter any specialty.
29. Rojas, "Invisible Ones," 1–2.
30. Taylor, *Archive*, 86.
31. Flores, "Oye Lo Boricua," 1.
32. Puerto Rico is packaged as a convenient Caribbean destination for both business and vacation travelers. No passports are needed. Money need not be exchanged. Low-cost carriers such as JetBlue offer frequent, affordable flights from the Northeast United States to the Caribbean for returning migrants and for those seeking a respite from the cold winter.
33. Duany, *Puerto Rican Nation*, illustrates how this narrative is represented in museum exhibits of cultural artifacts and how the narrative is deployed in Puerto Rican politics.
34. Flores, "Oye Lo Boricua," 2.
35. Ibid.
36. Lipsitz, *Dangerous Crossroads*; Roach, *Cities of the Dead*; Gilroy, *Black Atlantic*.
37. Eperjesi (*The Imperialist Imaginary*) and Wilson (*Reimagining the American Pacific*) call this space the American Pacific.
38. Gramsci, Hoare, and Nowell-Smith, *Prison Notebooks*, 10.
39. Ibid., 340.
40. Pineau, "Teaching Is Performance."
41. Aquino, "Curses and Blessings," 153.
42. Chen and Omatsu, *Teaching*.
43. Baroma, personal communication.
44. Mercado, personal communication.
45. Morales, personal communication.
46. Merina, personal communication.
47. Habermas, *The Philosophical Discourse of Modernity*, idealizes the public sphere as a site free from institutional regulation enabling the realization of true democratic practices. Fraser, "Rethinking the Public Sphere," critiques Habermas's theorization of the public sphere by illustrating how the state regulates the public sphere; Fraser suggests the formation of separate public forums for different subaltern groups.
48. Fischer, "Song is Unfinished," 292.
49. Dolan, *Utopia in Performance*, 91–92.
50. Figueroa, personal communication.

51. Lefebvre, *Production of Space.*
52. Sandoval, *Methodology*, 31.
53. Lowe, *Immigrant Acts.*
54. Yoneyama, *Hiroshima Traces*, describes how third-generation Koreans in Japan formed coalitions with people of different backgrounds to advocate for antidiscrimination and the construction of Japanese citizenship, and for civil rights independent of nationality.
55. Taylor, *Archive.*
56. Flores, "Oye Lo Boricua," 5.
57. Briggs, *Reproducing Empire.*
58. Welfare Poets, "Drop the Bomb."
59. Ibid.
60. Ramirez, personal communication.
61. Welfare Poets, "Drop the Bomb."
62. Ramirez, personal communication.
63. Ibid.
64. Ibid.
65. Santilla, personal communication.
66. Merina, personal communication.
67. Soriano, personal communication.
68. *La Enkanto.* CD, 2001.
69. Santilla, "Mirror Images."
70. Candelaria, "La Malinche."
71. Native Guns, "Work It."
72. Foucault et al., *Society Must Be Defended.*
73. Ibid.
74. There is a ritual for welcoming new poets to the stage at the Nuyorican Poets Cafe's open room every Friday night. The audience is prompted to simultaneously yell "virgin" to acknowledge the poet's first time at the Nuyorican.
75. For more on Urban Word NYC, see their Web site, http://www.urbanwordnyc.org
76. Rojas, *In Front of the Class.*
77. Ibid.
78. Ibid.
79. Morales, personal communication.
80. Macedo, "Colonialism."
81. Zentella, *Growing Up Bilingual*, 268.
82. Melendez, personal communication.
83. Ebojo, personal communication.

Conclusion

Portions of this conclusion originally appeared in *Transnational Crossroads: Remapping the Americas and the Pacific*, edited by Camilla Fojas and Rudy P. Guevarra Jr., used by permission of the University of Nebraska Press. Copyright 2012 by the Board of Regents of the University of Nebraska.

1. For a relational history of Filipino and Puerto Rican plantation workers in the early twentieth century, see Poblete, *Islanders in the Empire*.

2. Here are two examples of such. Smolenyak, "What Race is Bruno Mars?" published in the mainstream news publication *Huffington Post*, celebrates Mars's diverse heritage, delineating his genealogy in more detail than Mars's own explanation of being half Puerto Rican and half Filipino. This article celebrates Mars's diverse heritage as emblematic of the United States' cultural roots, even referencing Barack Obama. De Castro, "Bruno Mars: The Fil-Am Artist with Universal Appeal," was published in a Filipino American news publication and claims Mars exclusively as Filipino American, though the author acknowledges Mars's father to be Puerto Rican.

3. Williams, *Marxism and Literature*.

4. My transcription of a Volkswagen advertisement entitled "Poet" in circulation from February 2007 to May 2007.

5. Dávila, *Latinos, Inc.*, 218.

6. Lee, *Orientals*.

7. Park, *Consuming Citizenship*, discusses the link between consumption and citizenship, and argues that second-generation Asian Americans assert their social citizenship through conspicuous consumption.

8. Williams, *Marxism and Literature*.

9. Ibid., 25.

10. Ibid.

11. Miller, "National Endowment"

12. Himmelstein and Zald, "American Conservatism."

13. Ardenne and Vale, "Art Market."

14. For an analysis of how the deregulation of the telecommunications companies in the United States influenced hip hop, see Cooper, "Hip Hop's Profane Victory."

15. More information about YouthSpeaks multiple programs can be found on their Web site, http://YouthSpeaks.org.

16. Gramsci, Hoare, and Nowell-Smith, *Prison Notebooks*.

17. Bascara, *Model Minority Imperialism*, xvi.

18. Associated Press, "Poets Invade Vieques."

19. Nadal, personal communication, 2006.

20. Fouron and Glick-Schiller, "Generation of Identity."

21. Ibid., 61.

22. Concordia, "Do You Want to Know."

23. Ibid.

24. Ibid.

25. Welfare Poets, "Drop the Bomb."

Bibliography

Acosta-Belen, Edna. *The Puerto Rican Woman: Perspectives on Culture, History, and Society*. Praeger, 1986.
Aguilar, Delia D. "Gender, Nation, Colonialism: Lessons from the Philippines." In *The Women, Gender, and Development Reader*, edited by Nalini Visvanathan, Lynn Duggan, and Laurie Nisonoff, and Nan Wiegersma, 309–16. Atlantic Highlands, N.J.: Zed, 1997.
———. *Toward a Nationalist Feminism*. Quezon City: Giraffe, 1998.
Algarín, Miguel, and Bob Holman. *Aloud: Voices from the Nuyorican Poets Cafe*. 1st ed. New York: Holt, 1994.
Anthias, Floya, and Nira Yuval-Davis. "Women and the Nation-State." In *Nationalism*, edited by John Hutchinson and Anthony D. Smith, 312–15. Oxford: Oxford University Press, 1994.
Aquino, Allan. "On the Curses and Blessings of War: Discussions for a Filipino American Experience Class." In Chen and Omatsu, *Teaching*, 153–59.
———. Personal communication, December 2005.
Ardenne, Paul, and Michel Vale. "The Art Market in the 1980s." *International Journal of Political Economy* 25, no. 2 (1995): 100–128.
Ashplant, T. G., Graham Dawson, and Michael Roper. *The Politics of War Memory and Commemoration*. Routledge Studies in Memory and Narrative. London: Routledge, 2000.
Associated Press. "Poets Invade Vieques." *Puerto Rico Herald*, May 4, 2002.
Aurthur, Kate. "The Budgets May Not Be Huge, but All the Expression Is Free." *New York Times*, June 11, 2006.
Bacevich, Andrew J. "What Happened at Bud Dajo: A Forgotten Massacre and Its Lessons." *Boston Globe*, March 12, 2006.
Bakhtin, M. M., and Michael Holquist. *The Dialogic Imagination: Four Essays*. University of Texas Press Slavic Series. Austin: University of Texas Press, 1981.
Banet-Weiser, Sarah. *The Most Beautiful Girl in the World: Beauty Pageants and National Identity*. Berkeley: University of California Press, 1999.

Baroma, Rebecca. Personal communication, December 2004.
———. "Solving the Sweetest Science." In *Tabo(o)*, edited by Claremont Graduate University Art Department, Claremont, Calif., 2000.
Baver, Sherrie L. *The Political Economy of Colonialism: The State and Industrialization in Puerto Rico*. Westport, Conn.: Praeger, 1993.
Bascara, Victor. *Model Minority Imperialism*. Minneapolis: University of Minnesota Press, 2006.
Benson-Arias, Jaime. "Puerto Rico: The Myth of the National Economy." In *Puerto Rican Jam: Essays on Culture and Politics*, edited by Frances Negrón-Muntaner and Ramón Grosfoguel, 77–92. Minneapolis: University of Minnesota Press, 1997.
Bhabha, Homi K. *The Location of Culture*. London: Routledge, 1994.
Bhatia, Sunil. *American Karma: Race, Culture, and Identity in the Indian Diaspora*. Qualitative Studies in Psychology. New York: New York University Press, 2007.
Blumentritt, Mia. "*Bontoc Eulogy*, History, and the Craft of Memory: An Extended Conversation with Marlon E. Fuentes." *Amerasia Journal* 24, no. 3 (1998): 75–90.
Bodey, Michael. "Lonely Planet Founders Finally Hand Over Their 'Baby' to BBC." *Australasian Business Intelligence*, February 20, 2011.
Bradley, Mark. *Imagining Vietnam and America: The Making of Postcolonial Vietnam, 1919–1950*. The New Cold War History. Chapel Hill: University of North Carolina Press, 2000.
Briggs, Laura. *Reproducing Empire: Race, Sex, Science, and U.S. Imperialism in Puerto Rico*. American Crossroads. Berkeley: University of California Press, 2002.
Brown, Joan L. "Constructing Our Pedagogical Canons." *Pedagogy* 10, no. 3 (2010): 535–53.
Bunten, Alexis Celeste. "Sharing Culture of Selling Out? Developing the Commodified Persona in the Heritage Industry." *American Ethnologist* 35, no. 3: 380–95.
Cabranes, José A. *Citizenship and the American Empire: Notes on the Legislative History of the United States Citizenship of Puerto Ricans*. New Haven: Yale University Press, 1979.
Candelaria, Cordelia. "La Malinche, Feminist Prototype." *Frontiers: A Journal of Women Studies* 5, no. 2 (1980): 1–6.
Caronan, Faye. "Colonial Consumption and Colonial Hierarchies in Representations of Philippine and Puerto Rican Tourism." *Philippine Studies* 53, no. 1 (2006): 32–58.
———. "Memories of U.S. Imperialism: Narratives of the Homeland in Filipino and Puerto Rican Homes in the United States." *Philippine Studies: Historical and Ethnographic Viewpoints* 60, no. 3 (2012): 337–66.
———. "Post/Colonial Immigration and Transnational Activist Practices: Filipino American and U.S. Puerto Rican Performance Poet Activism." Chapter 1 in *Transnational Crossroads: Remapping the Americans and the Pacific*, edited by Camilla Fojas and Rudy P. Guevarra Jr., 33–56. Lincoln: University of Nebraska Press, 2012.
Chen, Edith Wen-Chu, and Glenn Omatsu. *Teaching about Asian Pacific Americans: Effective Activities, Strategies, and Assignments for Classrooms and Communities*. Critical Perspectives on Asian Pacific Americans Series. Lanham, Md.: Rowman and Littlefield, 2006.
Chuh, Kandice. *Imagine Otherwise: On Asian Americanist Critique*. Durham, N.C.: Duke University Press, 2003.
Clay-Warner, Jody, and Jennifer McMahon-Howard. "Rape Reporting: 'Classic Rape' and the Behavior of Law." *Violence and Victims* 24, no. 6 (2009): 723–43.

Concordia, Johneric. September 2005.
———. *Do You Want to Know? The Next Best Thing.* 2005. CD.
Cooper, Brittney. "Hip Hop's Profane Victory: How Corporations Co-opted Black Cool." *Salon.com.* Available at http://www.salon.com/2014/06/10/hip_hops_profane_victory_how_corporations_co_opted_black_cool (accessed June 13, 2014).
Corretjer, Juan Antonio. "Albizu Campos and the Ponce Massacre." In *Latino/a Thought*, edited by Rodolfo D. Torres and Francisco Hernandez Vazquez, 377–404. Lanham, Md.: Rowman and Littlefield, 2009.
Cowie, Elizabeth. *Recording Reality, Desiring the Real.* Visible Evidence. Minneapolis: University of Minnesota Press, 2011.
Crenshaw, Kimberle. "Mapping the Margins: Intersectionality, Identity Politics, and Violence against Women of Color." *Stanford Law Review* 43, no. 6 (1991): 1241–99.
Cullen, Jim. *The American Dream: A Short History of an Idea That Shaped a Nation.* New York: Oxford University Press, 2003.
Dávila, Arlene M. *Barrio Dreams: Puerto Ricans, Latinos, and the Neoliberal City.* Berkeley: University of California Press, 2004.
———. *Latinos, Inc.: The Marketing and Making of a People.* Berkeley: University of California Press, 2001.
De Castro, Cynthia. "Bruno Mars: The Fil-Am Artist with Universal Appeal." *Asian Journal* January 5, 2011, available at http://web.archive.org/web/20110109090928/http://www.asianjournal.com/aj-magazine/midweek-mgzn/8386-bruno-mars-the-fil-am-artist-with-universal-appeal.html (accessed September 10, 2014).
de la Cruz, Pennie Azarcon. *Filipinas for Sale: An Alternative Philippine Report on Women and Tourism.* Manila: Aklat Filipino, 1985.
de Olivares, José, and William Smith Bryan. *Our Islands and Their People as Seen with Camera and Pencil.* 3 vols. St. Louis: Thompson, 1904.
Dery, Luis Camara. *From Ibalon to Sorsogon: A Historical Survey of Sorsogon Province to 1905.* Quezon City: New Day, 1991.
Dolan, Jill. *Utopia in Performance: Finding Hope at the Theater.* Ann Arbor: University of Michigan Press, 2005.
Dominguez, Robert. "Smits' P.R. Job Narrates New Film for Perez." *Daily News*, June 10, 2006.
Duany, Jorge. *The Puerto Rican Nation on the Move: Identities on the Island and in the United States.* Chapel Hill: University of North Carolina Press, 2002.
Duara, Prasenjit. *Rescuing History from the Nation: Questioning Narratives of Modern China.* Chicago: University of Chicago Press, 1995.
Ebojo, Alfie. Personal communication, October 10, 2005.
Emecheta, Buchi. *The Rape of Shavi: A Novel.* 1st ed. New York: Braziller, 1985.
Eperjesi, John R. *The Imperialist Imaginary: Visions of Asia and the Pacific in American Culture.* Reencounters with Colonialism: New Persepctives on the Americas. Hanover, N.H.: Dartmouth College Press / University Press of New England, 2005.
Escobar, Arturo. *Encountering Development: The Making and Unmaking of the Third World.* Princeton Studies in Culture/Power/History. Princeton, N.J.: Princeton University Press, 1995.
Espiritu, Yen Le. *Asian American Women and Men: Labor, Laws, and Love.* The Gender Lens Series. 2nd ed. Lanham, Md.: Rowman and Littlefield, 2008.

———. *Body Counts: The Vietnam War and Militarized Refuge(es)*. Berkeley: University of California Press, 2014.

———. *Home Bound: Filipino American Lives across Cultures, Communities, and Countries*. Berkeley: University of California Press, 2003.

———. "Multiple Identities of Second-Generation Filipinos." In *The Second Generation: Ethnic Identity among Asian Americans*, edited by Pyong Gap Min, 19–52. Critical Perspectives on Asian Pacific Americans Series. Walnut Creek, Calif.: AltaMira, 2002.

Eviota, Elizabeth U. *The Political Economy of Gender: Women and the Sexual Division of Labour in the Philippines*. London: Zed, 1992.

Fanon, Frantz. *Toward the African Revolution*. Pelican Books. Harmondsworth: Penguin, 1970.

Ferro, Christine, Jill Cermele, and Ann Saltzman. "Current Perceptions of Marital Rape: Some Good and Not-So-Good News." *Journal of Interpersonal Violence* 23, no. 6 (June 1, 2008): 764–79.

Figueroa, Jose Angel. Personal communication, January 27, 2006.

Findlay, Eileen. *Imposing Decency: The Politics of Sexuality and Race in Puerto Rico, 1870–1920*. American Encounters/Global Interactions. Durham, N.C.: Duke University Press, 1999.

Fischer, Maisha T. "'The Song Is Unfinished': The New Literate and Literary and Their Institutions." *Written Communication* 21, no. 3 (2004): 290–312.

Flores, Juan. *Divided Borders: Essays on Puerto Rican Identity*. Houston, Tex.: Arte Público, 1993.

Flores, Shaggy. "Oye Lo Boricua." In *Sancocho: A Book of Nuyorcian Poetry*, Springfield, Mass.: Dark Souls, 2001.

Foucault, Michel, Mauro Bertani, Alessandro Fontana, François Ewald, and David Macey. *Society Must Be Defended: Lectures at the Collège De France, 1975–76*. 1st Picador pbk. ed. New York: Picador, 2003.

Fouron, Georges E., and Nina Glick-Schiller. "The Generation of Identity: Redefining the Second Generation within a Transnational Social Field." In *Migration, Transnationalization, and Race in a Changing New York*, edited by Héctor R. Cordero-Guzmán, Robert C. Smith, and Ramon Grosfoguel, 58–86. Philadelphia: Temple University Press, 2001.

Frake, Charles O. "Abu Sayyaf: Displays of Violence and the Proliferation of Contested Identities among Philippine Muslims." *American Anthropologist* 100, no. 1 (1998): 41–54.

Francisco, Luzviminda. "The First Vietnam: The U.S.-Philippine War of 1899." *Bulletin of Concerned Asian Scholars* 5, no. 4 (December 1973): 2–15.

Fraser, Nancy. "Rethinking the Public Sphere: A Contribution to the Critique of Actually Existing Democracy." In *Habermas and the Public Sphere*, edited by Craig Calhoun, 109–42. Studies in Contemporary German Social Thought. Cambridge, Mass.: Massachusetts Institute of Technology Press, 1992.

Gantar, Jure. *The Pleasure of Fools: Essays in the Ethics of Laughter*. Montreal: McGill-Queen's University Press, 2005.

George, William H., and Lorraine J. Martinez. "Victim Blaming in Rape: Effect of Victim and Perpetrator Race, Type of Rape, and Participant Racism." *Psychology of Women* 26, no. 2 (June 2002): 110–19.

Gilligan, Eugene. "Puerto Rico Succeeds in Balancing Act." *Commercial Property News* 22, no. 3 (March 2008): 21–22.

Gilroy, Paul. *The Black Atlantic: Modernity and Double Consciousness*. Cambridge, Mass.: Harvard University Press, 1993.

Go, Julian. *American Empire and the Politics of Meaning: Elite Political Cultures in the Philippines and Puerto Rico During U.S. Colonialism*. Politics, History, and Culture. Durham, N.C.: Duke University Press, 2008.

———. "The Chains of Empire: State Building and 'Political Education' in Puerto Rico and the Philippines." In *The American Colonial State in the Philippines: Global Perspectives*, edited by Julian Go and Anne L. Foster, 182–216. American Encounters/Global Interactions. Durham, N.C.: Duke University Press, 2003.

Goldberg, David Theo. *Racial Subjects: Writing on Race in America*. New York: Routledge, 1997.

Gonzales, Juan. "Puerto Rico Had Never Seen Anything Like It: The Meaning of the General Strike." *The Progressive* 62, no. 9 (September 1998): 24–28.

Gonzalez, Vernadette V. "Military Bases, 'Royalty Trips,' and Imperial Modernities: Gendered and Racialized Labor in the Postcolonial Philippines." *Frontiers: A Journal of Women Studies* 28, no. 3 (2007): 28–59.

Gonzalves, Theodore. "We Hold a Neatly Folded Hope." *Amerasia* 21, no. 3 (1995): 155–74.

Goodno, James. "Casino, Hotels Replace U.S. Military in the Philippines." *Hotel and Motel Management*, August 15, 1994, 6–8.

Goodno, James B. *The Philippines: Land of Broken Promises*. Politics in Contemporary Asia. London: Zed, 1991.

Gordon, Avery. *Ghostly Matters: Haunting and the Sociological Imagination*. Minneapolis: University of Minnesota Press, 1997.

Gramsci, Antonio, Quintin Hoare, and Geoffrey Nowell-Smith. *Selections from the Prison Notebooks of Antonio Gramsci*. 1st ed. New York: International Publishers, 1972.

Griggers, Camilla, Sari Raissa Lluch Dalena, National Commission on Culture and the Arts (Philippines), Pennsylvania Council on the Arts, and Newsreel. *Memories of a Forgotten War*. Video recording. New York: Third World Newsreel, 2001.

Grosfoguel, Ramón. *Colonial Subjects: Puerto Ricans in a Global Perspective*. Berkeley: University of California Press, 2003.

Habermas, Jürgen. *The Philosophical Discourse of Modernity: Twelve Lectures*. Studies in Contemporary German Social Thought. Cambridge, Mass.: MIT Press, 1987.

Hagedorn, Jessica Tarahata. *Dogeaters*. 1st ed. New York: Pantheon, 1990.

Haraway, Donna. "Situated Knowledges: The Science Question in Feminism and the Privilege of Partial Perspective." *Feminist Studies* 14, no. 3 (1988): 575–99.

Harrison, David. "Tourism to Less Developed Countries: The Social Consequences." In *Tourism and the Less Developed World: Issues and Case Studies*, edited by David Harrison. London: Belhaven, 1992.

Hilfrich, Fabian. *Debating American Exceptionalism: Empire and Democracy in the Wake of the Spanish-American War*. New York: Palgrave, 2012.

Hilsdon, Anne-Marie. *Madonnas and Martyrs: Militarism and Violence in the Philippines*. Women in Asia. New South Wales: Allen and Unwin, 1995.

Himmelstein, Jerome L., and Mayer Zald. "American Conservatism and Government Funding of the Social Sciences and the Arts." *Sociological Inquiry* 54, no. 2 (April 1984): 171–87.

Hoganson, Kristin L. *Fighting for American Manhood: How Gender Politics Provoked the Spanish-American and Philippine-American Wars*. Yale Historical Publications. New Haven, Conn.: Yale University Press, 1998.

Homiak, John P. "A Body in the Archives: A Review of *Bontoc Eulogy*." *American Anthropologist* 102, no. 4 (2000): 887–91.

Honig, Bonnie. "Immigrant America? How Foreignness 'Solves' Democracy's Problems." *Social Text* 25, no. 56 (Autumn 1998): 1–27.

hooks, bell. "Representing Whiteness in the Black Imagination." In *Cultural Studies*, edited by Lawrence Grossberg, Cary Nelson, and Paula Treichler, 338–46. London: Routledge, 1992.

Horwitz, Steven, and Michael J. McPhillips. "The Reality of the Wartime Economy: More Historical Evidence on Whether World War II Ended the Great Depression." *Independent Review* 17, no. 3 (Winter 2013): 325+.

Ignacio, Abraham Flores. *The Forbidden Book: The Philippine-American War in Political Cartoons*. San Francisco: TBoli, 2004.

Isaac, Allan Punzalan. *American Tropics: Articulating Filipino America*. Critical American Studies. Minneapolis: University of Minnesota Press, 2006.

Izon, Noel, dir. "An Untold Triumph: America's Filipino Soldiers." ICT, 2002.

Janer, Zilkia. "Creating a National Womanhood." Chapter 2 in *Puerto Rican Nation-Building Literature: Impossible Romance*, 32–50. New Directions in Puerto Rican Studies. Gainesville: University Press of Florida, 2005.

Javellana-Santos, Julie. "Over 2,000 OFWs Are in U.S. Army Bases in Iraq." *Arab News*, April 22, 2004. Available at http://www.arabnews.com/node/248094 (accessed August 6, 2014).

Jennings, Louise, and Cynthia Potter Smith. "Examining the Role of Critical Inquiry for Transformative Practices: Two Joint Case Studies of Multicultural Teacher Education." *Teachers College Record* 104, no. 3 (2002): 456–81.

Johnson, Chalmers. *Blowback: The Costs and Consequences of American Empire*. New York: Holt, 2004.

Jones, Garrett Steadman. "The Specificity of U.S. Imperialism." *New Left Review* 60 (March–April 1970): 59–86.

Justice, Benjamin. "Education at the End of a Gun: The Origins of American Imperial Education in the Philippines." In *American Post-Conflict Educational Reform: From the Spanish-American War to Iraq*, edited by Noah W. Sobe, 19–52. New York: Palgrave Macmillan, 2009.

Kessler, Richard J. "Marcos and the Americans." *Foreign Policy* 63 (Summer 1986): 40–57.

Kim, Claire Jean. *Bitter Fruit: The Politics of Black-Korean Conflict in New York City*. New Haven, Conn.: Yale University Press, 2000.

Kim, Jodi. *Ends of Empire: Asian American Critique and the Cold War*. Critical American Studies. Minneapolis: University of Minnesota Press, 2010.

Kim, Wonik. "Rethinking Colonialism and the Origins of the Development State in East Asia." *Journal of Contemporary Asia* 39, no. 3 (2009): 382–99.

Koshy, Susan. "The Fiction of Asian American Literature." *Yale Journal of Criticism* 9, no. 2 (1996): 35–65.

La Enkanto. *In Our Blood: Filipino American Spoken Word from Los Angeles.* 2001. CD, track 11.
Lee, Robert G. *Orientals: Asian Americans in Popular Culture.* Asian American History and Culture. Philadelphia: Temple University Press, 1999.
Lefebvre, Henri. *The Production of Space.* Oxford: Blackwell, 1991.
Lewis, Oscar. *La Vida: A Puerto Rican Family in the Culture of Poverty—San Juan and New York.* New York: Random House, 1966.
Lipsitz, George. *Dangerous Crossroads: Popular Music, Postmodernism, and the Poetics of Place.* London; New York: Verso, 1994.
Love, Eric Tyrone Lowery. *Race over Empire: Racism and U.S. Imperialism, 1865–1900.* Chapel Hill: University of North Carolina Press, 2004.
Lowe, Lisa. *Immigrant Acts: On Asian American Cultural Politics.* Durham, N.C.: Duke University Press, 1996.
Lustre, Napoleon. Conditions (An Unrestricted List), *In Our Blood: Filipino American Spoken Word From Los Angeles.* CD, track 3.
Macdonald, Myra. "Demonizing Islam." In *Exploring Media Discourse,* 151–73. Understanding Media. London: Arnold, 2003.
Macedo, Donaldo. "The Colonialism of the English Only Movement." *Educational Researcher* 29, no. 3 (April 2000): 15–34.
Maeda, Daryl J. *Chains of Babylon: The Rise of Asian America.* Critical American Studies. Minneapolis: University of Minnesota Press, 2009.
Makow, Henry. *A Long Way to Go for a Date.* Winnipeg: Silas Green, 2000.
Matuštík, Martin Joseph. *Specters of Liberation: Great Refusals in the New World Order.* SUNY Series in Radical Social and Political Theory. Albany: State University of New York Press, 1998.
McCaffrey, Katherine T. *Military Power and Popular Protest: The U.S. Navy in Vieques, Puerto Rico.* New Brunswick, N.J.: Rutgers University Press, 2002.
McClintock, Anne. *Imperial Leather: Race, Gender and Sexuality in the Colonial Contest.* London: Routledge, 1995.
McCoy, Alfred W., and Francisco A. Scarano. *The Colonial Crucible: Empire in the Making of the Modern American State.* Madison: University of Wisconsin Press, 2009.
Melendez, Jesus Papoleto. Personal communication, January 17, 2006.
Mercado, Nancy. Personal communication, February 2006.
Merina, Dorian. Personal communication, December 2004.
Merrill, Dennis. "Negotiating Cold War Paradise: U.S. Tourism, Economic Planning, and Cultural Modernity in Twentieth-Century Puerto Rico." *Diplomatic History* 25, no. 2 (Spring 2001): 179–214.
Miller, Stuart Creighton. *"Benevolent Assimilation": The American Conquest of the Philippines, 1899–1903.* New Haven, Conn.: Yale University Press, 1982.
Miller, Toby. "The National Endowment for the Arts in the 1990s: A Black Eye on the Arts?" *American Behavioral Scientist* 43, no. 9 (June 2000): 1429–45.
Morales, Anthony. Personal communication, January 2006.
Morreall, John. *Taking Laughter Seriously.* Albany: State University of New York, 1983.
Muñiz, Humberto García. "Goliath against David: The Battle for Vieques as the Last Crossroad?" *Centro Journal* 13, no. 1 (2001): 129–43.

Muñoz, José Esteban. *Disidentifications: Queers of Color and the Performance of Politics*. Cultural Studies of the Americas. Minneapolis: University of Minnesota Press, 1999.

Mydans, Seth. "4 Marines to Begin Defense in Rape Trial in Philippines." *New York Times*, September 11, 2006.

Nadadur, Ramanujan. "Illegal Immigration: A Positive Economic Contribution to the United States." *Journal of Ethnic and Migration Studies* 35, no. 6 (July 2009): 1037–52.

Nadal, Lenina. Personal communication, February 9, 2006.

Native Guns. *Work It, Barrel Men*. 2006. CD, Track 13.

Neumann, A. Lin. "Tourism Promotion and Prostitution." In Schirmer and Shalom, *Philippines Reader*, 182–87.

Ngai, Mae M. *Impossible Subjects: Illegal Aliens and the Making of Modern America*. Politics and Society in Twentieth-Century America. Princeton, N.J.: Princeton University Press, 2004.

Nieto, Sonia, and Patty Bode. *Affirming Diversity: The Sociopolitical Context of Multicultural Education*. 6th ed. Boston: Pearson, 2012.

Nill, Andrea Christina. "Latinos and SB 1070: Demonization, Dehumanization, and Disenfranchisement." *Harvard Latino Law Review* 14 (2011): 35.

Noor, Farish A. "Uncle Sam to the Rescue? The Political Impact of American Involvement in ASEAN Security and Political Issues in the Wake of 9/11." In *With Us or Against Us: Studies in Global Anti-Americanism*, edited by Denis Lacorne and Tony Judt, 207+. CERI Series in International Relations and Political Economy. New York: Palgrave-McMillan, 2005.

Ocampo, Anthony C. "Are Second-Generation Filipinos 'Becoming' Asian American or Latino? Historical Colonialism, Culture and Panethnicity." *Ethnic and Racial Studies* (February 2013): 425–45.

Okamura, Jonathan Y., and Amefil R. Agbayani. "Pamantasan: Filipino American Higher Education." In *Filipino Americans: Transformation and Identity*, edited by Maria P. P. Root, 183–97. Thousand Oaks, Calif.: Sage, 1997.

Palumbo-Liu, David. "Introduction." In *The Ethnic Canon: Histories, Institutions, and Interventions*, edited by David Palumbo-Liu, 1–27. Minneapolis: University of Minnesota Press, 1995.

———. *The Deliverance of Others: Reading Literature in a Global Age*. Durham, N.C.: Duke University Press, 2012.

Park, Lisa Sun-Hee. *Consuming Citizenship: Children of Asian Immigrant Entrepreneurs*. Asian America. Stanford, Calif.: Stanford University Press, 2005.

———. "Continuing Significance of the Model Minority Myth: The Second Generation." *Social Justice* 35, no. 2 (2008): 134–44.

Parreñas, Rhacel Salazar. *Children of Global Migration: Transnational Families and Gendered Woes*. Stanford, Calif.: Stanford University Press, 2005.

Parvulescu, Anca. *Laughter: Notes on a Passion*. Short Circuits. Cambridge, Mass.: MIT Press, 2010.

Peffer, Randall S. *Puerto Rico*. Lonely Planet Regional Guides. Oakland, Calif.: Lonely Planet, 1999.

Perdomo, Willie. "Spotlight at the Nuyorican Poets Café." In *Step into a World: A Global Anthology of the New Black Literature*, edited by Kevin Powell, 351–52. New York: Wiley, 2000.

Perez, Rosie, and Liz Garbus. *Yo soy Boricua, pa'que tu lo Sepas!* Videocassette (Digital Betacam). 2006.
Pietri, Pedro. *Puerto Rican Obituary.* New York: Monthly Review Press, 1974.
Pineau, Elyse Lamm. "Teaching Is Performance: Reconceptualizing a Problematic Metaphor." *American Educational Research Journal* 31, no. 1 (March 1994): 3–25.
Poblete, JoAnna. *Islanders in the Empire.* Urbana: University of Illinois Press, 2014.
Pratt, Mary Louise. *Imperial Eyes: Travel Writing and Transculturation.* London: Routledge, 1992.
Raman, Parvathi. "Signifying Something: Che Guevara and Neoliberal Alienation in London." In *Enduring Socialism: Explorations of Revolution and Transformation, Restoration and Continuation*, edited by Harry G. West and Parvathi Raman, 250–70. Oxford: Berghahn, 2008).
Ramirez, Ray. Personal communication, January 19, 2006.
Redonidez, Rachel. "Rapist's Transferral Exposes Arroyo's True Agenda—Continuous Rape of the Country Is the Cost of Unconditional Us Subservience." *Bagong Alysang Makabayan (BAYAN)-USA News* (2006).
Reincke, Nancy. "Antidote to Dominance: Women's Laughter as Counteraction." *Journal of Popular Culture* 24, no. 4 (Spring 1991): 27–37.
Richter, Linda K. "After Political Turmoil: The Lessons of Rebuilding Tourism in Three Asian Countries." *Journal of Travel Research* 38, no. 1 (August 1999): 41–45.
Rizal, José, and Harold Augenbraum. *El Filibusterismo.* Penguin Classics. New York: Penguin, 2011.
Rizal, José, Ma. Soledad Lacson-Locsin, and Raul L. Locsin. *Noli Me Tangere.* Shaps Library of Translations. Honolulu: University of Hawai'i Press, 1997.
Roach, Joseph R. *Cities of the Dead: Circum-Atlantic Performance.* The Social Foundations of Aesthetic Forms. New York: Columbia University Press, 1996.
Rocamora, Rick, Bill Filner, Kim Komenich, and Rene P. Ciria-Cruz. *Filipino World War II Soldiers: America's Second-Class Veterans.* 1st ed. San Francisco, Calif.: Veterans Equity Center, 2008.
Rodriguez, Dylan. *Suspended Apocalypse: White Supremacy, Genocide, and the Filipino Condition.* Minneapolis: University of Minnesota Press, 2010.
Rodriguez, Robyn Magalit. *Migrants for Export: How the Philippine State Brokers Labor to the World.* Minneapolis: University of Minnesota Press, 2010.
Rodriguez-Perez, Katherine. "Reports on the Ponce Massacre: How the U.S. Press Protected U.S. Government Interests in Puerto Rico in the Wake of Tragedy." Honors thesis, Wesleyan University, Middletown, Conn.
Rodríguez-Fraticelli, Carlos. "Albizu Campos: Strategies of Struggle and Strategic Struggles." *Centro Journal* 4, no. 1 (1991–92): 25–33.
Rojas, Bonafide. Personal communication, March 2006.
———. "Invisible Ones." In *Pelo Bueno: A Day in the Life of a Nuyorican Poet*, 62–63. Arlington, Va.: Dark Souls, 2004.
———. "In Front of the Class." In *Learn Then Burn*, edited by Tim Stafford and Eric Brown, 11–14. Long Beach: Write Bloody, 2010
Rowland, Ashley. "Korea-Based U.S. Soldier Gets 3 Years in Prison for Rape Conviction." *Stars and Stripes*, February 10, 2012.

Rowland, Ashley, and Yoo-Kyong Chang. "SOFA Scrutinized after Rash of Crimes by U.S. Troops in Korea." *Stars and Stripes*, November 22, 2011.

Rowthorn, Chris, Greg Bloom, Michael Day, Michael Grosberg, and Ryan ver Berkmoes. *Philippines*. Lonely Planet Country Guides. 8th ed. Melbourne, Australia: Lonely Planet, 2003.

Rusing, James. "Interview with President William McKinley." *Christian Advocate*, January 22, 1903, 17.

Russell, Brenda L. *Battered Woman Syndrome as a Legal Defense: History, Effectiveness and Implications*. Jefferson, N.C.: McFarland, 2010.

Salomon, Larry. "Movement History: Ethnic Studies Movement." *Third Force*, December 31, 1997, 35.

Samuels, Shirley. *Romances of the Republic: Women, the Family, and Violence in the Literature of the Early American Nation*. New York: Oxford University Press, 1996.

Sandoval, Chela. *Methodology of the Oppressed*. Theory out of Bounds. Minneapolis, MN: University of Minnesota Press, 2000.

Sanger, David E. "Bush Cites Philippines as Model in Rebuilding Iraq." *New York Times*, October 19, 2003.

Santiago, Esmeralda. *América's Dream*. 1st ed. New York: HarperCollins, 1996.

Santiago-Valles, Kelvin. "The Sexual Appeal of Racial Differences: U.S. Travel Writing and Anxious American-ness in Turn-of-the-Century Puerto Rico." In *Race and the Production of Modern American Nationalism*, edited by Reynolds J. Scott-Childress, 127–48. New York: Garland, 1999.

Santilla, Faith. "Mirror Images." In *Legacy to Liberation: Politics and Culture of Revolutionary Asian Pacific America*, edited by Fred Ho, Carolyn Antonio, Diane Fujino and Steve Yip, 361–62. San Francisco: AK, 2000.

———. Personal communication, November 19, 2004.

Schirmer, Daniel B., and Stephen Rosskamm Shalom. *The Philippines Reader: A History of Colonialism, Neocolonialism, Dictatorship, and Resistance*. 1st ed. Boston: South End, 1987.

Schoorman, Dilys, and Ira Bogotch. "Moving beyond 'Diversity' to 'Social Justice': The Challenge to Re-Conceptualize Multicultural Education." *Intercultural Education* 21, no. 1 (2010): 79–85.

Sexton, Jared. *Amalgamation Schemes: Antiblackness and the Critique of Multiracialism*. Minneapolis: University of Minnesota Press, 2008.

Sharpe, Jenny. *Allegories of Empire: The Figure of Woman in the Colonial Text*. Minneapolis: University of Minnesota Press, 1993.

Sheth, Niraj. "BBC to Aquire 75% Stake in Publisher Lonely Planet." *Wall Street Journal*, October 2, 2007. Available at http://online.wsj.com/news/articles/SB119127618987245594 (accessed September 10, 2014).

Smolenyak, Megan. "What Race Is Bruno Mars?" *Huffington Post*, November 12, 2012. Available at http://www.huffingtonpost.com/megan-smolenyak-smolenyak/what-race-is-bruno-mars_b_2116984.html.

Soriano, Aquilina. *What about My Story*? In *Our Blood: Filipino American Spoken Word from Los Angeles*. 2001. CD, track 12.

Soriano, Irene Suico. Personal communication, October 29, 2004.

Sparrow, Bartholomew H. *The Insular Cases and the Emergence of American Empire*. Landmark Law Cases and American Society. Lawrence: University Press of Kansas, 2006.

Spence, Louise, and Vinicius Navarro. *Crafting Truth: Documentary Form and Meaning*. New Brunswick, N.J.: Rutgers University Press, 2011.

Spivak, Gayatri. "Can the Subaltern Speak?" In *Marxism and the Interpretation of Culture*, edited by Cary Nelson and Lawrence Grossberg, 271–313. Chicago: University of Illinois Press, 1988.

"Statistical Yearbook." United Nations. New York: United Nations, 2003.

Sturdevant, Saundra Pollock, and Brenda Sturdevant. *Let the Good Times Roll: Prostitution and the U.S. Military in Asia*. New York: New Press, 1993.

Tadiar, Neferti Xina M. *Things Fall Away: Philippine Historical Experience and the Makings of Globalization*. Post-Contemporary Interventions. Durham, N.C.: Duke University Press, 2009.

Tan, Amy. *The Joy Luck Club*. New York: Putnam, 1989.

Tannock, Stuart. "Is 'Opting Out' Really an Answer? Schools, Militarism, and the Counter-Recruitment Movement in Post–September 11 United States at War." *Social Justice* 32, no. 3 (101) (2005): 163–78.

Taylor, Diana. *The Archive and the Repertoire: Performing Cultural Memory in the Americas*. Durham, N.C.: Duke University Press, 2003.

Tinker, George E., and Mark Freeland. "Thief, Slave Trader, Murderer: Christopher Columbus and Caribbean Population Decline." *Wicazo Sa Review* 23, no. 1 (Spring 2008): 25–50.

"Tourism." *Institutional Investor*, October 1998, 22–23(D).

Truettner, William H., Nancy K. Anderson, National Museum of American Art (U.S.), Denver Art Museum, and St. Louis Art Museum. *The West as America: Reinterpreting Images of the Frontier, 1820–1920*. Washington: National Museum of American Art / Smithsonian Institution Press, 1991.

Tschofen, Monique Y. "Post-Colonial Allegory and the Empire of Rape." *Canadian Review of Comparative Literature* 22, no. 3 (1995): 501.

Turner, Ronald. "The Dangers of Misappropriation: Misusing Martin Luther King Jr.'s Legacy to Prove the Colorblind Thesis." *Michigan Journal of Race and Law* 2, no. 1 (1996).

"U.S. Closes Vieques Test Range." *BBC*, February 10, 2003. Available at http://news.bbc.co.uk/1/hi/world/americas/2743395.stm (accessed August 6, 2014).

Vergara, Benito M. *Displaying Filipinos: Photography and Colonialism in Early 20th Century Philippines*. Quezon City: University of the Philippines Press, 1995.

Walker, Lenore E. *The Battered Woman Syndrome*. 2nd ed. New York: Springer, 2000.

Ween, Lori. "This Is Your Book: Marketing America to Itself." *PMLA* 118, no. 1 (2003): 90–102.

Williams, Raymond. *Marxism and Literature*. Marxist Introductions. Oxford: Oxford University Press, 1977.

Wilson, Rob. *Reimagining the American Pacific: From South Pacific to Bamboo Ridge and Beyond*. New Americanists. Durham, N.C.: Duke University Press, 2000.

Winter, Bronwyn. "Guns, Money, and Justice." *International Feminist Journal of Politics* 13, no. 3 (2011): 371–89.

Wolf, Diane L. "'There's No Place Like 'Home': Emotional Transnationalism and the Struggles of Second-Generation Filipinos." In *The Changing Face of Home: The Transnational Lives of the Second Generation*, edited by Peggy Levitt and Mary C. Waters, 255–94. New York: Sage, 2002.

World Travel and Tourism Council. "Travel and Tourism Economic Impact 2014: Philippines." WTTC, 2014. Available at http://92.52.122.233/site_media/uploads/downloads/philippines2014.pdf (accessed September 10, 2014).

World Travel and Tourism Council. "Travel and Tourism Economic Impact 2014: Puerto Rico." WTTC, 2014. Available at http://92.52.122.233/site_media/uploads/downloads/puerto_rico2014.pdf (accessed September 10, 2014).

Yoneyama, Lisa. *Hiroshima Traces: Time, Space, and the Dialectics of Memory*. Twentieth-Century Japan. Berkeley: University of California Press, 1999.

Yuh, Ji-Yeon. *Beyond the Shadow of Camptown: Korean Military Brides in America*. Nation of Newcomers. New York: New York University Press, 2002.

Zentella, Ana Celia. *Growing Up Bilingual: Puerto Rican Children in New York*. Malden, Mass.: Blackwell, 1997.

Zimmerman, Eugene. "The Old Yank." *Judge*, August 13, 1898.

Index

Page numbers in italics refer to illustrations.

Afghanistan War, 101, 114, 153–54
African Americans: African Puerto Ricans, 89, 118, 129; hip hop and, 120, 146; Latino racialization and, 117, 120, 140; multiculturalism and, 1; pedagogy of resistance and, 125, 128; as Philippines military residents, 35; poetry of resistance and, 117, 126–30; racial categorization of, 155n4. *See also* civil rights discourse
Albizu Campos, Pedro, 95–98, 100, 117
American Tropics, 3
América's Dream (Santiago): benevolent assimilation in, 18; clean/dirty motif and, 40; colonial legacy in América's lineage, 33–34; consumption of ethnicity and, 21–23; counterhegemonic stance in, 30, 150; economic dependency in, 18; fascination with U.S. commodities/culture in, 54–55; migration to U.S. in, 43–44, 119; as minority literature, 17; neocolonialism as rape in, 18, 47–48, 50–53, 55–61, 69–71; objectification of local culture, 38–39; production and marketing of, 44–45, 51–52, 73, 144; representation of tourism in, 23; safety/danger motif and, 36, 40; subversion of stereotypes in, 40; tourist industry in, 30–32, 43
Anthias, Floya, 48
anti-imperialism. *See* decolonization; imperialism/colonialism; resistance

Aquino, Alan, 122–25
Aquino, Benigno, Jr., 61–65, 67–68
Armenia, 117
Asian Americans: Asian American literature, 14–15; Asian American subjectivity, 16; counterhegemonic narrative and, 20; cultural critique and, 2; Filipino solidarity with racialized Asians, 115–16; model minority discourse and, 14, 16, 146, 157n48; opportunity/mobility discourse and, 157n44; performance poetry of, 134, 145–46; racial categorization of, 12–13, 140, 155n4
Asian Pacific Economic Cooperation forum (APEC), 133
Aspiras, José, 31
assimilation: benevolent assimilation narrative, 4–5; Filipino-American assimilation, 14–15; immigration and assimilation narratives, 149–50; unassimilability as cultural critique, 2. *See also* benevolent assimilation
authenticity: authentic postcolonial others, 21–22; heritage persona, 41; local culture as tourist commodity, 38–39; memory as speculative reenactment and, 77–78, 80–86, *84*; Puerto Rican cultural nationalism initiative, 55–59; travel guides and, 24. *See also* frontier/savage imagery; otherness

Baez, Anthony, 117
Bakhtin, Mikhail, 88
Balagtasan Collective, 131–34
Banet-Weiser, Sarah, 64
Baroma, Rebecca, 114–16, 123–25
Bascara, Victor, 149
Bataan death march, 114–15
Bell Trade Agreement, 6
benevolent assimilation: economic development narrative and, 17; as heterosexual romance, 18, 47–48, *49*, 60–61, 73–74, 78–86, 161n29; overview of mechanisms of, 143; public education and, 19–20, 105–6; U.S. exceptionalist policies and, 4–5, 85–86. *See also* assimilation; imperialism/colonialism; neocolonialism; paternal benevolence
Bhabba, Homi, 106
Bhatia, Sunil, 157n48
Black Panthers, 117
Bontoc Eulogy (Fuentes), 78
Briggs, Laura, 6–7
British Broadcasting Corporation, 25
Bunten, Celeste, 41
Bush, George W., 7, 160n15

Chavez, Cesar, 128
Chuh, Kandice, 16
citizenship status: ambiguous identity and, 2, 5; economic status and, 43; freedom of travel/migration, 13–14, 43; military benefits, 9; multiculturalism as displacement of, 16; Puerto Rican disenfranchisement, 90–91; Puerto Rican racial identity and, 28
civil rights discourse: model minority discourse and, 14; multiculturalism co-optation of, 16, 88; racial progress narrative and, 98. *See also* African Americans
Clark Special Economic Zone, 33
class: class solidarity with oppressed minorities, 113–14, 134–35, 151; CUNY tuition strike and, 151; Film Palace workers in *Dogeaters*, 37; menial labor in *América's Dream*, 33–34; meritocracy, 2, 3, 92–95, 118–19; opportunity/mobility discourse and, 92–95; U.S. immigration quotas and, 108. *See also* economy; meritocracy
Clinton, Hilary, 100
colonialism. *See* imperialism/colonialism

commemoration: Enola Gay exhibit, 11; "Posters from the Division of Community Education of Puerto Rico, 1949–1989," 12; Puerto Rico and Philippines Memorial, *8*, 9; "Singgalot" Filipino experience exhibit, 11–12; "West as America" exhibit, 11. *See also* history
commodification: of ethnic literature, 1–2; fascination with U.S. commodities/culture, 53–55; local culture as tourist commodity, 38–39; manufacture of U.S.-market commodities, 135; of performance poetry, 145–48. *See also* economy
commonwealth status: cultural nationalism and, 163n30; disavowal of empire and, 102–3; familial illegitimacy and, 76, 79–80, 87, 89–91, 101, 103–4; Smithsonian presentation of, 12; sovereignty restrictions and, 5–6; stealth imperialism and, 7–8; U.S. Congress representation, 6, 100
Concordia, Joneric, 143, 152–53
cultural critique. *See* resistance
cultural identity: agency in tourist industry resistance, 43; Asian American subjectivity, 16; class solidarity with stigmatized minorities, 113–14; differential consciousness and, 127; of Filipino and Nuyorican poets, 109; Filipino colonialism and, 112–13; heritage persona, 41; Puerto Rican cultural nationalism initiative, 55–59; reclamation of sexual/political agency, 70; renunciation of colonial name, 59–60. *See also* citizenship status; disidentification; Filipino identity; Puerto Rican identity
cultural nationalism: commonwealth status and, 163n30; economic incorporation and, 50, 69; multiculturalism and, 89, 99–101; Operation Serenity, 55–59, 87–89, 100; Original Pilipino Music (OPM), 65; political vs. cultural nationalism, 55–57, 70, 87–88, 100; Puerto Rican femininity and, 57, 59–60
cultural production, 3, 9–10, 38
culture of poverty thesis, 92–93, 164n42

Dalena, Sari, 77. See also *Memories of a Forgotten War*
Dávila, Arlene, 146
decolonization: familial illegitimacy and, 76, 79–80, 87, 89–91, 101, 103–4; performance

poetry and, 19–20, 106–7, 120–22, 140; Philippine independence and, 5–6, 75, 76, 101; renunciation of colonial name, 59–60; U.S. imperial vs. colonial view of, 150. *See also* resistance

de la Cruz, Alison, 134

Diallo, Amadou, 117

disidentification: defined, 111–13; critical thinking skills and, 107; critique of power hierarchies, 113, 122, 150; with exceptionalist narrative, 19–20, 114–16, 119–22, 125–26; Filipino racial identity and, 13, 112–13; filtering of historical narratives, 117; with multiculturalism discourse, 118; solidarity with oppressed minorities, 111–12, 114, 116–17; with U.S. racial hierarchy, 123–26, 150. *See also* cultural identity; resistance

documentary film: funding and distribution constraints, 103; memory as speculative reenactment in, 78, 80–86, *84*; presumed realism of, 73–74

Dogeaters (Hagedorn): benevolent assimilation in, 18; consumption of ethnicity and, 21–23; counterhegemonic stance in, 30, 149–50; economic dependency in, 18; fascination with U.S. commodities/culture in, 54–55; Marcos administration depiction in, 36–38, 50, 61–64; migration to U.S. in, 43–44; as minority literature, 17; neocolonialism as rape in, 18, 47–48, 50–53, 61–62, 64, 66–71; production and marketing of, 44–45, 51–52, 73, 144; sex tourism in, 31–32, 34–35, 41–42; tourist industry in, 23, 30, 43

Dolan, Jill, 126

Ebojo, Alfie, 147

economic development narrative: as exceptionalism, 17, 23; Marcos martial law and, 37–38; *Our Islands and their People* and, 25–27. *See also* economy; imperialism/colonialism

economy: culture of poverty thesis, 92–93, 164n42; economic sovereignty/dependency, 17–18, 24; ethnic studies canon and, 21; marketplace limitations on resistance, 103; meritocracy, 2, 3, 92–95, 118–19; military recruitment practices and, 91–92; neocolonial transformation in Puerto Rico, 91; opportunity/mobility discourse, 2–3, 92–95, 118–19, 157n44, 164n39, 164n41; Puerto Rico commonwealth status, 31; sexual colonialism and, 28; tourist economy, 35–38. *See also* class; commodification; economic development narrative

education: ESL language classes, 125; fostering of international solidarity, 124; genealogy of global power in, 122–25, 140–41; hegemonic historical narratives in, 106; as medium for decolonization, 19–20, 106–7, 120–22; paternal colonial education, 105–6; performance poetry as pedagogy, 126, 136–38; "Posters from the Division of Community Education of Puerto Rico, 1949–1989," 12

Escobar, Arturo, 37–38

Espiritu, Yen Le, 109, 155n3, 155n5, 157n44, 165n17

Estrada, Joseph, 133

ethnicity: class solidarity with stigmatized minorities, 113–14; consumption of ethnicity and, 21–23; ethnic specificity, 127; ethnic studies curricula, 5, 157n4; of Filipino and Nuyorican poets, 109; minority literature discourse, 17, 45–46, 157n4; Puerto Rican Day Parade, 87–88, 99–100; solidarity with racialized ethnicities, 115–16, 120, 128–29; superficial difference discourse, 3; workforce diversity and, 21. *See also* multiculturalism

exceptionalism: ambiguous citizenship status and, 2; Bataan death march and, 114–15; benevolent assimilation and, 4–5, 85–86, 112; commemorative narratives and, 10–11; commonwealth status as disavowal of empire, 102–3; cultural critique and, 9–10; economic development narrative and, 17, 23; gendered exceptionalism, 4; hegemonic construction of, 50–51, 85–86, 89–90, 140–41; historical legitimacy and, 125; infantilization discourse, 4; military intervention and, 114–15; multiculturalism and, 89–90, 111–12; neocolonial transformation of, 71, 73; opportunity/mobility discourse and, 94–95, 118–19, 157n44, 164n39, 164n41; Philippine independence and, 5–6, 75, 76, 101, 114; selective traditions and, 144. *See also* imperialism/colonialism

familial illegitimacy, 76, 79–80, 87, 89–91, 101, 103–4
Figueroa, José Angel, 126
Filipino identity: American Tropics discourse and, 3; citizenship status and, 2, 5; class solidarity with stigmatized minorities, 113–14; cultural invisibility and, 15–16; of Filipino and Nuyorican poets, 109; racial categorization and, 12–13, 78; solidarity with racialized Asians, 115–16, 120. See also cultural identity; Los Angeles Filipinos; Philippines
Filipino performance poetry: "Conditions (an unrestricted list)" (Lustre), 112–14; "Do You Want to Know?"(Concordia), 152–53; genealogy of global power in, 110–12; history of, 139–40; housing activism and, 132–33; Los Angeles Filipino history and, 131–32; "Mirror Images" (Santilla), 133–34; Philippine-Filipino American collaboration, 151–52; poetry commodification and, 147–49; poetry communities, 126–27, 131–34, 135; "Solving the Sweetest Science" (Baroma), 114–16; "What About My Story?" (Soriano), 105–7; "Work It" (Kiwi), 134–35. See also performance poetry
Fischer, Maisha, 126
Flores, Juan, 15
Flores, Shaggy, 117–20, 128
Foucault, Michel, 4, 10, 106–7, 135
Fouron, Georges E., 151
France, 7
frontier/savage imagery: in *Our Islands and their People*, 26–27; Puerto Rican jíbaro image, 119–20; safety/danger motif and, 36, 40; unruly orphaned children imagery, 105; World's Fair presentation of Filipinos, 78. See also authenticity; otherness
Fuentes, Marlon, 78

Gabriela (Filipino feminist organization), 70
Gandhi, Mahatma, 117
gaze, 38–39, 41–42
gender: consumption of femininity in the Young Miss Philippines pageant, 64–66; exceptionalist women's rights discourse, 71; Gabriela (Filipino feminist organization), 70; gendered exceptionalism, 4; guidebook depiction of Filipino women, 27–28; nationalist discourse and, 48, 50–51; sexual colonialism and, 28. See also sexuality
genealogy of global power, 19, 106–7, 121–25, 135
Glick-Schiller, Nina, 151
globalization: imperialism and, 6–7; manufacture of U.S.-market commodities, 135; multiculturalism and, 149; reproduction of colonial capitalism, 43–44; U.S. hegemonic trade relationships and, 23; WTO protests, 134–35
Goldman, Emma, 117
Gonzalez, Vernadette, 33
Gordon, Avery, 9, 81
Gramsci, Antonio, 107, 121, 140
Griggers, Camilla Benilao, 77–82, 85. See also *Memories of a Forgotten War*
Guatemala, 135
Guevara, Che, 97–98, 128

Hagedorn, Jessica, 141. See also *Dogeaters*
Harrison, David, 33
hegemony: commodity gratification and, 145–48; cultural construction of rape and, 50–51; economic development narrative and, 37–38; exceptionalism discourse and, 2–3, 50–51, 85–86, 89–90, 140–41; explicit vs. implied critique and, 76, 102; historical legitimacy and, 20, 103–4, 106, 125; institutional power and, 10; legitimization of knowledge and, 4, 10; multiculturalism discourse and, 1–2; packaging of anticolonial critique, 1–2, 12, 45–46, 99–100; postracial hegemony, 111; racial progress narrative and, 98–99; selective traditions and, 20, 144; tourist gaze and photography, 38–39; in travel guides, 30
hip hop, 108, 120, 145–46
history: colonial nostalgia, 33; counter-hegemonic narrative and, 20; genealogy of global power, 19, 106–7, 121–25, 140–41; historical amnesia, 2, 75, 123–25; historical legitimacy as hegemony, 20, 103–4, 125; memory as speculative reenactment, 77–85, 102–3; mixed heritage narrative and, 89–90; museum representation and, 95–97, 96; poetic historical narration, 116–17; ritual

performance as alternative history, 107–8; selective traditions and, 20, 144; slam poetry as anti-historical, 147. *See also* commemoration
Hoganson. Kristin L., 159n2
Hosseini, Khaled, 149
Hughes, Langston, 1

imperialism/colonialism: benevolent assimilation and, 4–5; commonwealth status as disavowal of empire, 102–3; cultural imperialism, 53–55, 64–65; European self-interest empire, 4; Filipino resistance to, 27; frontier/savagery imagery and, 26–27, 78; globalization and, 6–7; history of Spanish colonization, 125; modernization and, 37–38; racialized settler colonialism, 124; rationale for territorial status, 5–6; reluctant intervention policy, 6; stealth imperialism, 7–9. *See also* benevolent assimilation; economic development narrative; exceptionalism; neocolonialism; paternal benevolence; postcolonialism
India, 160n5
Iraq War, 7, 101, 102–3, 114, 153–54
Isaac, Allan, 3, 15, 42, 62
Israeli-Palestinian conflict, 124

Japan, 112–15
Joy Luck Club (film, 1993), 149

Kabataang Maka-Bayan, 152
Kim, Jodi, 16, 20
King, Martin Luther, Jr., 97–99
Kite Runner, The (Hosseini), 149
Kiwi, 131, 134–35
Kochiyama, Yuri, 128
Koshy, Susan, 14–15

LA Enkanto Kollective, 131–32
Latin Americans: Latino racialization, 117, 120, 140; Latino stereotypes, 13–14; Spanish language stigmatization, 138
Lavoe, Hector, 130
Lebrón, Lolita, 117
literature: Asian American literature, 14–15; commodification of ethnic literature, 1–2; minority literature discourse, 17, 45–46, 157n4; Puerto Rican American writing, 15

Lonely Planet: Philippines: cultural consumption in, 44; depiction of Filipino people, 27; exotic paradise imagery and, 26. *See also* travel guides
Lonely Planet: Puerto Rico: cultural consumption in, 44; exotic paradise imagery, 26; Puerto Rican racial harmony in, 28; westward expansion rhetoric in, 26–27. *See also* travel guides
Los Angeles Filipinos: anti-exceptionalist coalitions, 116, 120; Asian Pacific Culture of, 120; critique of institutionalized history, 121; poetry communities, 126–27, 131–34; socioeconomic status of, 108–9. *See also* Filipino identity; Philippines
Love, Eric Tyrone Lowery, 156n16
Lowe, Lisa, 2, 16, 127
ludic multiculturalism, 111
Lustre, Napoleon, 112–13, 116

Maldonado, Adal, 150
Marcos, Ferdinand: corruption of, 36–37; development of tourism, 31–32; opposition to, 62–63; representation in *Dogeaters*, 36–38, 50, 61–64; sexual violence against opposition, 67; U.S. support for, 50, 61–62, 70
Marcos, Imelda, 36–37
Mars, Bruno, 143–44, 150, 168n2
Mastuśik, Martin, 111
Matos Rodríguez, Félix, 91
McClintock, Anne, 48
McMillan, Terry, 71
Meléndez, Jesús Papoleto, 138–39
Memories of a Forgotten War (Griggers and Dalena): familial illegitimacy in, 76, 79–80, 87; marginalization of, 145; memory as speculative reenactment in, 77–85, *84*, 102–3, 123; overview, 75–76; paternal benevolence and, 18–19, 101–2; Philippine-American War violence in, 80–86, *84*; production and marketing of, 77–78, 103; resistance to appropriation in, 20, 97, 150
memory. *See* commemoration; history
Mercado, Nancy, 124–25
Merina, Dorian, 125, 147
meritocracy, 2, 3, 92–95, 118–19. *See also* class; economy
Mexico: deportation initiatives and, 13; Filipino history/identity and, 113, 116, 125,

133; Filipino labor coalitions and, 114; NAFTA and, 133

migration: escape from violence in *América's Dream*, 59; exceptionalism and, 118–19; generational experience and, 108–9; immigration and assimilation narratives, 149–50; Operation Bootstrap and, 55–59, 92–93, 108; Puerto Rican agricultural jíbaro image and, 119–20; Puerto Rican racial stereotyping and, 14; transnational migration studies, 155n3; U.S. as refuge for women, 71; U.S. imperialism and, 2–3, 15

military (U.S. military): availability of U.S. commodities and, 53–54; citizen military benefits, 9; exceptionalism and, 114–15; as haunting of colonial wars, 52–53; military rape cases, 48, 159n2, 160n7; Philippine-American War, 76–77, 80–86, *84*; Philippines prostitution and, 27–28, 35; presence in Puerto Rico, 32, 91; presence in the Philippines, 15; racism in, 119; recruitment practices, 91–92, 163n34, 163n36; treatment of Filipino veterans, 115; Vieques bomb testing, 117, 129, 150, 160n15. *See also* United States

Morales, Anthony, 125, 138

Mujeres de Maiz, 134

multiculturalism: Bruno Mars as packaging of, 143–44; civil rights discourse and, 16, 88; critical education and, 125; cultural nationalism and, 89, 99–101; ethnic specificity and, 127; exceptionalism and, 89–90, 111–12; Filipino progress narrative and, 88; globalization and, 149; ludic multiculturalism, 111; minority literature discourse, 17; mixed heritage narratives, 28, 89–90; model minority discourse and, 16, 157n48; packaging of anticolonial critique, 1–2, 45–46, 73; Puerto Rican mixed heritage narrative, 89–90; selective traditions and, 144; superficial difference discourse, 3. *See also* ethnicity

Muñoz, José Esteban, 111, 113

Muñoz Marin, Luis, 55, 100, 118

Nadal, Lenina, 151

Namesake, The (film, 2007), 149

neocolonialism: authenticity-convenience tandem and, 29; cheap labor as feature of, 33; exceptionalist narrative and, 7; fascination with U.S. commodities/culture, 53–55; global capitalism and, 43–44; neocolonialism as rape, 18, 47–48, 50–53, 55–62, 64, 66–71, 159n2, 160n5, 160n7, 161n53; opportunity/mobility discourse and, 2–3, 92–95, 118–19; silence of colonial genealogy, 53; tourist industry and, 43; trade agreements and, 133; transformation of colonial infrastructure, 33, 91; transnationalism and, 59–60. *See also* benevolent assimilation; imperialism/colonialism

Nicaragua, 117

North American Free Trade Agreement (NAFTA), 133

Nuyorican performance poetry: "At the Head of the Class" (Rojas), 137–38; critique of institutionalized history, 121; "Drop the Bomb" (Ramirez), 129, 153; ethnic identity and, 108–9; genealogy of global power in, 110–12, 121; history of, 139; "One Man's Fight for Love" (Rojas), 116–17; open mic events, 136; "Oye Lo Boricua" (Flores), 117–19, 128; performances spaces, 127–30; poetry commodification and, 1–2, 147–49; poetry communities, 126–27, 130, 135; "Puerto Rican Obituary" (Pietri), 13, 93–94; "Spotlight at the Nuyorican Poets Café" (Perdoma), 1. *See also* Nuyoricans; performance poetry

Nuyoricans: Anthony Baez death, 117; Black Atlantic culture of, 120; CUNY tuition strike, 151; ethnic identity of, 109, 127; pollution of neighborhoods, 129; Puerto Rican Day Parade, 87–88, 99–100; Young Lords, 98–99. *See also* Nuyorican performance poetry

organic intellectualism, 107, 121, 140

otherness: authentic postcolonial others, 21–22; ethnic literature curricula and, 157n4; racial othering of Puerto Ricans, 28–29; tourist subordination of local other, 38; travel guides and, 24. *See also* authenticity; frontier/savage imagery

Our Islands and their People: cultural consumption in, 21–23, 39–40, 44; description of purpose, 25–26; economic development narrative and, 17, 25–27; Filipino savagery in, 27; presentation of colonial other in, 24; Puerto Rican racial harmony in, 28

Palmer, Fay, 95
Palumbo-Liu, David, 21, 157n4
Pataki, George, 100
paternal benevolence: consent to colonial rule and, 112; deconstruction of, 74, 101–2; denial of imperialism and, 18–19; ubiquity of, 74; Uncle Sam figure in, 74, 75; unruly orphaned children imagery, 105. See also benevolent assimilation; imperialism/colonialism
Perdomo, Willie, 1–2, 138
Perez, Rosie, 76, 86–94, 141. See also *Yo soy Boricua, pa'que tu lo Sepas!*
Perez, Sixto, 89–90
performance poetry: activist collaboration and, 152–54; Asian American poetry, 134; commodification of, 145–46; cultural assets available to, 140–41; decolonization initiatives and, 19–20, 106–7, 120–22, 140; genealogy of global power in, 110–12, 121, 140–41; overview, 107–8, 126; poetry communities, 126–27, 130–31; public arts funding, 136, 139, 147–48; repertoire vs. archive and, 107, 126, 128; spoken-word and slam poetry, 146–48. See also disidentification; Filipino performance poetry; Nuyorican performance poetry
Philippines: anti-imperialism and, 2; assassination of Benigno Aquino Jr., 61–65, 67–68; Bell Trade Agreement, 6; Clark Special Economic Zone, 33; economic dependency narratives, 24; Filipino American literature, 14–15; Gabriela (Filipino feminist organization), 70; independence status, 5–6, 75, 76, 101, 143; Manila Film Festival, 36–38, 42; Marcos development of tourism, 42; Marcos government corruption, 36–37; martial law period, 24, 30, 31, 37–38, 42, 50, 61–62; mixed heritage narrative, 89–90; as model postcolonial nation, 7; Muslim minority in, 27; People Power Movement, 68; Philippine-American War, 76–77, 80–86, 84, 123; Philippine-Filipino American activist collaboration, 151–52; resistance to U.S. colonization, 27; Spanish colonization, 13, 23, 41, 112–13; territorial status of, 5; U.S. military presence, 15, 27–28, 30–31, 35, 112–13. See also Filipino identity; Los Angeles Filipinos
photography, 38–39

Pietri, Pedro, 13, 93–94, 150
poetry. See performance poetry
postcolonialism: authentic postcolonial others, 21–22; economic development narrative and, 17; economic privilege and, 25–26, 32, 39–40; Philippines as model postcolonial nation, 7; postcolonial tourism, 24–25; travel guides and, 24, 29. See also imperialism/colonialism
Pratt, Mary Louise, 31–32
Puerto Rican identity: citizenship status and, 2, 5; cultural invisibility and, 15–16; Latino stereotypes and, 13–14; Puerto Rican femininity and, 57, 59–60; Puerto Rican racial identity and, 28, 94, 120. See also cultural identity
Puerto Rico: activist collaboration and, 151; anti-imperialism and, 2; commonwealth status, 5–8, 75–76; cultural nationalism initiative (Operation Serenity), 55–59, 87–89, 100; economic dependency narratives, 24; industrialization (Operation Bootstrap), 55–59, 92–93, 108; mixed heritage narrative, 28, 89–90; Ponce Massacre, 95–98, 96; Taíno legacy in, 34, 89; territorial status of, 5; U.S. military presence, 32, 91; Vieques as *América's Dream* setting, 32; Vieques bomb testing, 117, 129, 150, 160n15. See also commonwealth status; Nuyoricans

race: annexation debate and, 156n16; Bonafide Rojas racial identity, 117; cultural invisibility and, 15–16; Filipino racial categorization, 12–13, 78; meritocratic hierarchy and, 3; postracial hegemony, 111, 143–44; Puerto Rican racial categorization, 28, 94, 119–20; Puerto Rican racial harmony, 28, 89–90, 118; racialization of Filipino natives, 27; racialized settler colonialism, 124; racial progress narrative and, 98–99; "Singgalot" Filipino experience exhibit, 11–12; solidarity with racialized minorities, 115–16, 120, 128–29; U.S. military racism, 119
Ramirez, Ray, 129–30, 153
religion: depiction of fundamentalist Islam, 71; Philippine Muslim minority, 27; religious depiction of social change, 62; weddings in *Memories of a Forgotten War*, 81–86
resistance: activation of local knowledges,

135–36; activist collaboration and, 152–54; agency in tourist industry resistance, 43; delegitimization of historical narrative, 125; differential consciousness and, 127; double-voiced discourse and, 89–90, 100–102; exceptionalism and, 9–10, 45, 85–86; explicit vs. implied critique, 76, 102; historic oppression and resistance, 116–17; humor and, 90, 163n32; marketplace pressures on, 103; *Memories of a Forgotten War* resistance to appropriation, 20; organic intellectualism, 107, 121, 140; packaging of anticolonial critique, 1–2, 12, 45–46, 99–100; Ponce Massacre and, 95–98, 96; sexualized anticolonialist narrative and, 47–48, 50–51; transformation of Daisy in *Dogeaters*, 68–69; unassimilability as cultural critique, 2. *See also* decolonization; disidentification
ritual performance, 107–8
Rodríguez, Dylan, 88–89, 100, 102
Rojas, Bonafide, 116–17, 137
Roosevelt, Franklin, 12

Samson, Cheryl, 147
Samuels, Shirley, 64
Sandino, Augusto, 117
Sandoval, Chela, 127
San Juan, E., Jr., 123–24
Santiago, Esmeralda, 141. *See also América's Dream*
Santiago-Valles, Kelvin, 161n29
Santilla, Faith, 131–35, 147
Schwarzenegger, Arnold, 136, 139
selective traditions, 20, 144
sexuality: benevolent assimilation as heterosexual romance, 18, 47–48, 49, 60–61, 73–74, 78–86, 161n29; cultural construction of rape, 50–51, 69, 161n35; familial illegitimacy, 76, 79–80, 87, 89–91, 101, 103–4; military rape cases, 48, 70–71; neocolonialism as rape, 18, 47–48, 50–53, 55–62, 64, 66–71, 159n2, 160n5, 160n7, 161n53; neocolonial power/control and, 41–42; prostitution in Puerto Rico vs. Philippines, 30–31; reclamation of sexual/political agency, 70; sex tourism, 31–32, 34–35, 41–42; sexual colonialism, 28; U.S. military presence and, 27–28, 35. *See also* gender
Shakur, Assata, 117

Sharpe, Jenny, 61, 160n5
Sharpton, Al, 100
Sierre Leone, 135
slam poetry, 146–48
Smits, Jimmy, 86
Soriano, Aquilina, 105–6
South Korea, 160n7
Spain: colonization of the Philippines, 13, 23, 41, 112–13; Gabriela and Malinche as revolutionary figures, 133; history of Spanish colonization, 125
spoken-word and slam poetry, 146–48
stealth imperialism, 7–9
subjugated knowledges, 10

Taino (Joel Bosch), 86
Taylor, Diana, 107, 117, 128
tourism: cheap labor as feature of, 33; clean/dirty motif and, 40; consumption of otherness and, 24, 29; economic development narrative and, 17; economic privilege and, 25–26, 32, 39–40; economic role of, 24–25; exotic paradise imagery, 26, 117–18; façade of cleanliness and, 36–37; heritage persona, 41; neglect of native economy, 35–38; political resistance and, 42–43; postcolonial economy and, 24–25; Puerto Rican tourist infrastructure, 31, 167n32; safety/danger motif and, 36, 40, 42–43; sex tourism, 31–32, 34–35, 41–42; subordination of local culture, 38; tourist desire and, 52; tourist gaze and photography, 38–39; tourist industry in *Dogeaters* and *América's Dream*, 23, 30–32, 43
travel guides: cultural consumption in, 21–23, 39–40, 44; economic development narrative and, 17; economic privilege and, 25–26, 32, 39–40; erasure of colonialism in, 35; frontier imagery in, 26–27; tourist desire and, 52. *See also Lonely Planet: Philippines*; *Lonely Planet: Puerto Rico*
Tschofen, Monique Y., 47, 52

United Kingdom, 160n5
United States: commonwealth representation in Congress, 6, 100; cultural construction of rape in, 50–51; exceptionalist policies, 4–5; fascination with U.S. commodities/culture, 53–55; occupation of Iraq and Afghanistan, 7, 101, 102–3, 114; Puerto Rican U.S. House

delegate, 6; reluctant intervention policy, 6; support for Marcos regime, 50, 61–62, 70. *See also* military

Valen, Terry, 131
Vera Cruz, Philip, 128
Vietnam War: Marcos support for, 24, 66; Philippine independence and, 114–15; Philippines prostitution and, 30–31; racialization of Asians in, 115–16; Vietnam as French colony, 7

Welfare Poets, 130
Wexler, Laura, 39
Williams, Raymond, 3, 12, 20, 144, 146–47
Winter, Bronywn, 160n7
World Trade Organization (WTO), 134–35
World War II: Bataan death march, 114–15; economic effects of, 91–92, 164n37; Enola Gay exhibit, 11; Filipino performance poetry on, 134; France-Vietnam status and, 7; military benefits and, 9; Philippine & Puerto Rican independence and, 5–6; Puerto Rico and Philippines Memorial, *8, 9*; treatment of Filipino veterans, 115

X, Malcolm, 128

Yo soy Boricua, pa'que tu lo Sepas! (Perez): anticolonial stance in, 97–100, 150; cultural critique in, 97–98, 102; familial illegitimacy in, 87, 89–91, 101, 103–4; multiculturalism discourse in, 89–90; opportunity/mobility discourse and, 92–95; overview, 75–76; paternal benevolence and, 18–19; Ponce Massacre and, 95–98, *96*; production and marketing of, 86–87, 144–45; Puerto Rican Day Parade, 87–88, 99–100; Young Lords treatment in, 98–99
Youth Speaks, 148
Yuval-Davis, Nira, 48

Zedillo Ponce de Leon, Ernesto, 133
Zentella, Ana Celia, 138
Zimmerman, Eugene, 73

FAYE CARONAN is an assistant professor of ethnic studies at the University of Colorado Denver.

The Asian American Experience

The Hood River Issei: An Oral History of Japanese Settlers in Oregon's
   Hood River Valley   *Linda Tamura*
Americanization, Acculturation, and Ethnic Identity: The Nisei Generation
   in Hawaii   *Eileen H. Tamura*
Sui Sin Far/Edith Maude Eaton: A Literary Biography   *Annette White-Parks*
Mrs. Spring Fragrance and Other Writings   *Sui Sin Far; edited by Amy Ling
   and Annette White-Parks*
The Golden Mountain: The Autobiography of a Korean Immigrant, 1895–1960
   Easurk Emsen Charr; edited and with an introduction by Wayne Patterson
Race and Politics: Asian Americans, Latinos, and Whites in a Los Angeles Suburb
   Leland T. Saito
Achieving the Impossible Dream: How Japanese Americans Obtained Redress
   Mitchell T. Maki, Harry H. L. Kitano, and S. Megan Berthold
If They Don't Bring Their Women Here: Chinese Female Immigration before Exclusion
   George Anthony Peffer
Growing Up Nisei: Race, Generation, and Culture among Japanese Americans
   of California, 1924–49   *David K. Yoo*
Chinese American Literature since the 1850s   *Xiao-huang Yin*
Pacific Pioneers: Japanese Journeys to America and Hawaii, 1850–80
   John E. Van Sant
Holding Up More Than Half the Sky: Chinese Women Garment Workers
   in New York City, 1948–92   *Xiaolan Bao*
Onoto Watanna: The Story of Winnifred Eaton   *Diana Birchall*
Edith and Winnifred Eaton: Chinatown Missions and Japanese Romances
   Dominika Ferens
Being Chinese, Becoming Chinese American   *Shehong Chen*
"A Half Caste" and Other Writings   *Onoto Watanna; edited by Linda Trinh Moser
   and Elizabeth Rooney*
Chinese Immigrants, African Americans, and Racial Anxiety in the United States,
   1848–82   *Najia Aarim-Heriot*
Not Just Victims: Conversations with Cambodian Community Leaders in the United
   States   *Edited and with an introduction by Sucheng Chan; interviews conducted
   by Audrey U. Kim*
The Japanese in Latin America   *Daniel M. Masterson with Sayaka Funada-Classen*
Survivors: Cambodian Refugees in the United States   *Sucheng Chan*
From Concentration Camp to Campus: Japanese American Students
   and World War II   *Allan W. Austin*
Japanese American Midwives: Culture, Community, and Health Politics   *Susan L. Smith*
In Defense of Asian American Studies: The Politics of Teaching
   and Program Building   *Sucheng Chan*
Lost and Found: Reclaiming the Japanese American Incarceration   *Karen L. Ishizuka*
Religion and Spirituality in Korean America   *Edited by David K. Yoo
   and Ruth H. Chung*

Moving Images: Photography and the Japanese American Incarceration
Jasmine Alinder
Camp Harmony: Seattle's Japanese Americans and the Puyallup Assembly Center
Louis Fiset
Chinese American Transnational Politics   Him Mark Lai, *edited and with an introduction by Madeline Y. Hsu*
Issei Buddhism in the Americas   *Edited by Duncan Ryûken Williams and Tomoe Moriya*
Hmong America: Reconstructing Community in Diaspora   *Chia Youyee Vang*
In Pursuit of Gold: Chinese American Miners and Merchants in the American West
Sue Fawn Chung
Pacific Citizens: Larry and Guyo Tajiri and Japanese American Journalism in the World War II Era   *Edited by Greg Robinson*
Indian Accents: Brown Voice and Racial Performance in American Television and Film
Shilpa S. Davé
Yellow Power, Yellow Soul: The Radical Art of Fred Ho   *Edited by Roger N. Buckley and Tamara Roberts*
Fighting from a Distance: How Filipino Exiles Helped Topple a Dictator
Jose V. Fuentecilla
In Defense of Justice: Joseph Kurihara and the Japanese American Struggle for Equality
Eileen H. Tamura
Asian Americans in Dixie: Race and Migration in the South   *Edited by Jigna Desai and Khyati Y. Joshi*
Undercover Asian: Multiracial Asian Americans in Visual Culture   *Leilani Nishime*
Islanders in the Empire: Filipino and Puerto Rican Laborers in Hawai'i
JoAnna Poblete
Virtual Homelands: Indian Immigrants and Online Cultures in the United States
Madhavi Mallapragada
Building Filipino Hawai'i   *Roderick N. Labrador*
Legitimizing Empire: Filipino American and U.S. Puerto Rican Cultural Critique
Faye Caronan

The University of Illinois Press
is a founding member of the
Association of American University Presses.

Composed in 10.5/13 Adobe Minion Pro
by Kirsten Dennison
at the University of Illinois Press
Manufactured by Cushing-Malloy, Inc.

University of Illinois Press
1325 South Oak Street
Champaign, IL 61820-6903
www.press.uillinois.edu